THE MEDIA AND ELECTIONS

A Handbook and Comparative Study

The European Institute for the Media Series

THE EUROPEAN INSTITUTE FOR THE MEDIA

Kevin • *Europe in the Media: A Comparison of Reporting, Representation, and Rhetoric in National Media Systems in Europe*

Noam/Groebel/Gerbarg • *Internet Television*

Lange/Ward • *Media and Elections: A Handbook and Comparative Study*

van Ginneken • *Collective Behavior and Public Opinion: Rapid Shifts in Opinion and Communication*

Published by Lawrence Erlbaum Associates, Publishers

THE MEDIA AND ELECTIONS

A Handbook and Comparative Study

Edited by

Bernd-Peter Lange
University of Osnabrück

David Ward
European Institute for the Media

 LAWRENCE ERLBAUM ASSOCIATES, PUBLISHERS
2004   Mahwah, New Jersey   London

Lawrence Erlbaum Associates, Inc., Publishers
10 Industrial Avenue
Mahwah, New Jersey 07430

Cover design by Kathryn Houghtaling Lacey

Library of Congress Cataloging-in-Publication Data

The media and elections : a handbook and comparative study / edited by
  Bernd-Peter Lange, David Ward.
       p. cm.
  Includes bibliographical references and index.
  ISBN 0-8058-4780-4 (cloth: alk. paper)
    1. Mass media-Political aspects—Europe—Case studies. 2. Elections—
Europe—Case studies. 3. Mass media policy—Europe. 4. Mass media—
Political aspects—United States. 5. Elections—United States. 6. Mass
media policy—United States. 7. Mass media—Political aspects—South
Africa. 8. Elections—South Africa. 9. Mass media policy—South Africa.
I. Lange, Bernd-Peter. II. Ward, David, 1966–
P95.82.E85M42 2003
302.23'094—dc22
                                                             2003065119
                                                             CIP

Books published by Lawrence Erlbaum Associates are printed on acid-free paper,
and their bindings are chosen for strength and durability.

Printed in the United States of America
10 9 8 7 6 5 4 3 2 1

Contents

Acknowledgments and Preface

The comparative study brings together academics and practitioners who work in the field of media and elections. They have provided a set of national case studies and an analysis of the legal and regulatory frameworks that are employed by nation-states to ensure that the media perform according to certain standards during election periods. In setting out the legal and regulatory framework, each chapter provides an account of the sociopolitical conditions and media environment in each of the countries and subsequently details the laws that govern the print and broadcast media during election campaign periods.

The book is based on the work of the Media and Democracy Programme (MADP) of the European Institute for the Media and has been organized by the Communication Policies Programme in cooperation with the MADP. The program has carried out over 40 media-monitoring missions over the past 10 years during elections in Eastern Europe and the former Soviet Union under a series of projects financed by the European Commission's Tacis program, the European Initiative for Democracy and Human Rights, and the Organization for Security and Co-operation in Europe (OSCE). A list of media-monitoring missions conducted by MADP is included at the end of this text.

Many thanks to Gillian McCormack, Head of the Media and Democracy Programme for the Commonwealth of Independent States (CIS), at the European Institute for the Media, who suggested many of the contributors for the chapters. Céline Delahaie, Deirdre Kevin, Emmanuelle Machet, Gabriele Parlmeyer, Santiago Perez Pardo, Eleftheria Pertzinidou, Martina Pohl,

Dusan Reljic, Amina Strothenke, Ljudmila Von Berg, and Verena Voss have also helped in immeasurable ways to bring the text to completion. Thanks also to Andrea Millwood-Hargrave for recommending a specialist on South Africa and Emily Wilkinson of LEA for her support over the past year and her efforts in ensuring that the EIM book series, of which this book is a part, has materialized.

The editors would also like to thank all of the contributors, some of whom produced their chapters under fairly tight deadlines. It has been a great pleasure to bring expertise from throughout the world together to produce this book. The editors would like to also express their gratitude to Nadine Simms of LEA for her editorial support in bringing the manuscript to completion.

—Bernd-Peter Lange
—David Ward

Introduction

David Ward

The collection of essays on media and elections gathered in this book have a dual purpose. First and foremost the essays are intended to provide a comparative overview of how the media is required to act by national law when arguably the media is most scrutinized, during elections to the institutions of government. Second, it is intended to provide for media monitors, professionals and academics who work within the field of media and elections, an overview of the body of law and regulations that are employed in different countries to provide for fairness in coverage of elections. In allowing the candidates access to the mass media, together with creating certain conditions that are understood to provide for balance, impartiality, and adequate coverage of an election to ensure that the citizenship has the necessary information to make an informed decision when they vote, nation-states are ipso facto recognizing the importance of the mass media in democratic life. Regulation and the nature of regulation is therefore crucial. A distinction is usually made between traditional and transitional democratic societies that appears to be premised on the fact that some countries have enjoyed long, stable democratic institutions, whereas others are only now developing such structures. In many ways the distinction is a simplification and one of the tasks of the book is to give an overview of how the media is regulated to ensure that elections are characterized by certain basic standards that are understood as providing fair and nondiscriminatory access and sufficient amounts of coverage dedicated to elections, while at the same time providing a critical account of these mechanisms.

Elections are one of the central instruments employed by nation-states to ensure that the democratic right of citizens and the will of the public are channeled into the political decision-making process. Periodically, citizens vote for the party or candidate that will represent them in a whole range of institutions that are designed to provide for deliberation through representation.

The mass media are a crucial component in this process and the dissemination of news and commentary, together with the nature of this information, are crucial for accountable and sustainable structures of governance. The media are instrumental to this process and the platform that they provide at election times remains a vital stage for the presentation of party ideologies as well as granting the public the opportunity to scrutinize and gather information on a broad array of manifestos presented by candidates for election.

THE MEDIA AND DEMOCRACY

The media's role in the democratic process is unquestionably central, and a democratic system of government that is not supported by a free, vibrant, and healthy media system represents a nominal rather than real system of democratic decision making. The very roots of democracy are understood as an active sphere of praxis with individuals participating in debate and argument about the nature of the basic structure of the society that they share. Indeed, the sphere of activity raises a whole set of questions about inclusion and participation that act as the basis of civil society. In many respects the Agora or the New England town hall meeting have provided a model for democratic deliberation and exchange within the system of republican government supported by representative systems of deliberation.

For modern-day societies the idea of public meetings where citizens come together to debate and vote on certain issues remains a model for democratic deliberation. However, the size of these societies means that not all of the population can all converge at a meeting point to make decisions about social and public life. Legal and constitutional frameworks provide a normative base for democratic governance; but without an informed, active, and participating electorate that provides for a dynamic and engaged civil society, the system cannot always automatically be sustained. It is the duty of a legitimate state to ensure the conditions that support such a vision of citizenship and the institutions, which are required to undertake certain activities in the public interest function to a standard that supports, rather than fails, to fulfill certain prerequisites to guarantee a working and healthy democratic system of government.

In this respect the constitutional rights of free speech and the organization of representative democracies form powerful arguments that suggest the mass media have a vital role to play in public and democratic life. The mass media of broadcasting and newspapers are today the most important sources of information and news about public life and they are, as a result, crucial to the democratic system of governance.

INTERNATIONAL PROTECTION OF THE MEDIA IN A DEMOCRATIC SOCIETY

The two most notable international instruments that have proclaimed the importance of the media in the democratic life of societies are the United Nations Declaration of Human Rights and the European Convention on Human Rights. As legal instruments, the texts represent two of the most ambitious and geographically far-reaching initiatives that attempt to set out a number of basic rights of the individual.

The UN Declaration states, "Everyone has the right to freedom of opinion and expression; this right includes freedom to hold opinions without interference and seek, receive and impart information and ideas through any media and regardless of frontiers" (Article 19, UN Declaration of Human Rights, 1948/1999). Among the range of rights afforded under the UN Declaration and the European Convention, the rights to freedom of thought and expression are seen as integral to freedom and inviolable rights that all individuals, regardless of their background, race, or religion, are entitled to under the rule of law.

In the preamble of the European Convention of Human Rights it states that the maintenance and further development of human rights and fundamental freedoms is possible only in a democratic society. By the same token, it also recognizes that as a precondition for a democratic society, societies must be built upon certain human rights that are respected and encouraged by democratic states, in order to grant citizens the rights conferred through citizenship. The bind between democracy and human rights is therefore one of symbiosis in that the rights granted in a democratic state can be achieved only through having a civic culture grounded in respect for, and understanding of, the right for all members of a community to participate in public life. In terms of the right to communicate, Article 10 of the European Convention of Human Rights states:

> 1. Everyone has the right to freedom of expression. The right shall include freedom to hold opinions and to receive and impart information and ideas without interference by public authority and regardless of frontiers. This Article shall not prevent States from requiring the licensing of broadcasting, television and cinema enterprises.

2. The exercise of these freedoms, since it carries with it duties and responsibilities, may be subject to such formalities, conditions, restrictions or penalties as are prescribed by law and are necessary for a democratic society, in the interests of national security, territorial integrity or public safety, for the prevention of disorder or crime, for the protection of health and morals, for the protection of reputation of rights of others, for preventing the disclosure of information received in confidence, or for maintaining the authority and impartiality of the judiciary. (Council of Europe [COE], 1995, p. 7)

Freedom of the media is not explicitly mentioned in Article 10, but it is guaranteed as part of the general right to freedom of expression. This has been supported in several legal judgments, which have stressed the importance of freedom for the press (see COE, 2001a). In the case *Sunday Times v. United Kingdom* (COE, 2001a), the European Court of Human Rights stressed the importance of the protection of political expression and of freedom of the press in general. It stated that it is incumbent on the media to "impart information and ideas concerning matters . . . of public interest. Not only do the media have the task of imparting such information and ideas: the public also has a right to receive them." In addition, the Court pointed out that it was "faced not with a choice between two conflicting principles but with a principle of freedom of expression that is subject to a number of exceptions which must be narrowly interpreted" (COE, 2001a).

In the Castells judgment, the Court underlined that "the pre-eminent role of the press in a state governed by the rule of law must not be forgotten" (Castells judgment, 1992; cited in COE, 2001a). The Court further recognized the importance placed on the freedom of the press in the following statement:

Freedom of the press affords the public one of the best means of discovering and forming an opinion on the ideas and attitudes of their political leaders. In particular, it gives politicians the opportunity to reflect and comment on the preoccupations of public opinion; it thus enables everyone to participate in the free political debate which is at the very core of the concept of a democratic society. (Castells judgment, 1992; cited in COE, 2001a, p. 12)

According to case law based on the European Convention of Human Rights, freedom of speech is inextricably linked to the freedom to publish in the public domain without coercion from the state, except under certain circumstances in the public interest. The European Court's interpretation of Article 10 therefore adopts a classical position in terms of constitutional law in that it perceives the freedom of the media to publish and disseminate a range of news and information to the public, as a cornerstone of the democratic system of government. Technically, at least in this respect, every member of society should have access to a range of viewpoints through the ability of all to have access to a multiplicity of different views and opinions that combine into a patchwork of information provided by mass media. Interference by the state, except on public-interest grounds, is deemed to infringe the right of free expression.

The idea that the media should be free from external interference is part of a long tradition in democratic countries and is rooted in the history of constitutional democratic structures. As an integral part of accountable government the media is perceived to act as a fourth estate, which watches over the government of the day in the public interest. It is also seen to be a central vehicle that informs the public about a whole range of public affairs on which political decisions are made within parliamentary structures. This enables citizens to make an informed choice on a variety of public matters and it empowers them to reflect upon, and reason about, decisions that affect public life and the political decision-making processes.

In large-scale societies, this necessarily entails having mass-communication structures that in turn necessitate mediated structures where public communication is channeled through a range of media, and therefore the range of that media, and access to the channels of communication for individuals and groups to express and receive opinions, is a crucial consideration as to the degree that the media are free from constraints and external pressures from both the state and commercial forces.

As the contributions to this book demonstrate, there are many models of democracy and equally many different ways that the mass media are legally established within the parameters of the system of government. Representative democracy is often seen as the solution for making a system of democratic deliberation into a workable and manageable framework for decision making. In electing representatives, the electorate are making a decision to invest their rights of deliberation to a representative who acts on their behalf in parliament and the other organs of government, and the nature of the mass media is fundamental in this relationship.

MEDIA AND ELECTIONS

In the contemporary world, the idea of elections without the mass media would be unthinkable as broadcast media and newspapers have become the primary site where an election is actually taken to the electorate. Candidates and parties standing for election all rely on the media to carry their manifestos and ideological messages to the general public. It is perhaps one of the most important public-interest functions of the media in the context of the democratic life of national citizens to not only report on politics generally, but also, during election campaigns when the electorate decide who will represent them in the institutions of government to provide a platform for discussion, representation, and debate.

In approaching the whole issue of elections, the mass media are required to perform certain public-interest objectives that not only require them to allow access to the media, but also oblige media outlets to provide certain conditions for candidates and parties to access the public through mass media. As the national examples in this book demonstrate, there are a myriad of different mechanisms employed to provide access to candidates to the mass media and regulatory instruments to support this access.

Two clear models are discernible. The first, a free-market model, has been employed essentially to regulate the press in all of the countries in this collection, where political coverage is regulated according to light-touch requirements. In most of these cases, negative regulation is employed to ensure that certain practices are not pursued by the press. Paid political advertising is banned in a number of countries and at the same time political coverage in general enjoys minimal regulation and a traditional model for freedom is the dominant paradigm. The press in most cases are highly partisan toward political parties in their coverage of the election campaigns, and again the patchwork model of a whole range of proprietors competing in a marketplace of ideas underpins the approach to the sector as a whole.

The second model is concerned with television and the differences in national approaches to the regulation of television, which is far more marked than the approach to the press. This model, unlike the one applied in the press sector, is not uniform and is marked by differences between countries that employ different models of television and radio broadcasting systems. As a consequence varying degrees of state regulation have evolved and a whole range of instruments been developed, which in most cases are used to support media freedom, but in some cases are used to the detriment of the liberty of the media. In the context of elections the rules that govern access are varied in each country, but nevertheless the same philosophical principle guides the regulation of television at election times as a public service, however this is defined.

CONCLUSION

The contributions in this book demonstrate the variety of national systems of democracy and the range of differences in how nations organize both their media systems and the rules that require elections to be covered according to certain normative standards in the mass media, which are characterized by hugely different approaches.

The chapters all attempt to follow a similar template; however, given the range of differences in the laws, media systems, and democratic models employed by the different countries, divergence is not only inevitable but in many ways represents the richness of putting together a comparative study. In the majority of contributions, the mass media are contextualized within the political and social environment and a summary of the media ecology is presented. This is followed by a comprehensive analysis of how the mass media are legally required to cover and grant access to candidates and parties during election periods.

The countries selected are by no means exhaustive in their geographic coverage. However, as one of the aims of this book was to give a critical account of not only developing democracies, but also developed democracies, the editors have attempted to strike a balance between a variety of countries that represent some of the problems and some of the successes in how the media cover elections.

As one of the contributors to this collection points out, there is no media system that does not have weaknesses (see Kaid and Jones, chap. 2, this volume), and it is perhaps at election times when these weakness are most visible. Even in the so-called mature democracies of the West, equality and fairness are not to be taken for granted and a sophisticated legal and regulatory system has been developed based on constitutional and normative principles that technically ensure elections are played out in the mass media according to certain criteria.

Another of the contributors points out that media systems and their subsequent relationship to the democratic process must be understood within the historical conditions within which certain notions of media freedom and autonomy have developed (see de Beer, chap. 4, this volume). The case of Russia is perhaps the most poignant example in this collection, and the shift from a state media model associated with state communism to a liberal model is characterized by fundamental and profound problems. The acquiescence of the media and journalists to the political elite demonstrates that the idea that a successful system of liberal democracy has supplanted alternative political ideologies is far from unproblematic. Communism may have collapsed in the late 1980s, however, a system of control and subservience pervades the media ecology, as it does in many other post-Soviet states.

In covering the contemporary legal framework and guidelines, and in reviewing the realities of how the media function at election times, the book aims to achieve a truly international set of comparative studies and commentaries. The contributions combine to give a wide overview of the area by providing a detailed description of the legal and regulatory instruments that govern how elections should be covered in the mass media. Furthermore, because each of the contributors holds extensive experience in this area, each is in a position to evaluate the current system and evaluate the performance of the system employed in their respective country.

The aim of the book, however, is also to provide a practical guideline so that it can be used as a guideline and a handbook, and in this respect the final chapter, by Bernd-Peter Lange, lays out a set of recommendations that can be used as a reference for professionals working in the field of media and elections and development.

REFERENCES

Council of Europe. (1995). *The European Convention on Human Rights.* Strasbourg, France: Author.

Council of Europe. (1999). *Recommendation No. R15 of the Committee of Ministers and the Member States on Measures Concerning Media Coverage of Election Campaigns.* Strasbourg, France: Author.

Council of Europe. (2001a). *Case law concerning Article 10 of the European Convention on Human Rights.* File Number 18. Strasbourg, France: Author.

Council of Europe. (2001b). *Cases of the European Court of Human Rights.* Retrieved from http://www.echr.coe.int/Eng/Judgments.htm

United Nations. (1999). *The Universal Declaration of Human Rights.* New York: Author. (Original work published 1948)

1

Italy

Teresa Perrucci
Marina Villa

THE ITALIAN POLITICAL SYSTEM

With the referendum of June 2, 1946, Italy became a parliamentary Republic. The Italian Parliament has two chambers, the Chamber of Deputies (630 members) and the Senate (315 members plus 11 Senators for life), which are elected for a 5-year term. The president of the Republic is elected for a 7-year term by an electoral college composed of members of the two chambers.

From 1948 to 1993, Italy had a purely proportional electoral system, which guaranteed an almost exact correspondence between the total votes and the seats assigned to parties. In the 1990s, this system was criticized because it was thought that it encouraged the fragmentation of parties, promoted instability in government, and prevented the voters from choosing directly the government. As a matter of fact, "one of the defining characteristics of Italian democracy during its first four decades was the large number of political parties. Throughout this period, there were at least seven significant parties, ranging from the far right to the left" (Bruneau et al., 2001, p. 70), even if one party, Christian Democracy (DC), often had the predominant position. Some minor parties that had not obtained as much as 5% of the total vote proved to be decisive in parliamentary alliances and in government coalitions. In this system, Italy has had weak center and center-left governments, or five-party governments (Lotti, 2002; Pasquino, 2002).

In 1993, after a referendum, Parliament voted an electoral reform based on a mixed system, that is, a plurality system with a proportional correction. The reform of the Senate elections, which was accomplished by abolishing some norms of the previous election laws, was initiated by the referendum of April 18, 1993. It was then completed on August 4, 1993, when Parliament passed Law 276. The reform of the Chamber of Deputies elections was also passed by Parliament on August 4, 1993, with Law 277, with the aim of applying the referendum principles to the Chamber. Three fourths of the members of the House and Senate are elected in single-member districts, whereas the rest are assigned by a proportional method based on the votes that parties receive in 27 regional constituencies.

The change in the electoral system came at a moment of crisis and of significant transformation in the political system, marking such a major break with the past that observers spoke of a transition to a "Second Republic." This great change represents the point of arrival of developments that brought about a substantial reduction of electoral choices related to subcultural or ideological bases. Along with these phenomena, there was an increase of disaffection toward traditional parties (Mannheimer & Sani, 1994). As one observer noted: "The deep social cleavages that strongly stabilized partisanship in the past have substantially eroded. In addition, function previously performed by the party organization appeared to be fulfilled by other instruments, such as television" (Sani & Segatti, 2001, p. 181).

In 1992, an inquiry by the public prosecutors of Milan uncovered a widespread system (called "Tangentopoli") of corruption and illicit financing of parties—a system that had involved many leaders governing Italy in previous decades (Bufacchi & Burgess, 2002). The forces representing the major political subcultures of the country, that is, the Catholic and the communist movement, disintegrated. Most historical parties disappeared from the scene and new forces appeared. The historical parties that disappeared from the political scene were the Socialist Party (PSI, founded in 1892), the Republican Party (PRI, 1895), the Communist Party (PCI, 1921), the Liberal Party (PLI, 1942), the Christian Democrats (DC, 1944), and the Social Democrat Party (PSDI, 1952).

In this context, the Northern League asserted itself as a "new, alternative, antisystem" party, with a manifesto based on the independence of northern Italy and the containment of immigration. There was also a second and more important novelty in the electoral line-up: *Forza Italia,* the party created in 1994 by Silvio Berlusconi, owner of a major editorial group (press, television, books, etc.). According to some observers, *Forza Italia* can be described as a "media-party" that, unlike those of the past, has neither a rooted organizational structure nor an ideological culture (Calise, 1996; Mazzoleni, 1995). It is a "light party," not territorially rooted and without structured internal communication and debate. As Mazzoleni (1998) described it, "Its inner hierarchy is similarly less structured.... However, *Forza Italia,* which is called 'the Premier's party', the media-party, has a strong highly-personalised leadership, taking its legitimacy from personal charisma, from the visibility assured by the media but also from the lack of an internal dialectic that can challenge it" (p. 69).

As a media-party, *Forza Italia* relies heavily on widespread communication activities (mostly in advertising) and the exploitation of the political marketing potentialities. The most frequently used medium is, of course, television. In January 1994, Berlusconi publicly declared that he was going to "enter the fray" in order to defend Italy from the Communist threat and to promote "a new Italian miracle-boom." For the launch of *Forza Italia,* he used a relentless advertising campaign to create awareness of his new party and to prepare for the first electoral test, the Parliamentary elections of 1994. In this election, only 2 months after its announced birth, the *Forza Italia* party got the most votes and the Berlusconi-headed coalition, which included two other parties, gained an absolute majority in the Chamber of Deputies.

According to Sani and Segatti (2001), this electoral earthquake of 1994 resulted in the following:

> [It] led to patterns of government formation that were decidedly different from those that characterized the First Republic throughout its four decades of existence. In contrast with the center-left to center-right coalitions of this period (which always included the centrists DC [Christian Democracy], and always excluded the principal parties occupying the left and right ends of the political continuum, the PCI and the MSI), and with the quasi-consociational practices of that period, especially the *lottizzazione,* which had given the DC, PCI, and PSI their own public television channels, the Berlusconi government included the post-fascist *Alleanza,* excluded the remnants of the DC, and adopted more majoritarian policies that had previously been embraced (attempting, for example, to dominate the public sector of television broadcasting completely). (p. 176)

However, the alliance between governing parties proved to be an unstable one. By the fall of 1994, the Berlusconi government was already in trouble and by the end of the year the Northern League left the coalition. After a caretaker government led by Lamberto Dini, in 1996 the president of the republic dissolved Parliament and called early elections. The parties of center-left united under the *Olive tree* coalition led by Romano Prodi and won the 1996 election, bringing the parties of the left to power.

This did not bring about more stability, however, but instead divisions within the center-left camp, especially between Rifondazione Comunista (a remnant of the old Communist Party) and the other members of the coalition. In 1998, Rifondazione decided to leave the parliamentary majority, causing the fall of the Prodi government. This was followed by weaker center-left governments led by D'Alema and Amato, which lasted until the spring of 2001 when elections were held once again. This time the center-right coalition (Alleanza Nazionale, Forza Italia, Northern League, and center-right parties) won the parliamentary elections. Thus, whereas for half a century Italy had been a democracy without alternation, in the brief span of 7 years government changed hands several times.

The electoral campaign of the 2001 elections was emblematic of the changes that have occurred in the last 10 years in Italy. Political marketing practices were extremely important—even for the Left, which in the past had been reluctant to use commercial techniques of communication. The leaders of the two major coalitions conducted a very personalized campaign—almost a "presidential one" à l'américaine—and used a variety of image-building strategies.

Television remained the most important medium, notwithstanding the restrictions on its use. After the election, there was an intense debate over the role played by television and the fairness of the information distributed to the public during the campaign (as we see later, the law regulates propaganda, but information hasn't strict rules). Accusations of biased coverage of the campaign by certain broadcasters were raised from both sides.

JOURNALISM AND POLITICS

Some features of current Italian journalism can only be understood by thinking about press history. This is because, from the beginning of its development, the Italian press has been characterized by two particular features: "literary criteria" (Murialdi, 1996) and its close link to politics. The literary criteria were apparent both in the use of elevated language and in a style oriented to elegance, even in a journalistic form, mainly directed toward a limited public. Today this practice proves to be argumentative, a style "which not only tries to recount events but also to give interpretation, comment, evaluation and consideration of the consequences. This approach has kept Italian journalism far away from the Anglo-Saxon model, which focuses on mere factual accounts" (Mancini, 2000, p. 20).

The primacy of politics in Italian journalism is due to the fact that, since its origins, the Italian press has been both a means of mobilization and a partisan voice. This phenomenon, which was reinforced during the Fascist period and later on during the Liberation period, partly continues today. "Italian journalism not only devotes a lot of space to politics; it is itself political journalism. It gives its opinion, it takes sides, as most of the single professionals do" (Mancini, 2000, p. 21).

The economic-structural bases of the literary and political qualities of Italian journalism are explained by the following facts. In Italy, there is no simple publisher, that is, someone who takes his or her profits only from publishing. Italian journalism is "historically an interventionist journalism in both senses: politically and economically" (Mancini, 1992, p. 10). This has happened because the main industrial state and private groups have become involved in journalism, publishing, and broadcasting (including television).

Some authors describe the current close link between journalism and politics, for both the printed press and television, as "backing up" or "parallelism." In this framework, laws that regulate the system play an important role. They defend not only press freedom and journalist independence, but also the correct working-out of electoral competition. The most important rules in both the press and television sectors deal mainly with (a) guaranteeing freedom of expression on the one hand, and the right to correct and pluralistic information on the other, (b) favoring transparency in the sector (including financial) and avoiding concentrations, (c) supporting the press with subsidies, and (d) regulating admittance to the journalistic profession and encouraging the introduction of professional ethical rules.

PRESS REGULATION

The judicial principle that has dominated the legislation since the end of fascist censorship is the right to information (or to news reporting), which is in accordance with the notion of press freedom as being the right of anyone practicing journalism. Indeed, Italy's Constitution recognizes press freedom as a basic value, and for this reason defends it with the following general rule concerning freedom of expression: "Everybody has the right to express his own thought freely in speech, writing and any other means of news transmission. Printing cannot be subjected to authorization or censorship" (Article 21).

The Constituent Assembly considered this topic so important that it immediately approved a law concerning printing (Law 47/1948). Here, precise obligations were established for people working in the sector in order to defend the right to information and news reporting.

The concern for journalistic independence and the defense of information and critical freedom also form the basic structure of the law established in 1963, which regulated access to journalism as a profession and indicated the requirements and methods for enrollment in the journalists' Register—regulation and admission were entrusted to the Journalists' Association (Law 69/1963). This law faithfully reflects mistrust of journalists as a class and shows how consensus was reached with this cooperative attitude adopted by the politicians of the time:

The very obvious consequence of this situation has been the failure to provide the association with a code of professional conduct.... The lack of such a code and the priority of the right to report news have created a vacuum in regulation. The law has tried to fill this vacuum each time the freedom of information as a right of journalists has come into conflict with other rights. (Papuzzi, 1998, p. 54)

The law established in 1948 has been changed over the years in order to provide efficient antitrust measures and to bring into existence a system of incentives and economic subsidies favoring journalistic publishing. At the same time, an effort has been made to deal with problems of transparency concerning press financing. For example, Law 416/1981, on the one hand, increases indirect subsidies to the press (fund for facilitating access to credit, tax-relief concessions, limits imposed on television advertising); before this time the press had largely been subsidized by direct or indirect payments (e.g., controlling the price of paper). It tries to guarantee financial transparency and avoid concentrations. On the other hand, the law of 1981 also established a guaranteeing authority, the Publishing Guarantor (watchdog), which would gain greater control and powers of sanctions with the television law of 1990, which is described later on.

With the evolution of the media, the necessity for anticoncentration norms for the press became urgent. Law 67/1987, for instance, intends to prevent any publisher from having a dominant position in the sector; that is, that through deeds of transfer, lease agreements, or credit ratings, as well as the transfer of shareholdings, an individual publishes or controls companies that publish dailies whose circulation in the previous year was 20% of the total newspaper circulation in Italy (or more than 50% in the same region or interregional area).

Law 223 on radio-television, described later, also introduces some limits for the processes of cross concentration in press and television. The latest law, Law 62 of 2001, regulates ownership and transparency, as well as doubles press subsidies.

THE REGULATION OF THE RADIO AND TELEVISION SECTORS

From the introduction of television in 1954 up until 1975, the TV system was characterized by a state monopoly exercised by a franchisee (RAI) under government control. Law 103/1975, New Norms on Broadcasting, was the first reform law of the television system. The prerequisite of the 1975 reform was the repeated intervention of the Constitutional Court, and especially Sentence 225, which described, as cited in Corasaniti (1992), the principles that every reform law affecting the state television system had to respect:

a) autonomy of directive organs of the franchisee as regards the power of the executive;
b) guarantee of impartiality of information;
c) recognition of Parliament's role in vigilance;
d) impartiality and respect of a professional code of conduct by journalists in the information field;
e) limitations of advertising profits so as not to harm the other information media;
f) guarantees of access for groups and associations (pluralism);
g) acknowledgement of the right to retrospective correction. (p. 191)

As previously mentioned, the criteria delineated by the Constitutional Court for the state television system were particularly concerned with the organization and the information activity of RAI, which had to respect *impartiality* and *political and social pluralism*. The Constitutional Court orientations were absorbed into Law 103/1975, which transfers, among other things, the central control of the aims, vigilance, and management of the state television service from the government to parliament. The law defines the state service as essential and of prominent general interest. It also determines the fundamental principles of the system: independence and impartiality open to the different political, social, and cultural trends present in the country. A specific "Parliamentary committee for the general aims and vigilance of television services" was created to realize these criteria and "given direct functions to ensure a real 'parliamentary government' of the service" (Corasaniti, 1992, pp. 191–192).

Law 103/1975 also provided for the creation of regional committees for the broadcasting service, with advisory remits for the regions, as regards:

• Regional broadcasting.
• The criteria of access to television for social groups.
• The right to retrospective correction.

On the explicit request of the Constitutional Court, Law 103/1975 was to be integrated through a subsequent regulation of the television system as a whole, that is, state and private. The new law was not passed until 1990, which means that for 15 years there was deregulation, or rather, a lack of effective regulation, which in a few years favored the transformation of the Italian television system from a monopoly regime to a mixed regime, strongly private based and subsequently competitive.

Because of this regulation vacuum, the end of the 1980s saw an intertwining of ownership in press, television, and advertising agencies; that is, concentration among the media developed. The Italian media scene, in the press, publishing, and television, is dominated by some groups that are real publishing giants. In the television sector, the most important are RAI and the Fininvest Group.

In the summer of 1990, the parliamentary debate on the law that regulates the television system, state and private, was concluded and Law 223/1990 was passed. Law 223/1990 gives a precise framework for concentration in the radio and television sector, fixing an average limit of the communication market resources that can be accumulated by individual economic entities. However, it puts limits on concentration between television and press dailies but not between television and periodicals. Additionally, the law recognized in radio and TV programs the character of general primary interest and defined the fundamental principles of the radio and television system, which are realized (a) with the participation of state and private entities, (b) in pluralism, impartiality, completeness, and objectivity of information, (c) in the openness to different opinions and political, social, cultural, and religious trends, and (d) in the respect of freedom and of the rights guaranteed by the Constitution.

The law transforms the Guarantor for publishing, created in 1981, into a Guarantor for broadcasting and publishing, with a remit including inspection, administration, and sanction functions with regard to the companies that work in the radio and television sector. Finally, some regional organisms with advisory functions were created, as well as the council of viewers and listeners.

The present system is composed of the radio and television state service (RAI) and a great number of both national and local private radio and television channels. RAI is a limited company that is totally state controlled. It exercises its functions based on a 20-year contract and a service agreement by which it carries out the contract, drawn up with the government (Ministry of Communications). The RAI and the private radio and television stations have to respect some fundamental principles such as pluralism, impartiality, and fairness of information. Vigilance and control over the RAI are exercised by the parliamentary committee for aims of and vigilance in the radio and television sector. Private broadcasters, national and local, are subject to the vigilance and control of the Authority for Guarantees in Communications.

THE REGULATORY AUTHORITIES

The parliamentary committee for the aims of and vigilance over radio and television services was created to let parliament supervise broadcasting activities, especially concerning information, which is considered particularly important for a democratic system. The committee is composed of 40 members (20 deputies and 20 senators) appointed by the speakers of the two chambers, on the basis of the suggestions of the parliamentary groups, so as to ensure proportional representation. The committee is renewed at the end of each legislature and wields its powers till the first meeting of the two new chambers. The committee's activity is devoted to the RAI and consists of general policy suggestions, resolutions, and detailed indications. The committee gives detailed indications when there are political events (i.e., elections),.through decisions about political discussion programs (TV and radio) so as to guarantee adequate propaganda time to all political and social forces according to the criterion of pluralist information. The committee aims to guarantee that all the opinions present in society can be expressed in radio and television programs. To guarantee the presence of all voices and opinions in society, the subcommittee for access regulates the access programs that RAI broadcasts. These informational programs are reserved for associations or bodies that address particular areas of political, social, or cultural interest, ultimately providing them access to TV programs where they can express their points of view.

The Authority for Guarantees in Communications, created by Law 249/ 1997, has its remit in telecommunications, television, and the press sector. The Authority is independent of any other institutional organ and each year it presents a report on its activity to the prime minister and to parliament. The organizational structure is made up of the president of the Authority and the following:

1. The council, composed of the president and eight committee members, whose activity concerns technological evolution, licenses and authorizations, antitrust powers, and cooperation with the parliamentary committee. The Authority president is appointed by the prime minister; the eight committee members are elected by the Senate and the Chamber of Deputies. The job lasts 7 years with no reappointments allowed.

2. The committee for infrastructures and networks, which has responsibility for the radio-wavelength spectrum (also regarding the national plan for sharing frequencies, decoder standards, etc.), interconnection between and access to telecommunication infrastructures, and the communication operators' register.

3. The committee for services and products, whose responsibilities concern above all the audiovisual field: services and products, program content, the state service franchisee, and different media audience shares. Each committee has a president and four members.

Referring to program content, "the law gives the Committee for services and products some responsibilities characterised by the need to reconcile the freedoms involved in broadcasting with the protection of values consti-

tutionally guaranteed, mostly in favour of the viewers and listeners" (Filippeschi, 1998, p. 241). These responsibilities concern advertising, protection
of minors and of language minorities, and pluralism. The Committee carries
out monitoring of radio and TV programs; it controls the correct publication and transmission of polls in the media, according to the stated rules.
The auxiliary bodies of the Authority are the National Council of Users
(viewers and listeners) and the Regional Committees for Communications.
These committees are functional bodies to which the Authority can delegate some of its responsibilities.

FURTHER CHARACTERISTICS OF THE RADIO AND TELEVISION SYSTEM

The Italian television system has some particular features, the first being
structural. In the national television channels, two entities have a very important position as regards the television network, such that everybody
speaks of a duopoly: the state television (RAI) and the commercial group
Mediaset. However, local broadcasters are characterized by their plurality:
Across the nation, there are hundreds of local television stations, with vari-
able and often very small audiences. In many cases, these television stations do not succeed in collecting enough advertising revenues to consolidate themselves and to expand. Consequently they have difficulty reaching
acceptable quality standards. A second feature of the Italian television system and, at a general level, the whole media system, is that it suffers from
the heritage of the close relationship between journalism and politics that
has regulated information for decades. In speaking about this phenomenon,
some authors have called it "a collateral approach" or "political parallelism," referring to this specific function of a mass of information at different
levels—organizational, economic, professional, thematic, and ideological—
which expresses itself in substantial support of the political institutional
class, more or less explicit, more or less marked (Mazzoleni, 1998).

As previously mentioned, Italian journalism is interventionist and the
principal industrial groups in the country have entered the field of journalistic publishing, thus favoring this strict relationship between politics and
information. As a consequence of this collateral attitude, electoral television communication was dominated by so-called *party logic,* as opposed to
media logic. The lack of a clear separation between information and politics
was particularly evident in the RAI in the 1980s. The passage of RAI control
responsibilities from government to Parliament (Law 103/75) introduced
the procedure of party distribution of TV top management between majority parties and the most representative groups in opposition (*lottizzazione,*

the share-out among parties). However, as Mancini (1992) pointed out, "the RAI, with its problems of patronage, i.e. 'share-out of top jobs,' is only the most transparent case of a procedure that has always made the journalist a political figure, and often a party one" (p. 11).

The aforementioned revolution caused by "Tangentopoli" has produced some profound changes not only in the party arena and the electoral framework, but also in the information field favoring some interesting emancipation attempts in the media system. Nevertheless, the present situation might be seen as characterized by the presence of some signs of continuity with the past, at least in the electoral campaigns. In particular, many observed the following:

> [The electoral campaigns of 2001] marked an important turning point in the crisis of Italian journalism, especially in television. Some people think that we are already at the end of a cycle that started at the beginning of the nineties, when the meeting between the innovative impulse of neo-television and the increasing wave of anti-politics had made a success of TV panel discussions (the electronic squares), opening a period of new relationships between politics and TV journalism. This period was characterised by the new capacity of journalism to exert its influence and by the progressive strengthening of the communication apparatus against the background of crisis in the traditional parties. (Roncarolo, 2002, pp. 51–52)

The developments in television, with its particular characteristics, were marked by a professional mixing of communication and politics, as well as by the long RAI monopoly and, especially, the lack of laws regulating broadcasting in the private and state system.

MEDIA COVERAGE OF ELECTIONS

Up until 1993, "the system of election campaign organisation was rather simple and approximate" (Bettinelli, 1995, p. 29). The regulations for this system comprised quite a large corpus of laws. Law 515 of December 10, 1993, on the regulation of election campaigns for the Chamber of Deputies and the Senate of the Republic answered the need to update the current regulations, whose framework, dating back to Law 212 of 1956, "was no longer considered suitable as a valid system of reference for regulating the matter" (Camera dei Deputati, 1995, p. 3).

Essentially, the new regulations were established for two reasons: the in-depth revision of the election system for both chambers, to be reformed mainly with a majority uninominal approach, and the adoption, in election campaigns, of the new means of mass communication, whose specific qualities had been almost completely neglected in the standing rules. Law 515/93 introduced substantial innovations:

1. It foresaw a detailed regulation of access to the media by candidates and political groups.
2. It replaced a series of limits on "election propaganda by means of adverts in dailies and periodicals, TV ads and other forms of radio-TV publicity" (section 2, par. 1) as well as on opinion polls which were forbidden "during the 15 days before the election date and until voting was over" (section 6, par. 1).
3. It regulated—and still does—a very important aspect of the question of the financing of election expenses (besides fixing the maximum for each candidate's expenses, Law 515/93 asserts that those expenses must be quantified in specific statements).
4. It also regulated private TV channels, both national and local.
5. It entrusted the guarantor for radio-TV and publishing with the job of defining the rules to be observed by communicators in broadcasting and publishing (those responsible for dailies and periodicals, franchisees, etc.) and of applying administrative and financial sanctions whenever norms and standing regulations were violated.

The elections of March 27, 1994, showed the limits of the regulations for election campaigns contained in the recent Law 515/93 and in particular showed that there was an "uncovered" period between the date fixed for election meetings and the official start of the campaign 30 days before voting. During this period, it was possible "by exploiting the media, above all radio and TV, to acquire dominant resources and positions" with prejudice to the equality of opportunity asserted for all contestants (Bettinelli, 1995, p. 20). Given the absence of regulations applying to this case, the Guarantor, who, as we said earlier, by Law 515/93, had powers to discipline and sanction, could only invite the private channels to apply, "in a virtually extended way," the rules of Law 515/93 (Bettinelli, 1995, p. 20). The Guarantor's invitation was ignored. As Valastro (2000) noted:

> The process of reform of the rules for political and electoral communication may be taken as beginning in 1995 when the Dini government presented a bill aimed at substituting the contents of law 515/93 (Bill A.C. 2065, developed by the Gambino-La Pergola-Crisci committee and presented to the Chamber 20th February 1995). But this initiative had no follow-up. Indeed, in the midst of parliamentary delays in approving this bill and seeing that there was an imminent election campaign (voting 23rd April 1995), the Dini government had to have recourse to a law-decree, 20th March, 1995, n°83, stating "Urgent rules for equality of access to means of information during electoral and referen-

dum campaigns", which partly repeated the contents of Bill n° 2065. The polemics that accompanied the government decree, and particularly the recourse to an emergency procedure, hindered its passing as a law despite repeated attempts to push it through. (p. 31)

Thus the system of *par condicio* (equal treatment) was set up (introduced by the so-called Gambino decree-law). This system answered the need to revise the rules of Law 515/93, which was considered incomplete and defective as regards the timeliness of corrective intervention and the need for an incisive framework for sanctions. One can obtain an interesting indication of the *par condicio* problems by going through the relevant decree-laws (d.-l.). For example, the d.-l. 19 of January 16, 1996, repeated the following obsolete decree-laws: d.-l. 83 of March 20, 1995; d.-l. 182 of May 19, 1995; d.-l. 289 of July 18, 1995; d.-l. 386 of September 18, 1995; d.-l. 488 of November 18, 1995.

The relationship between the media system and political questions at both election times and normal times is presently controlled by Law 28/2000, titled "Instructions for Equality of Access to Means of Information During Election and Referendum Campaigns and for Political Communication." The parliamentary progress of this law, which came into force at the time of the local elections and referendum of spring 2000, was accompanied, as outlined previously, by a long, heated debate, due to the intrinsic problems of the matter as well as to the distinctions between political positions.

There is almost universal agreement on the need for a legislative solution to this issue, from sections 21 and 49 of the Constitution. However, an argument commenced immediately over the constitutional acceptability of the "solutions that, concretely, law n° 28/2000 has taken over" (Caretti, 2000, p. 14). In particular, questions were asked as to "the superabundance of rules leading the legislators to fix limits and vetoes which seem difficult to apply and control and thus difficult for fixing sanctions" and "doubts were raised about that part of the law which seems to concern watching over the impressionability of the electorate when subjected to particular techniques of political propaganda," that is, independently controlled messages (Caretti, 2000, p. 14). It is worth mentioning that the opportunity for a fresh intervention by the legislators was suggested at the same time as the new law was coming into force.

THE LAW OF 2000 ON POLITICAL COMMUNICATION

Law 28/2000 regulates the relationship between media systems and political matters at both election and normal times so as to "guarantee equality of treatment and impartiality for all political matters" (section 1, par. 1). The extension of the regulation to nonelection periods is, as Zaccaria (2000) stressed, an important novelty, which "prefigures the formation of some bodies of general importance" (p. 10). Law 28/2000 specifies the three types of forms of expression that are allowed: *political communication, independently controlled political messages,* and *information.*

Political Communication

Audiovisual political communication is defined as "radio and television broadcasting of programmes containing political opinions and judgements." Concerning this, we must state that according to some writers, by using the term political communication, "the legislators only wished to adopt a new term" to indicate what previous regulation had dealt with as propaganda (Gobbo, 2000, p. 21). Forms in which political communication can be expressed are also foreseen, such as party political broadcasts, debates, roundtable discussions, the presentation of contrasting political programs, confrontations, interviews, and every other kind of broadcast where the expression of political opinions and judgments is important. Radio stations and TV channels must ensure, impartially for all political persons and matters, access to political information and communication; national radio and TV franchisees are compelled to offer political programs that are free for candidates and parties.

Independently Controlled Messages (Free or Paid): A Kind of Publicity?

The political independently controlled message, free or paid, is, together with political communication, a new genre, regulated precisely and rigorously. It is compulsory for state broadcasters to broadcast these messages whereas it is optional for private broadcasters; national channels may only broadcast free messages whereas local channels, once they have also offered free program time for political communication, may sell time at a 50% discount on current prices for advertisements. Independently controlled messages are not calculated as part of the mass of normal advertisements but they must conform to precise rules: They must show the expression of a political policy or opinion; they must last from 1 to 3 minutes on TV and from 30 to 90 seconds on radio; they must not interrupt programs; they must be placed separately and be broadcast in suitable magazine-programs; nobody may broadcast more than one message in the same program; each of these transmissions must bear the title "free independently controlled message" or "paid independently controlled message."

Moreover, as Besi (2000) pointed out, the law introduces an explicit relationship between political communication and independently controlled messages because on national radio and television, channel time for the messages must not exceed 25% of the total length of political communication programs in one week and in the same band of viewing time; furthermore, there must not be more than two magazine programs during each day's program schedule. Program space for independently controlled messages (on an equal-treatment basis for political matters and persons) in each magazine program is divided by drawing lots. The parliamentary vigilance committee and the Authority for guarantees in communications, each with its own remit, set up rules and adopt eventual further regulations for controlling political communication and independently controlled messages.

The aforementioned information about independently controlled messages raises questions as to the relationship between these messages and normal advertisements. In this respect, one can suggest that by introducing a new formula, that is, the independently controlled message, together with a precise definition of its possible contents and limits, the legislators wanted to "ban advertising in its most penetrating forms so as to encourage a more reasoned and reasonable form of advertising" (Besi, 2000, p. 66). Starting from a judgment, according to which independently controlled messages must not be like commercial advertisements, but should, rather, accompany political ones (Court of Cassation, Sentence 477/98), Besi singled out the main factors that the two forms have in common: The aim of both is the creation of consensus; there is an absence of discussion; the broadcast is made at the client's request. Besi also hypothesized that the messages are "less persuasive than real adverts not so much because of their brevity but because they are placed within a magazine programme. This placement largely reduces or even wipes out the effectiveness a message may possess" (p. 68).

A novelty introduced by Law 28/2000 is that besides fixing the start of the campaign on the day when the electoral meetings begin, that is, 15 days before the time stipulated in the previous law, the campaign period is divided into phases. These phases are tied to: (a) the start of political communication in its anticipated forms (the date for calling election meetings) and the broadcasting of independently controlled messages (the date for presenting candidates); and (b) the allotment of broadcasting time among political parties. As regards this allotment, which is regulated by the parliamentary committee and the Authority within the limits of their remit, the following points are articulated:

- Between the calling of election meetings and the date for presenting candidates, broadcasting times are allotted among the politicians and parties present in the entities to be reelected and among those of the two chambers of the national Parliament or the European assembly.

- Between the date for presenting candidates and the closure of the election campaign, the time available on air or on TV is allotted on the principle of equal opportunity between the competing groups of parties (eventual coalitions) and the electoral lists of candidates for constituencies involving at least a quarter of the electors registered on the relevant voting lists—with the exception of the eventual presence of candidates representing language minorities.

- For ballots or referenda, the time allotment is on an equal basis among the candidates for a ballot, as it is for the different approaches to a referendum.

Another notable factor of Law 28/2000 can be found in the criteria controlling the broadcasting of independently controlled messages on local channels. Above all, as opposed to the national channels, local ones may broadcast paid political messages at both normal and election times. Second, the local channels that broadcast free messages during election times can ask for state reimbursement. The radio stations retain at least a third of the sum given. As Signori (2000) pointed out, the reimbursements are without doubt modest but "this shows the legislators' wish not to make the fact that the message is free for the clients (a fact that is its indispensable basis) meaningless as a gesture" (p. 90). Another rule is that the total time devoted to paid, independently controlled messages must, in the space of the week, be equal to that of the free ones.

Information

Let us turn our attention now to the third form of expression addressed in Law 28/2000, that is, information. The legislators acknowledged that the rules for political communication do not apply at normal times to information programs (newscasts, in-depth surveys, investigative programs, etc.), because the information proposed to be disseminated by a program maker using his or her own approach "is free and cannot be subject to ties either of content or of manner" (Besi, 2000, p. 53). In any case, for the time of the election campaign, the law states that the parliamentary committee and the Authority have to define the specific criteria to which, in information programs, state and private franchisees must conform. Moreover, it establishes the following:

- In any broadcast, it is forbidden to give, even indirectly, indications of how to vote or show one's preference in an eventual election.

- Producers and presenters must behave correctly and impartially in running programs so as not to influence, even surreptitiously, the electors' free choice.
- In broadcasts that are the responsibility of a specific newspaper or journal, the presence of candidates, representatives of parties or political movements, Members of Parliament (MPs), and members of regional juntas, councils or local bodies must be limited exclusively to the need to ensure completeness and impartiality of information. The presence of such persons is forbidden in all other broadcasts.

On the basis of rules implementing Law 28/2000, issued by the parliamentary committee and Authority during the local elections and referendums in the year 2000, "there remains a general compulsion to impartiality which marks the information broadcasts of RAI (the state radio-TV service) and of the private channels and stations. One can also say that TV and radio newscasts are free of specific regulation" (Besi, 2000, p. 120).

The political experience of the local election campaign in 2000, and particularly in relation to *Porta a Porta* ("Door to Door," a RAI discussion program), showed that it was not always easy to tell the difference between information programs and political communication. In the case of *Porta a Porta,* the vigilance Committee and the Authority gave two different interpretations—the first declared it an information program and the second a type of political communication. This difficulty in making a sharp, precise distinction between information programs and political communication is probably one of the weak links in the legislation, posing, above all, problems as to sanctions.

As regards the press, Law 28/2000 asserts that at election times, publishers and editors of dailies and periodicals can distribute election messages either free or paid. Moreover, the law:

- Specifies the allowed forms of political message.
- Imposes on publishers who intend to distribute political messages the duty of giving immediate communication of their intentions so as to allow candidates and political groups access under conditions of equality.
- Specifies that communications must be made according to the methods and contents laid down by the Authority.

The allowed forms of political message are:

- Announcements of debates, roundtable discussions, lectures, and speeches.

- Presentation of the manifestos of electoral lists, groups of candidates, or lone candidates.
- Articles comparing various candidates.

POLITICAL POLLS

Concerning political and electoral polls, Law 28/2000 gives the Authority alone the power to impose criteria for their publication. At normal times, the poll results can only be published if they are accompanied by precise indications such as who conducted the poll, who requested it and paid for it, the sampling criteria, the methods for collecting information and the final data processing, the number of people interviewed, the questions answered, the percentage of no-answers to each question, and the date of the poll. During the campaign period, and precisely 15 days before the day of the elections, it is forbidden to publish or broadcast results of polls on the eventual vote and on the electors' political preferences.

SANCTIONS

Law 28/2000 gives the Authority the job of prosecuting (on its own account or on the basis of accusations from those involved) those who transgress the law or the rules laid down by the Authority and the vigilance committee. The Authority, also using the relevant regional committees for communications, local inspectors of the Communications Ministry, and the Revenue Guard Corps, sets up a procedure of complex, precisely organized interventions that must be brought to a conclusion in a very short time (brief preliminary investigation, rebuttal of facts, eventual acceptance of counterdeductions within 24 hours after the accusation, sanctions applied within 48 hours after the ascertained violation). The sanctions are intended to reassert the balance among the political parties.

To conclude, one should stress that Law 28/2000 was subject to counterappeals in the course of ordinary administrative jurisprudence—similarly, the question of constitutional legitimacy as regards the *par condicio* was raised in the Constitutional Court.

CONCLUSION

Reviewing the information herein, it is clear that the two latest laws on media election campaigns—Laws 515/93 and 28/2000—have given concrete answers to single specific aspects of political propaganda, such as pegging expenses for election campaigns, making such expense statements transparent, defining the parameters to give equal rights of access to information media, and excluding the forms that are too pervasive in communication. Despite such legislative interventions, some writers think that "the present norms still seem full of gaps as regards the framework of not strictly political thought . . . , a state of 'normative uncertainty' still weighs on the information field, hindering the full realization of authentic news, cultural and so political pluralism" (Gobbo, 2000, p. 28).

The persistence of general problems depends, at least partly, on the delay in law making (remember that private TV was regulated for the first time in 1990). However, there are still other gray zones, including those of organization. Concerning this, it is worth recollecting that current regulation gives the remit of controlling information matters to various bodies without, however, foreseeing adequate means of connection among these organs (Cimenti, 2000). As regards this question, there are various examples available. At present, vigilance and control are the responsibility of two institutions, the parliamentary vigilance committee for RAI and the Authority for Warranties in Communication, which, besides dealing with private broadcasters is also active as regards state franchising. And again, the imprecise regulation of the relationship between the Ministry of Communications and the Authority leads to an overlapping of competence as regards franchising. Added to this uncertainty in regulation and to the inefficiencies in organization, we must mention at least two further problems, that is, (a) the makeup of national TV schedules, which is characterized by programs that cannot always be easily defined as to genre and form, and (b) the nature of programs with political guests and representatives.

As regards the latter aspect, it must be said that rather than being limited to information and political communication programs, the presence of political actors on TV seems widespread in programs of various types (sport, entertainment, talk shows, etc.). This fact makes the monitoring (for vigilance and control), which is in the Authority's brief, extremely difficult and complicated. Elsewhere in this chapter, we referred to the role of TV anchors and presenters and their importance in information programs (see Further Characteristics of the Radio and Television System).

Moreover, concerning the relationship on television between media and politics, one must stress that there is a heated debate in progress about the role of the aforementioned TV anchors in information programs—with special attention being paid to the RAI, the state TV service. This criticism came out strongly during the 2001 election campaign. It was directed at two programs, which had become representative, whose presenters were accused of partisanship. Because, understandably, such debate deals with important general principles, such as freedom of speech and pluralism, it would be wrong to limit the discussion to single broadcasts.

TABLE 1.1
General Legal Obligations of the Mass Media
for the Transmitting of Political Material

---

1) POLITICAL INFORMATION: Newscasts, in-depth surveys, investigative programs, etc., that are the responsibility of a specific newspaper or journal.

General criteria	Impartiality and equal treatment for all political persons and matters. Information proposed by a program maker with his or her own approach is free and cannot be subject to ties either of content or of manner. The presence of candidates, representatives of parties or political movements, MPs, and members of regional juntas, councils, or local bodies must be limited exclusively to the need to ensure completeness and impartiality of information.
Obligations:	
Radio and TV	It is forbidden to give, even indirectly, indications of how to vote or show one's own preference in an eventual election. Producers and presenters must behave correctly and impartially.
Press	No specific rules.

---

2) POLITICAL COMMUNICATION (PROPAGANDA): Party political broadcasts, debates, roundtable discussions, the presentation of contrasting political programs, confrontations, interviews, and "every other kind of broadcast where the expression of political opinions and judgments is important."

General criteria	Impartiality and equal access for all political persons and matters.
Obligations:	
Public radio and TV	Compulsory; free.
Private national radio and TV	Compulsory; free.
Private local radio and TV	Facultative; free.
Press	No specific rules.

---

3) POLITICAL ADVERTISING

Obligations:	
Radio and TV	Not permitted.
Press	Permitted with restrictions (see Item 5).

---

4) TV INDEPENDENTLY CONTROLLED MESSAGES: Messages that show the expression of a political policy or opinion. They don't interrupt programs; they are placed separately and are broadcast in suitable magazine programs. They last from 1 to 3 minutes on TV and from 30 to 90 seconds on radio; each of these transmissions has the title "free independently controlled message" or "paid independently controlled message."

General criteria	Equal access.
Obligations:	
Public radio and TV	Compulsory; free (channel time for the messages must not exceed 25% of the total length of political-communication programs in one week and in the same band of viewing time; there must not be more than two magazine programs during each day's program schedule).

(Continued)

TABLE 1.1
(Continued)

Private national radio and TV	Facultative; free ((channel time for the messages must not exceed 25% of the total length of political-communication programs in one week and in the same band of viewing time; there must not be more than two magazine programs during each day's program schedule).
Private local radio and TV	Facultative; free and paid (once they have also offered free program time for political communication). Sell time at a 50% discount on current prices for advertisements. The channels that broadcast free messages during election times can ask for state reimbursement. Local channels may broadcast paid political independently controlled messages at both normal and election times, only if they have transmitted free messages. The total time devoted to paid messages must, in the space of the week, be equal to that of the free ones.

5) POLITICAL MESSAGES IN THE PRESS: Announcements of debates, roundtable discussions, lectures, speeches; presentation of the manifestos of electoral lists, groups of candidates, or lone candidates; articles comparing various candidates.

General criteria	Equal access.
Obligations	Facultative. Free and paid.
	Publishers who intend to distribute political messages have the duty of giving immediate communication of their intentions so as to allow candidates and political groups access in conditions of equality. Communications must be made according to the methods and contents laid down by the Authority.

6) POLITICAL POLLS

General criteria	The poll results can only be published if they are accompanied by precise indications: who conducted the poll, who requested it and paid for it, the sampling criteria, the methods for collecting information and the final data processing, the number of people interviewed, the questions answered, the percentage of no-answers to each question, the date of the poll.

Obligations	
Radio, TV, and the press	15 days before the day of the elections, it is forbidden to publish or broadcast results of polls on the eventual vote and on the electors' political preferences.

7) OTHER RADIO AND TV PROGRAMS

General criteria	The presence of candidates, representatives of parties or political movements, MPs, members of regional juntas, councils, or local bodies is forbidden in all other broadcasts during electoral period.

ACKNOWLEDGMENTS

Teresa Perrucci is responsible for the sections on authorities, the characteristics of radio and television, media coverage, and the review of the law of 2000. Marina Villa is responsible for the sections on the Italian political system, the regulation of the press and of the radio and television sector, journalism and politics, and Table 1.1. The authors would like to thank Giacomo Sani for his constructive comments on the first section of the chapter.

REFERENCES

Besi, A. (2000). Commento analitico alla legge 22 febbraio 2000, n. 28 [Analytic comment on the law 22 February 2000, n. 28]. *DRT, 1,* January–March, 44–56.

Bettinelli, E. (1995). *Par condicio: Regole, opinioni, fatti* [Par condicio: Rules, opinions, facts]. Torino, Italy: Einaudi.

Bruneau, T. S., Diamandouros, N. P., Gunther, R., Lijphart, A., Morlino, L., & Brooks, R. A. (2001). *Democracy, southern European style.* In N. P. Diamandouros & R. Gunther (Eds.), *Parties, politics, and democracy in the new southern Europe* (pp. 16–82). Baltimore: Johns Hopkins University Press.

Bufacchi, V., & Burgess, S. (2002). *L'Italia contesa: da Mani Pulite a Tangentopoli* [Italy contended: From Mani Pulite to Tangentopoli]. Rome, Italy: Carocci.

Calise, M. (1996). *Il partito mediale* [The media party]. In S. Bentivegna (Ed.), *Comunicare politica nel sistema dei media* [Communicating politics in the media system] (pp. 215–236). Genova, Italy: Costa & Nolan.

Camera dei Deputati–Servizio studi. (1995). *Parità di accesso ai mezzi di informazione durante le campagne elettorali* [Equal access to information media during electoral campaigns] (A.C. 2065–1663–1717), n. 204, XII legislatura–March.

Caretti, P. (2000). Introduzione [Introduction]. *DRT, 1,* January–March, 13–15.

Cimenti, A. (2000). *Informazione e televisione. La libertà vigilata* [Information and television. Freedom under surveillance]. Rome: Laterza.

Corasaniti, G. (1992). *Vecchie e nuove regole giuridiche per la professione* [Old and new jurisdiction for the journalistic profession]. In F. Chiarenza, G. Corasaniti, & P. Mancini (Eds.), *Il giornalismo e le sue regole. Un'etica da ritrovare* [Journalism and its rules] (pp. 173–224). Milan, Italy: ETASLIBRI.

Filippeschi, F. (1998). *La nuova Autorità per le garanzie nelle comunicazioni* [The new Authority for Guarantees in Communications]. In R. Zaccaria (Ed.), *Diritto dell'informazione e della comunicazione* [Information and communication law] (pp. 234–248). Padova, Italy: Cedam.

Gobbo, M. (2000). *Par condicio. DRT, 1,* January–March, 15–31.

Lotti, L. (2002). *I partiti della Repubblica* [The Republican parties]. Firenze, Italy: Le Monnier.

Mancini, P. (1992). La nuova struttura del sistema dell'informazione giornalistica [The new structure of journalistic information system]. In F. Chiarenza, G. Corasaniti, & P. Mancini (Eds.), *Il giornalismo e le sue regole. Un'etica da ritrovare* [Journalism and its rules] (pp. 156–172). Milan, Italy: ETASLIBRI.

Mancini, P. (2000). *Il sistema fragile* [The fragile system]. Rome: Carocci.

Mannheimer, R., & Sani, G. (1994). *La rivoluzione elettorale* [The electoral revolution]. Milan, Italy: Anabasi.

Mazzoleni, G. (1995). Towards a videocracy? Italian political communication at a turning point. *European Journal of Communication, X,* 3, 291–319.

Mazzoleni, G. (1998). *La comunicazione politica* [Political communication]. Bologna, Italy: Il Mulino.

Murialdi, P. (1996). *Storia del giornalismo italiano* [Italian journalism history]. Torino, Italy: Gutemberg.

Papuzzi, A. (1998). *Professione giornalista* [Profession: Journalist]. Rome: Donzelli.

Pasquino, G. (2002). *Il sistema politico italiano* [The Italian political system]. Bologna, Italy: University Press.

Roncarolo, F. (2002). Fra autoreferenzialità e guerriglia mediale. La campagna elettorale 2001 nella stampa quotidiana [Between self-reference and media guerrilla warfare. The 2001 electoral campaign]. *Comunicazione Politica, 3*(1), Spring, 51–79.

Sani, G., & Segatti, P. (2001). Antiparty politics and the restructuring the Italian party system. In N. P. Diamandouros & R. Gunther (Eds.), *Parties, politics, and democracy in the new southern Europe* (pp. 153–182). Baltimore: Johns Hopkins University Press.

Signori, N. (2000). Commento analitico alla legge 22 febbraio 2000, n. 28 [Analytic comment to the law 22 February 2000, n. 28]. *DRT, 1,* January–March, 85–114.

Valastro, A. (2000). L'iter normativo della disciplina di riforma della comunicazione politica sui mezzi di informazione [The normative process of the reform law on political communication in information media]. *DRT, 1,* January–March, 31–33.

Zaccaria, R. (Ed.). (1998). *Diritto dell'informazione e della comunicazione* [Information and communication law]. Padova, Italy: Cedam.

Zaccaria, R. (2000). Premessa [Introduction]. *DRT, 1,* January–March, 9–10.

2

United States of America

Lynda Lee Kaid
Clifford A. Jones

The conduct of modern elections in the United States of America guarantees that the relationship between media and politics is a symbiotic one. An informed electorate is not possible without information, and information is the business of the media. Lance Bennett (1996) described the significant role that the news media play in our system of governance and pointed out that the media actually control "democracy's most important product: political information" (p. xii). To understand candidates and their messages, citizens rely on the media. As democratic theory suggests (Berelson, 1966; Kelley, 1960), a prime requirement for self-governance is the ability of citizens to make informed decisions; and to make these decisions—such as who we will elect to be the leader of our nation—we need relevant information.

Though the media are conduits of information in a modern democracy, they are much more than simple purveyors of messages. In the American system, media election content provided directly by candidates, parties, and interest groups is an important aspect of the media's role in democracy. The media also play an important role as the source of independent election information, as they seek to provide the electorate with objective information about the political process and its major actors.

In this chapter, we describe this multifaceted process, a process in which both media and candidates/parties have potentially equal access to information outlets and where there is a constant struggle for supremacy in the "marketplace of ideas."

BACKGROUND AND CONTEXT OF MEDIA
AND ELECTIONS IN THE UNITED STATES

The United States has experienced a proliferation in the number and type of media. There are now approximately 1,600 daily newspapers, over 7,000 weekly newspapers, some 11,000 magazines and journals, 12,500 radio stations, and 1,500 television stations (Franklin, Anderson, & Cate, 2000).

Most voters derive the majority of their information about candidates, issues, and elections from television, and only limited numbers of voters rely primarily on information from newspapers or other print media, particularly in national elections. During the recent national election in 2000, the three primary networks' (ABC, NBC, CBS) nightly news programs collectively devoted 17 hours and 8 minutes to coverage during the primary season (January 1 to June 5), 13 hours and 25 minutes during the "hot phase" of the general election campaign (September 4 to November 6), and 21 hours 30 minutes during the post-election period (November 8 to December 12) (Center for Media and Public Affairs, 2000). This ranged from 4 minutes to about 12 minutes per night per network out of a nightly newscast of 30 minutes. Increasingly, voters in the United States also rely on cable news networks and on newscasts on local television stations for their political information ("TV Viewership," 1996).

Political participation in any governmental system can take many forms. However, voter turnout in elections is an important measure of the level of political engagement in any democracy. In the United States, election turnout levels were disappointingly low in the last half of the 20th century. Voter turnout in the 1996 election (48.8%) was the nation's lowest rate of participation since 1924 (Skiba, 1996). Although the 2000 elections turnout rate was somewhat higher, only 51% of the eligible electorate cast their ballots in the historic race (Gans, 2000).

Voting, however, is but one measure of civic participation. Putnam (1995) argued that "by almost any measure, Americans' direct engagement in politics and government has fallen steadily and sharply over the last generation, despite the fact that average levels of education—the best individual level predictor of political participation—have risen sharply throughout this period" (p. 68). This decline in civic participation has been accompanied by an increase in levels of political cynicism and distrust in government (Lipset & Schneider, 1987; Miller, 1974; *The Washington Post*/Kaiser Family Foundation/Harvard University Survey Project, 1997). However, political observers have noted that the September 11, 2001, terrorist attacks on the United States resulted in a dramatic increase in levels of government trust (Sander & Putnam, 2002). It is, of course, not clear how strong this reversal trend will be, how long it will continue, and whether it will result in an increase in turnout levels for subsequent presidential and other elections.

POLITICAL AND ELECTORAL SYSTEM STRUCTURE

The United States is a federal system of government taking the form of a republican democracy. The national or Federal government has the basic power to regulate elections for Federal office, and the 50 states regulate elections for state office, subject to U.S. constitutional requirements, with the autonomy of counties, municipalities, and other local governmental units varying according to the legal provisions in force in the respective states.

In practice, even Federal elections are administered by the states subject to legal requirements that Federal law may impose with regard to elections for Federal office. Most states administer elections on a countywide basis with the casting of ballots (via various manual, mechanical, or electronic means) and actual counting being carried out by voting subdivisions known as precincts, of which there are about 186,000. In some states, ballots, procedures, and voting methods are uniform for all counties; in others, each county has discretion concerning, for example, which vote-counting system—paper ballots, punch-card machines, mechanical-lever machines, optical scanning, or direct electronic recording equipment—to employ, choosing from among those systems specified by the state.

The only Federal offices for which citizens vote on a national basis are the President and Vice President, who seek election as a team for a 4-year term. Even this choice is not truly a direct election in that voters actually select "electors" in each state who then, as members of the Electoral College, cast their ballots for president. This system and its implications are described in more detail later. The national legislature, known as the United States Congress, is bicameral and is comprised of the U.S. Senate and the U.S. House of Representatives. There are 100 senators, 2 from each of the 50 states. The House is composed of 435 representatives who are apportioned among the states according to population. A decennial national census is taken (most recently in 2000), and House seats are adjusted following the census to account for population shifts. This reapportionment process is under way now with some states gaining seats and others losing seats in accordance with the census results.

The citizens of each state vote (on a statewide basis) for that state's two senators (whose 6-year terms are staggered so that both seats are not normally open in the same year). Each state is divided into House districts, and the citizens of each district vote only for their own district's representative. The term of a House member is 2 years, and the terms are not staggered, so that all House members seek reelection every 2 years. Federal elections take place in November of even-numbered years. In the 2004 Federal election, one third of Senate seats will be on the ballot; all House seats will be on the ballot. The next presidential election will be in 2004.

There is a highly developed Federal judicial system involving 1 to 4 federal district courts in each state, 13 federal courts of appeal, and the United

States Supreme Court. Federal judges are not elected but are appointed by the president for life upon good behavior in order to assure their independence, and judicial appointments must be confirmed by the Senate before a federal judge takes office.

The Federal government in the United States is a government of delegated powers. The U.S. Constitution delegates certain powers to the Federal government and reserves others to the states or to the people (Amend. 10, U.S. Constitution). In general, powers relating to currency, interstate and foreign commerce, foreign affairs, national defense, and others are assigned to the Federal government. Traditional local laws and "police" powers are generally the province of the states and their local governmental units. The U.S. Constitution contains a Bill of Rights (the first 10 Amendments) including the First Amendment, which provides in part that "Congress shall make no law . . . abridging the freedom of speech or of the press; or of the right of the people peaceably to assemble, and to petition the government for a redress of grievances." All state constitutions contain similar provisions or in some cases even more expansive ones.

At the state level there is wide variation in electoral systems. In some states, only the governor and lieutenant-governor stand for office on a statewide basis. In others, state officials such as the state attorney general, secretary of state, state Supreme Court judges, state treasurer, state auditor, and various other officials may be elected on a statewide basis according to the constitution and laws of the respective state. All state legislatures except one (Nebraska) are bicameral, but all state legislative districts, whether House or Senate, are allocated in proportion to population. In general, following the Federal example, there are fewer Senate districts than House districts, and state Senate terms of office are often of greater length than equivalent House terms, but this is not legally required by Federal law. The U.S. Constitution requires that states have a republican form of government (U.S. Constitution, art. IV, sec. 4), but the details are left up to the individual states. None of the states of the United States have a parliamentary system.

Many, but not all, states hold their "main" elections (those in which statewide candidates such as governor are chosen) in the so-called "off-years," even-numbered years in which there is no U.S. Presidential race. This permits more attention to be focused on the state candidates rather than the presidency. In presidential election years, state offices having 2-year terms (often state representative posts) and federal House of Representative (U.S. Congress) seats are held at the same time as the presidential election. States hold state elections in conjunction with federal elections for efficiency, voter turnout, and cost-saving reasons.

In some states, the state judiciary are appointed and in others elected. In some states, at least some judges are initially appointed and then later run on a "retention" ballot in which voters decide whether to retain the judge in office or not, without considering an opposing candidate. At times, some judicial offices in a state are appointed, and others in the same state are elected. Some state judicial officers are elected for specific terms; others are appointed for life. Where the judicial office is elected, the races are partisan in some states and nonpartisan in others.

Americans vote in a hodgepodge of some 3,141 counties with over 10,000 local jurisdictions (municipalities, townships, special districts, etc.) in the 50 states. In a given election year a large state may have 1 to 10 statewide offices on the ballot, 100–200 state legislative offices, over a thousand municipal or local offices, and up to 53 Congressional offices in addition to the President/Vice President. The number of offices at stake and candidates on the ballot is remarkable compared to some systems.

PARTY SYSTEM AND POLITICAL CLIMATE
IN THE UNITED STATES

The United States is dominated by two major parties, the Democratic Party and the Republican Party. At the time of this writing (2003), the president of the United States, George W. Bush, is a Republican. The Senate is composed of 48 Democrats, 51 Republicans, and 1 independent (who famously defected from the Republican Party during his term in office in 2001), and the Republicans thus control the Senate. The Republican Party controls the House by a relatively small margin (23 votes). Historically, the party that holds the presidency tends to lose seats in the Congress in midterm elections, but this did not occur in 2002.

Because the United States does not have a parliamentary system, the presidency does not depend on the president's party controlling any part of Congress, and party losses do not result in the resignation of a government. For example, from 1994 through 2000, the Republicans controlled both the House and Senate while a Democrat, Bill Clinton, held the presidency.

Third parties often field a candidate for president and sometimes candidates in lower races. Independent candidates also often run for office at all levels, but they are not often successful at higher levels or in any federal elections. An unusual event occurred in the state of Minnesota in 1998 when independent candidate Jesse Ventura won election as governor. Third-party or independent candidates have been unsuccessful in winning office at the presidential level, but they have at times influenced the outcome. In 1992 and 1996, Ross Perot's unsuccessful candidacy (Reform Party) apparently drew votes from the Republicans, allowing Bill Clinton to win the White House over George H. W. Bush and Bob Dole, respectively. In 2000,

Green Party candidate Ralph Nader may have won enough otherwise Democratic votes to hand the election to George W. Bush over Al Gore.

LEGAL AND REGULATORY REQUIREMENTS
FOR ELECTIONS

The timing of federal elections is determined by federal law, but almost all election administration is carried out by state and local governments. State law dictates the requirements for a political party to appear on the ballot, usually by means of obtaining a certain required number of signatures on a petition or by virtue of having previously qualified to appear on the ballot. Unlike in some systems, political parties do not have control over which candidates may stand for the party. Though a party organization may endorse a given candidate for that party's nomination and provide support, any individual may register as a member of that party and seek that party's nomination. Accordingly, there are normally two or more candidates for each party's slate of candidates in major races, and primary elections are held unless only one candidate files.

The precise procedure is laid down in each state's law, but typically by a certain date such as July 1 of an election year political hopefuls file documents initiating their campaigns. This normally leads to contested primary elections, and the candidate receiving the majority of votes cast becomes the party's nominee in the general election. If three or more candidates file and no single candidate obtains more than 50% of the vote, there is a "runoff" primary election between the two candidates with the highest vote totals.

In the general election held the first week in November, if held in even numbered years, each party's candidates and any independent candidates appear on the ballot. The candidate receiving the largest number of votes cast, even if less than a majority, is elected. There are no runoff elections in the general election.

Uniquely in the presidential election, the popular vote does not directly determine the outcome of the race. The Constitution provides for each state to choose electors in the manner designated by the state legislature (U.S. Constitution, art. II, sec. 1), and the electors cast their vote for president. Thus, technically a vote for president in any state is a vote for electors who are then expected to vote for that candidate when the body known as the Electoral College meets in December. In other words, there is no U.S. Constitutional right to vote for president, only for electors (*Bush v. Gore,* 2000). In theory, a state could choose its electors by means other than popular election, but none do so now. Electors are expected to vote for the candidate for whom they stood in the election, and they normally do, but it is possible for an elector to vote differently when the Electoral College count is taken. Each state in the United States has a number of electoral votes calculated as 1 vote for each U.S. senator and each member of the House of Representatives in its congressional delegation, plus 3 electoral votes for the District of Columbia, for a total of 538.

In order to win the presidency, a candidate must win 270 of the 538 electoral votes. Because reapportionment of Congressional delegations occurs only every 10 years, and because 48 states apportion all electoral votes on a "winner take all" basis regardless of the margin of victory, it is quite possible for a candidate to win the popular vote without winning the electoral vote. This happens only occasionally, but it occurred most recently in the 2000 election where Bush and Cheney received 271 electoral votes to 267 for Gore and Lieberman, but lost the popular vote by 50,996,582 to 50,456,062.

The use of electors (modeled after the Holy Roman Empire) is specified in Article II of the original U.S. Constitution of 1787. Though proposals to eliminate it and go to direct popular vote have been made, this requires a constitutional amendment, which has never passed Congress and been submitted to the states for a vote. In the 2000 presidential election, the Republican-controlled Florida legislature was considering selecting a slate of electors by vote of the legislature, but the U.S. Supreme Court's judgment in *Bush v. Gore* (2000) halted further action.

MEDIA SYSTEM: MEDIA FREEDOM
AND THE RULE OF LAW

The Legal Framework Guaranteeing
Media Freedom and Rights to Free Speech

In the United States, the print press operate with few legal restrictions on organization, institutional structure, or content. The First Amendment guarantee of a free press under the U.S. Constitution ensures that in general the press are not subject to any controls on structure or content. The principal exceptions would be (a) federal or state rules on anticompetitive practices (antitrust law) or federal laws that restrict ownership of media, (b) state laws on libel that provide for media responsibility by discouraging the printing of false and libelous information, and (c) state laws that protect the privacy of individuals to a limited extent.

Broadcast media, on the other hand, are subject to a more complex regulatory system under the supervision of the Federal Communications Commission (FCC), which administers the Federal Communications Act (FCA) of 1934 (and revisions). The access provision of this legislation (Sec. 312) requires that a licensed broadcast station must provide reasonable access to, or permit purchase of, a reasonable amount of time for the use of the station by all legally qualified candidates for federal elective office (National Association of Broadcasters, 1988, 2000). The term *use* is defined as meaning that the candidate must appear on the air (in television this can be by picture or voice or both). This requirement can be satisfied by the candidate's being "readily identifiable to a substantial degree by the listening or viewing audience." Consequently, it is not necessary for the candidate to appear or play any substantial role in the advertisement.

In addition, the FCA requires that in allocating time (or allowing its purchase) for candidates, stations must adhere to the Equal-Time Provision (Sec. 312b), providing essentially equal time access to all candidates. Stations must also sell this time at what is called "the lowest unit charge." This requirement, which is very unpopular with broadcasters, requires that the station must sell the advertising time to candidates at the lowest rate it has charged other commercial advertisers during the preceding 45 days, even if that rate is part of a discounted package rate (National Association of Broadcasters, 2000).

Reinforcing the Federal Election Campaign Act (FECA, 1971) requirement for sponsor identification in ads, the FCC also requires that political ads carry a disclaimer indicating the sponsoring entity. However, in administering the FCA, the FCC allows no station censorship of the content of political advertising. Although many stations have tried to gain exceptions to this principle, the FCC and the courts have generally held firm on this point, maintaining that the First Amendment to the U.S. Constitution prohibits any restraint on the content or format of political speech. For this reason, stations themselves are held to be exempt from any claim of libel or slander arising from an advertisement broadcast on their station (WMUR-TV, Inc., 1996).

It is important to remember that the foregoing rules related to candidate access and equal opportunity literally apply only to candidates for federal office. However, the FCC advises stations to apply similar rules to state and local candidates. On the other hand, the right to equal access does not apply to issue advertising or to party advertising. Thus, if an independent political-interest group or individual or an organized political party seeks to purchase time, broadcast stations need not allow such purchase (National Association of Broadcasters, 2000).

STRUCTURAL FRAMEWORK FOR THE MEDIA

The traditional "big three" commercial television networks, Columbia Broadcasting System (CBS), National Broadcasting Company (NBC), and American Broadcasting Corporation (ABC), who once commanded nearly 100% of the national audience among them, now account for less than 50%. Other national networks now include Fox Television (Fox), Warner Brothers (Warner), and United Paramount Network (UPN) plus 162 national cable networks. Nineteen cable networks have over 65 million subscribers. Approximately 97% of American homes have access to cable, and 69% actually subscribe (Franklin et al., 2000). Direct satellite broadcasts are also available in many areas of the country. Seventy-eight percent of American cable systems carry 30 programming channels or more. High-definition television broadcasting (HDTV) is still in the early stages in the United States, although all commercial channels are supposed to broadcast HDTV signals exclusively by 2006 (Jones, 1998). There is considerable doubt that this goal will be achieved.

In addition, the Public Broadcasting Service (PBS), a noncommercial interconnection service (technically not a network, as it does not engage in broadcasting), distributes national programming to approximately 150 educational station licensees. These licensees are often owned by state governments or universities. However, PBS has only a minor audience share. PBS was not created until 1967, when Congress created the Corporation for Public Broadcasting, a nonprofit corporation that coordinates the PBS. It receives its funding primarily from congressional budget appropriations. The individual public station licensees obtain their funding by a combination of methods including sponsorship (distinct from advertising) and charitable contributions from viewers.

The structure of the broadcast media differs in the United States from that in most European countries in that local station licensees are the broadcasters who distribute programming received from the networks. The national networks themselves do own a limited number of local stations, but it is the local stations that are the actual broadcasters. Local stations join a network by signing affiliation agreements with a network. Some stations are "independent" in the sense that they are not network affiliates but obtain programming from a variety of sources.

It is simple to describe the requirements that govern media outlets in the United States in regard to coverage of political candidates and elections: There are no rules that require fair, equal, or balanced news coverage. All news outlets, whatever their means of distribution, may cover elections in any way they deem appropriate. This applies basically to all newspapers, magazines, television stations, cable outlets, satellite distributors, Internet programmers, and all other forms of information distribution. As with any information dissemination, political or not, any outlet would be subject to liability claims for news coverage that was found by the courts to be libelous or invasive of privacy.

Neither federal nor state law in the United States imposes any specific programming obligations on television or radio broadcasters. As a condition of holding a federal license, broadcasters are required to operate "in the public interest, convenience, and necessity," but there is no more specific regulation of program content. In the course of licensing proceedings, stations may promise to engage in a certain amount of public service announcements or represent that they will provide certain types of program coverage, but no specific programming requirements are provided for by law. The FCC does not cancel or fail to renew broadcasting licenses based on the content of programming.

REGULATORY AUTHORITIES

The two main regulatory bodies that govern media and elections in the United States are the FCC and the Federal Election Commission (FEC). Both bodies operate as executive agencies, appointed by the president for finite, often renewable, terms. The FEC has an equal number of Democrats and Republicans, which is thought to make it a nonpartisan (or at least bipartisan) body. However, some observers have suggested that this balance has often resulted in deadlock or compromise, preventing any serious penalty or judgment against either side of the political spectrum (Jackson, 1990). In order to enforce its fines and orders, the FEC must take a candidate to court and obtain a judgment if the subject does not accept the agency's ruling. The FEC's decisions are subject to judicial review in the federal courts.

The FCC, on the other hand, lacks a specific partisan base, as its appointments are made from among experienced broadcasters with no attempt to balance partisan identification. The FCC is usually judged, therefore, to be less partisan in its administration of broadcast law that relates to elections. Decisions of the FCC are subject to judicial review in the federal courts.

THE ENVIRONMENT FOR JOURNALISTS

In general, journalists in the United States operate in an environment free from regulation of all but the most serious abuses. Prior restraints of publication or broadcasts are virtually unknown except in the area of pretrial publicity in criminal prosecutions where they are exceedingly rare. Such restrictions may be achieved only by a very compelling showing in court by the government. Because the courts have imposed very high burdens on plaintiffs seeking to establish libel when the plaintiff is a "public figure" (*New York Times v. Sullivan,* 1964), including requiring proof that false defamatory statements were made with actual malice, the environment in which journalists cover campaigns is one that is virtually free of restrictions or fear of government retaliation. Political candidates are always public figures for the purpose of the *New York Times* decision.

MEDIA COVERAGE OF ELECTIONS

Media Behavior in Election Campaigns

In this symbiotic relationship between the media and candidates/parties, Kaid, McKinney, and Tedesco (2000) suggested that "political campaigns provide an excellent benchmark for assessing how the media are executing their role of civic dialogue facilitator" (p. 12). Historically, in the United States the print media have been viewed as providing relatively transparent indicators of their political leanings. Like media outlets in many democratic systems, newspapers and magazines have often had a political or ideological identity and have felt free to express it in editorial content and in overt endorsements of political candidates and parties. Though academic research often addresses such questions, there has never been any real concern about findings that one newspaper or another supported or favored one candidate or another.

Alternatively, concerns about potential partisanship in the broadcast media have been of greater concern, both politically and as a matter of policy. Because the original broadcasting outlets were awarded licenses to broadcast over the "public's airwaves," the FCA of 1934 mandated that they do so in the "public interest, convenience, and necessity." This doctrine, which derived from the notion of the broadcast frequency spectrum as one of scarcity, suggested that broadcast entities had to be particularly careful in their guardianship of objectivity and in the provision of diversity of viewpoints. From these principles there developed a strong presumption in the first 50 years of political broadcasting that the electronic media has special obligations to ensure that coverage of political candidates and parties was fair and equal. As a result of this presumption about objectivity and fairness in the broadcast media, political observers and scholars have generally held the broadcast media to higher standards of partisan objectivity.

Objectivity in reporting has long been a tenet of fair journalism. Iyengar and Kinder (1987) identified three guiding standards for journalists: independence, balance, and objectivity. Independence from political allegiance or pressure, balance in length and content of coverage, and informative and complete, rather than judgmental language and tone, are goals that are not always achieved. Many studies have addressed the question of how well the media perform their responsibilities in reporting presidential campaigns. In particular, political communication scholars have focused much of their efforts on such issues as the amount, tone, and fairness of campaign reporting (e.g., Hanson, 1992; Patterson, 1993, 1994); the degree to which news reports focus on strategy and "horse race" aspects of a campaign, as opposed to issue reporting (e.g., Robinson & Sheehan, 1983); the framing of media interpretations; the shrinking sound bite (Hallin, 1992); the dramatic, or horse-race, nature of political coverage; as well as possible causes contributing to voter apathy. For example, poll reporting has become an increasingly salient topic for academic researchers and civic organizations. Finally, other analysts have examined the degree to which campaign news features the actual messages of candidates versus a "journalist-centered" style of reporting in which journalists provide their interpretation of the campaign (Lichter & Noyes, 1995; Patterson, 1993).

Researchers began the systematic study of network news coverage of political content in the 1970s. These early studies did not provide much support for charges that the major news networks in the United States were exhibiting overt political bias (Frank, 1973; Hofstetter, 1976; Robinson & Sheehan, 1983). However, these early studies have been supplanted in recent campaigns by more serious criticisms of news coverage. Researchers have charged that the networks demonstrate a bias in their coverage of some candidates over others, an outcome that seemed to work particularly against Republicans in the 1988–2000 races (Center for Media and Public Affairs, 2000; Lichter & Noyes, 1995; Lichter, Noyes, & Kaid, 1998). More generally, it has been charged that the major television networks exhibit a distinct leftist bias (Goldberg, 2001).

Recent findings on media content of political campaign stories have not cast the media in a favorable light. In *Out of Order* (Patterson, 1993) and *Feeding Frenzy* (Sabato, 1991), television and print journalists alike are criticized for having an attack, or pack, mentality that is eroding respect for politicians and the political system.

The Presidential Election of 2000 and the Media

The media's handling of the 2000 presidential election did little to enhance the public's confidence in this important democratic institution. The overall coverage continued to be characterized by shortened candidate sound bites, more emphasis on media covering themselves, rather than candidates, and more coverage of polling and strategies than of issues (Center for Media and Public Affairs, 2000). However, the failings of the overall campaign coverage were quickly eclipsed by the media's handling of election-night reporting. The media mistakenly predicted Al Gore as the winner of a tight race, only to later retract that prediction in the early hours of the morning, giving the election win to Bush, then quickly withdrawing that pronouncement to leave the election in a contested state. After much hand-wringing and soul-searching, this media blunder was blamed on faulty exit polling (Owen, 2001). Even the election-night-reporting debacle was soon overshadowed by a media frenzy that focused on the contested election in Florida. As one commentator noted, "The media gave the candidates low marks, the public gave the media low marks, and the Florida fallout diminished the image of the political system" (Owen, 2001, p. 124).

ACCESS TO THE MEDIA

Conditions of Free Media Access in the United States

There is no general system of free access to the media for political candidates and parties outside of the news coverage that is at the discretion of the media organizations. It should be recalled that political parties in the United States do not occupy the position of prominence they do in countries with parliamentary election systems. Though it has periodically been proposed that broadcasters be required to provide free broadcasting time to candidates for office as the "price" of their license to use the airwaves, this has never been implemented on a systematic basis.

Under the equal-time provision of the FCA, if a broadcaster provides free time to a candidate for elective office, it must provide equal (free) time to that candidate's opponent. The usual consequence is that broadcasters as a rule do not provide free time to any political candidates as such. However, at the national level, networks often cover major policy addresses by the president and the annual State of the Union message as part of news coverage. In these circumstances, the opposing political party is usually given time to air a "response," but this is not due to the president's status as a candidate (Foote, 1990).

In the 1996 presidential election, the Free TV for Straight Talk Coalition, an independent group of political observers, organized a campaign that resulted in certain networks voluntarily providing free broadcasting time in limited amounts to the major presidential candidates (incumbent President Bill Clinton and then-Senator Robert Dole) (Holtz-Bacha, 1999; "Imagine a Presidential Campaign," 1996). Several networks, including CBS, NBC, Fox, CNN, and PBS, provided the two major-party presidential candidates with varying amounts of free time for broadcasts of prescribed length and format (Mifflin, 1996). Studies of these "free time" broadcasts indicated that they were only slightly more issue oriented than paid political advertising and still contained a substantial number of negative attacks (Holtz-Bacha, 1999). There were two major differences in these broadcasts and the paid advertising in 1996. First, the free-time broadcasts were longer (usually 2–5 minutes in length) than normal paid spots in U.S. elections, which generally average 30–60 seconds (Kaid & Johnston, 2001). Second, the free-time broadcasts did result in the candidates themselves being the major speakers. In contrast, paid advertising for presidential candidates has increasingly featured anonymous announcers. In all general-election spots from 1952 through 1996, for instance, only 37% of the paid spots featured the candidate as the major speaker, and in 1996 Clinton and Dole were the main speakers in only 5% of their paid spots (Kaid & Johnston, 2001).

Despite the advantages of longer and more candidate-centered broadcasts, the free-time spots were little watched and little remembered by the public. A national telephone survey after the election in 1996 found that just over half (55%) of the U.S. public had even heard about the free-time advertising slots, and only 20% said they had seen any of them (Kaid et al., 2000). Nor is the U.S. voter typically favorable to such potential for the future. Focus group respondents are often outraged at the possibility of providing free-time spots (Kaid et al., 2000), and one national survey by an international association of promotion and marketing professionals (PROMAX, 1997) found that 61% of respondents said they would not support free-time proposals. With so little public support or apparent result, this voluntary experiment in free time was not repeated in the 2000 election.

As part of the transition from analog broadcasting to digital broadcasting or HDTV, existing broadcasters have been allocated additional spectrum to provide both analog and digital signals until 2006, when it is envisaged that analog broadcasting will cease (provided certain conditions are met) and only digital signals will be aired (Jones, 1998). It was proposed by then-Vice President Al Gore that the licensees receiving this spectrum capacity should be required to air free political advertisements in partial return. Although the FCC has not so far attempted to do so, this remains a possible if unlikely scenario.

The result of the essential absence of free access for political parties is that all parties, including new parties such as the emergent Ralph Nader-led "Greens" in the 2000 Presidential election have only such access as is generated by news coverage or they are able to purchase. One of the main opportunities for candidates to get free time is to participate in candidate debates. At the presidential level, candidate debates were first held between Richard Nixon and John F. Kennedy in the 1960 election. Presidential debates were not held again until the 1976 election between Gerald Ford and Jimmy Carter, but they are now a regular feature in U.S. presidential elections, including the state primary elections.

In the 1992 presidential election, Reform Party candidate Ross Perot was included by the organizers in the debates along with George H. W. Bush and Bill Clinton, but he was excluded from the debates between Clinton and Dole in 1996. Candidate debates represent one of the few ways in which a candidate can get free time, and third-party candidates such as Perot have mounted legal challenges to their exclusion from the events. Such challenges have been uniformly unsuccessful. Equal-time requirements are not triggered because the broadcasters are considered engaged in news coverage of an event organized by others. One principal reason third-party candidates are usually excluded from debate participation is because the major-party candidates (Democratic and Republican) will normally not consent to debate if others are included.

Debates are now organized and conducted by an entity known as the Presidential Debate Commission, a nonprofit, bipartisan, independent organization. The Commission determines which candidates are eligible to participate in debates based on objective criteria that are established in advance. A candidate wishing to participate in the presidential debate must demonstrate a serious possibility of success through measures such as opinion poll standings, proportion of vote in prior elections, and other viability criteria. However, no candidate is required to participate in debates organized by this independent commission.

There is no provision for free access for political parties or allocation of media coverage among the parties. It would be considered that any attempt by the federal or a state government to allocate coverage in the press or in broadcasting among the political parties on an equal or proportionate basis would infringe the First Amendment's protections of the freedom of the press. For example, in the press area, the U.S. Supreme Court has held that a Florida law requiring that a political candidate be given a right to reply to a newspaper editorial unconstitutionally infringed the First Amendment right to a free press (*Miami Herald Pub. Co. v. Tornillo,* 1974). In *Buckley v. Valeo* (1976), the Supreme Court ruled that spending restrictions designed to equalize the amount of advertising by political candidates were unconstitutional as violations of the First Amendment.

The 1974 amendments to FECA established a system of partial public funding for presidential candidates, but this does not apply to U.S. House or U.S. Senate candidates. This system does not provide any free access, but it does provide public funding to qualifying candidates that may be used to fund paid access. Political parties that qualify also receive funding to support their national nominating conventions in presidential elections. These conventions normally are covered by the broadcast media at least in part, and key speeches are often broadcast as news events.

Paid Access to the Media

In the United States, the primary form of political television outside of news broadcasts has been paid access in the form of "spot" advertising by candidates, parties, and independent groups or individuals. A spot advertisement typically ranges from 30 or 60 seconds to 5 minutes, with the shorter lengths being most common. Candidates sometimes will produce and air longer programs, such as the 30-minute offerings by Ross Perot in the 1992 presidential campaign. The use of candidate-centered paid advertising (and candidate-centered campaigns) has been a distinctive feature of the American political campaign process. Neither federal nor state law limits the number or length of political broadcasts, speeches, rallies, newspaper advertisements, pamphlets, or flyers a candidate or party may distribute or hold in the course of a campaign. Any such limits would be regarded as direct restraints on the quantity of political speech.

Consequently, the paid political commercial has become the dominant form of communication in political campaigns (Kaid, 1999a). The first presidential campaign to use this form of candidate campaigning was Dwight Eisenhower in 1952, and every presidential campaign since that time has relied increasingly on this format (Kaid & Johnston, 2001; West, 1993). Presidential candidates now spend the majority of their campaign budgets on such paid media advertising; in the 2000 election Al Gore and George W. Bush and their respective parties spent over $240 million for spot ads in the general-election campaign (Devlin, 2001). Although these paid advertisements in the United States are often criticized, research has shown that the spots are, in fact, predominantly characterized by issue content (Kaid, 1999b; Kaid & Johnston, 2001). Paid advertisements in the United States are also frequently cited for their negative tone and content. Though candidates have always felt free to criticize their opponents in all types of political speech, it is true that the paid spots in U.S. campaigns at all levels have been more negative in the past two decades (Kaid & Johnston, 2001; West, 1993). However, researchers have concluded that voters learn much more about issues in campaigns from political spot advertising than from campaign news or from debates (Just, Crigler, & Wallach, 1990; Patterson & McClure, 1976).

Because paid advertising has become so dominant in the electoral system of the United States, journalists now cover political advertising, just as they do speeches, rallies, campaign appearances, debates, and other candidate campaign activities. This particular type of news coverage has been labeled as "adwatch" coverage (Kaid, Gobetz, Garner, Leland, & Scott, 1993; Kaid, Tedesco, & McKinnon, 1996; West, 1993). Through this form of coverage, print and broadcast outlets attempt to "police" political spot ads and to provide voters with information about the accuracy and truthfulness of paid candidate messages (Broder, 1989).

REGULATION OF PAID MEDIA ACCESS
IN THE UNITED STATES

Because of the First Amendment protections for free speech, press, and assembly in the U.S. Constitution, the attempts to affect the conduct of campaigning through paid broadcasting has most often taken the form of regulation of the process by which candidates and parties raise money and make expenditures in support of election campaigns. This is because direct restrictions on political broadcasting would be patently unconstitutional. Donations of money to political candidates and their expenditures represent forms of political "speech" and free association that may be restricted only for compelling reasons, a conclusion that initially may not appear obvious, but is amply justified (Jones & Kaid, 1976). Political campaigns, especially at the presidential level, are for the most part carried out through the mass media and have been so conducted for many years. The relationship between political communication in the modern age and the raising and spending of money has therefore assumed U.S. Constitutional dimensions:

> Virtually every means of communicating ideas in today's mass society requires the expenditure of money. The distribution of the humblest handbill or leaflet entails printing, paper, and circulation costs. Speeches and rallies generally necessitate hiring a hall and publicizing the event. The electorate's increasing dependence on television, radio and mass media for news and other information has made these expensive modes of communication indispensable instruments of effective political speech. (*Buckley,* 1976, p. 19)

The *Buckley* court considered that making a contribution of money to a candidate, like joining a political party, served to affiliate a person with a candidate and to enable like-minded persons to pool their resources in furtherance of common political goals (*Buckley,* 1976, p. 22). The right of free association is a " 'basic constitutional freedom' . . . that is 'closely allied to freedom of speech and a right which, like free speech, lies at the foundation of a free society.' . . . In view of the fundamental nature of the right to associate, governmental 'action which may have the effect of curtailing the freedom to associate is subject to the closest scrutiny' " (*Buckley,* 1976, p. 25).

Underlying the American model of political campaign communication are the U.S. constitutional guarantees of free speech and freedom of association, which secure the rights of citizens to band together to support political candidates of their choosing and express that support in various forms from bumper stickers to electronic advertising (*Buckley,* 1976). Any regulations of political campaign processes therefore must be carefully crafted and narrowly focused to avoid conflict with the First Amendment.

The Federal Election Campaign Act of 1971 ('FECA') provided the first serious attempt to regulate federal elections. It has been amended several times, most substantially in 1974 (following the Watergate scandal involving the Nixon administration), in 1976 after several provisions were declared unconstitutional in *Buckley,* and most recently in March 2002, by the Bipartisan Campaign Finance Reform Act (BCRA, 2002). The BCRA amendments became effective on November 6, 2002. FECA's key elements include the following:

1. It required the disclosure of amounts and sources of contributions to candidates and political committees and the disclosure of independent expenditures. Reports are filed with the FEC, and they are publicly available over the Internet at www.fec.gov. The BCRA added new disclosure requirements concerning "electioneering communications" discussed later (BCRA, 2002).

2. It established contribution limits. Specific limits were set in the 1974 amendments at $1,000 per election (primary and general elections counted separately) to federal candidates by individuals, $20,000 per year on contributions to national political parties, and $5,000 per year to state and local parties. Effective with the BCRA amendments in 2002, the limits on contributions to candidates rise to $2,000 per election, and the limits are now indexed to inflation so they automatically will increase in the future. Under the BCRA amendments, the limits on contributions increase to $25,000 per year in the case of national parties and to $10,000 per year in the case of state or local parties. Aggregate contribution limits rise under BCRA from $25,000 per year to $95,000 per 2-year election cycle, of which only $37,500 may be contributed to candidates (as distinct from parties) over the 2 years.

3. It set limits on contributions by political action committees (PACs) of $5,000 per election to candidates, and annual limits on contributions by PACs of $5,000 to other outside PACs and state and local parties, and $15,000 annually to national parties. There is no annual aggregate limitation on PAC contributions.

4. It set expenditure limits (now invalid) on total candidate spending and on spending of a candidate's personal funds. These rules were declared unconstitutional in *Buckley* (1976). Accordingly, candidates may spend unlimited amounts of personal funds. However, in BCRA (2002), it is provided (Sec. 304 and 318) that Senate and House candidates running against candidates proposing to spend substantial amounts of personal funds will be allowed to receive contributions in excess of the contribution limits up to six times the normal limits and have limits on party "coordinated" expenditures removed. This so-called "millionaires provision" has been challenged as unconstitutional in *McConnell v. Federal Election Commission,* a lawsuit by U.S. Senator Mitch McConnell and others, now pending in federal court.

5. It established limits on expenditures for radio and television advertising by candidates. These specific limits were eliminated in the 1974 amendments, but general expenditure limits remained until declared unconstitutional in *Buckley* (1976). They are no longer in force.

6. It set limits on "independent" expenditures ($1,000) advocating or opposing election of a candidate. These were declared unconstitutional in *Buckley* (1976) and are no longer in force.

7. It banned corporate and labor union contributions, except through PACs. PACs are generally organized by employers (often but not always cor-

porations) or labor unions, or they may be nonconnected. A corporate or union PAC may solicit contributions from its employees or members, which are then pooled and contributed to political candidates. These funds are not considered corporate or union (i.e., general treasury funds derived from profits or union dues) funds and do not violate the statutes prohibiting such contributions. Contributions to PACs are voluntary. FECA 1971 created the framework that allowed PACs to exist. Prior to FECA, there were in place (and still are) separate statutory bans on direct contributions to candidates for federal office by corporations and labor unions.

8. It created the FEC.

9. It established a system of partial public funding of presidential campaigns and party conventions by a voluntary "tax check-off" system in which taxpayers may designate on their federal income tax returns that $3 (originally $1) of their tax liability should go to the Presidential Election Campaign Fund.

Buckley involved a constitutional challenge to certain provisions of the FECA amendments of 1974 which, inter alia, placed limits on the amounts of funds candidates could spend in support of their elections, limits on the amount of funds that could be expended by independent persons supporting or opposing candidates, and limits on expenditures by candidates of their personal funds in support of their elections. These limits on campaign expenditures by candidates and others were held to "heavily burden core First Amendment expressions" because they represented "substantial rather than merely theoretical restraints on the quantity and diversity of political speech" (*Buckley,* 1976, p. 19). Accordingly, they were unconstitutional as violations of the First Amendment.

The *Buckley* decision in 1976 substantially altered the campaign finance landscape as envisaged by Congress in FECA 1971 and the 1974 amendments. Three of the major features listed earlier were declared unconstitutional—limits on candidate spending, limits on independent spending, and limits on expenditures of candidates' personal funds. Though one goal of the legislation had been to limit the allegedly skyrocketing cost of election campaigns, the *Buckley* decision found such limitations to be impermissible: "The First Amendment denies government the power to determine that spending to promote one's political views is wasteful, excessive, or unwise" (*Buckley,* 1976, p. 57).

There can be no doubt that if broad restrictions on campaign spending are unconstitutional because they limit the quantity of political expression (i.e., limit the number of political broadcasts), direct prohibitions or limitations on televised political advertisements would be similarly unlawful. In the original FECA in 1971, Congress had included specific limits on the amount of dollars that could be expended on television advertising, but these were repealed in the 1974 amendments before they ever took effect (Jones, 2000), in favor of the general expenditure restrictions that were found unconstitutional in *Buckley*.

The *Buckley* decision did uphold expenditure limitations in the context of the public funding of presidential election campaigns created in the 1974 amendments to FECA. Under the presidential funding scheme, candidates are allowed to choose whether to participate in public funding. Those who do not participate do not receive public funds but are not restricted as to the amounts that may be expended on their campaign. Those who do participate receive "matching" public funds during the primary in proportion to certain eligible private contributions that they receive and "full" funding during the general-election campaign (private contributions may not be accepted).

Candidates who are participants in the public funding system are limited in the amounts they may spend during the primary season. In the general election, candidate spending is limited to the amount of the public grant. The Court distinguished the expenditure limits imposed in the public funding system from those declared unconstitutional on the basis of voluntary consent by the participants:

> Congress may engage in public financing of election campaigns, and may condition acceptance of public funds on an agreement by the candidate to abide by specified expenditure limitations. Just as a candidate may voluntarily limit the size of the contributions he chooses to accept, he may decide to forgo private fundraising and accept public funding. (*Buckley*, 1976, p. 57, n. 65)

The original 1974 presidential spending limits were $10 million per candidate in the primary and $20 million in the general election. FECA provided that expenditure limits were inflation adjusted, so that in the 2000 presidential election the spending limit was approximately $40.536 million in the primary and approximately $67.56 million (per candidate) in the general election.

In sum, there are no federal legal limits imposed on paid access to the media except in the case where a presidential candidate chooses to accept public funding. Several states have adopted some form of public financing for some candidates at the state level and some of these schemes involve spending restrictions for state candidates accepting state funds. Generally, the only restriction on paid access is the ability of candidates or parties to raise funds and the willingness of broadcasters to sell advertising slots. Political parties are limited in the amounts they can spend advocating election of candidates if the broadcasts are made in coordination with a federal candidate to the amount that parties may contribute to candidates (e.g., for U.S. Senate candidates, $35,000 under the BCRA, up from the previous limit of $17,500). In other words, coordinated expenditures by political parties are considered contributions (which may be limited) to the candidates.

In the years since the original FECA legislation and the landmark *Buckley v. Valeo* (1976) Supreme Court decision in 1976, the 50 individual states have adopted various forms of campaign legislation to regulate political campaign contributions, funding, disclosure, and conduct to govern state and local elections for offices below the federal level (e.g., races that are not for president, U.S. House, or U.S. Senate). Much of this legislation is modeled after the federal law, but there is no requirement that individual states adopt any particular code or system, and, in practice, there is a great deal of variation among the states as to the specific requirements that govern state and local elections.

CURRENT ISSUES RELATED TO PAID ACCESS

The BCRA (2002) raises a host of issues that impinge upon the rules governing paid access to the broadcast media. Prior to the passage of these amendments to FECA, it was widely predicted that a number of the new legal provisions would likely be found unconstitutional. Within 6 weeks of the signing into law of the BCRA, six lawsuits challenging its constitutionality had been filed. These lawsuits will not finally be decided before 2004. However, two issues of the many raised in these lawsuits deserve comment here.

Express Advocacy and "Electioneering Activity." The original FECA (1971 and the 1974 amendments) purported broadly to regulate all spending "in connection with," or "for the purpose of influencing" a federal election, or "relative to" a federal candidate. One of the issues faced by the Court was whether these statutory phrases were so vague and overly broad that they provided an unconstitutional lack of notice to persons potentially affected by the FECA. The statute did not define "in connection with" an election or "relative to a candidate."

In order to avoid declaring these provisions of FECA unconstitutional as too vague and overbroad, *Buckley* held that "explicit words of advocacy of election or defeat" are required in order to bring the expenditures within the reach of the statute. The Court listed certain explicit advocacy terms (nonexhaustively) as satisfying the strict "express advocacy" test: " 'vote for,' 'elect,' 'support,' 'cast your ballot for,' 'Smith for Congress,' 'vote against,' 'defeat,' 'reject' " (*Buckley,* 1976, p. 44, n. 52). The Court considered that such precision was required to avoid "chilling" speech involving public discussion of political issues:

The distinction between discussion of issues and candidates and advocacy of election or defeat of candidates may often dissolve in practical application. Candidates, especially incumbents, are intimately tied to public issues involving legislative proposals and governmental actions. Not only do candidates campaign on the basis of their positions on various public issues, but campaigns themselves generate issues of public interest. (*Buckley,* 1976, p. 42)

The result of the *Buckley* decision has been to free "issue advocacy" advertisements from regulation as either contributions or expenditures: "So long as persons and groups eschew expenditures that, in express terms advocate the election or defeat of a clearly identified candidate, they are free to spend as much as they want to promote the candidate and his views" (*Buckley,* 1976, p. 45). In 1976, Congress amended the statute to conform to the *Buckley* case interpretation. Title 2 U.S.C. 434(e) obligates any "person . . . who makes contributions or independent expenditures expressly advocating the election or defeat of a clearly identified candidate" in an amount exceeding $100 in any calendar year to file with the FEC a statement containing the information required of contributors of more than $100 to a candidate or political committee.

In several subsequent decisions, federal courts have ruled that advertisements lacking words of express advocacy are not regulated by FECA, and sponsors of such advertisements are not required to file disclosure statements with the FEC (CLITRIM, 1980; MCFL, 1986; Furgatch, 1987; Faucher, 1991; Christian Action Network, 1995; Maine Right to Life, 1996). Such ads are characterized as "issue ads" because they ostensibly address issues rather than advocate for or against election of candidates. BCRA establishes a new category of messages dubbed "electioneering communications" and seeks to bring them within the Constitutional reach of FECA and its amendments.

The BCRA views ads lacking express advocacy as a loophole and attempts to prohibit, discourage, or punish such ads. BCRA prohibits corporations and labor unions from running or indirectly financing electioneering communications identifying or targeting a federal candidate within 60 days of a federal general election (BCRA, 2002, Sec. 203). Electioneering communications that are coordinated with a candidate are treated as contributions and limited in accordance with the contribution limits (BCRA, 2002, Sec. 202).

Section 201 of BCRA (2002) requires interest groups, political organizations, and other persons not already banned from making electioneering communications to file disclosure reports if they spend over $10,000 on broadcast electioneering communications within 60 days of a federal general election and 30 days of a primary election. Persons making such communications must disclose the name of the person buying broadcast time, the election, the names of candidates identified in the ad, names and addresses of all donors contributing over $1,000, and all disbursements over $200. BCRA Section 204 prohibits tax-exempt nonprofit organizations from running "targeted" (electioneering) communications within 60 days of a general election or 30 days of a primary.

However, lower federal courts have already struck down similar requirements at the state level on First Amendment grounds (e.g., *Right to Life of Michigan, Inc. v. Miller*, 1998; *Planned Parenthood Affiliates of Michigan, Inc. v. Miller*, 1998; *Vermont Right to Life v. Sorrell*, 2000; and *Perry v. Bartlett*, 2000). These BCRA provisions similarly may be declared invalid unless the Supreme Court chooses to overrule *Buckley*. Moreover, it has been argued that because BCRA bans corporations and unions from electioneering communications but permits it for other entities, it violates the equal-protection guarantee of the Fifth Amendment (Bopp & Coleson, 2002).

Soft Money Contributions. "Soft money" is money contributed (usually to political parties) that is not subject to the "hard" limits (e.g., formerly $1,000, now $2,000 per election) of the FECA (Corrado, Mann, Ortiz, Potter, & Sorauf, 1997). The genesis of soft money was an FEC ruling that permitted national political parties to receive contributions and make expenditures for nonfederal (e.g., state election) purposes that would be prohibited under FECA.

The relatively low contribution limits upheld in *Buckley* resulted in increases in PAC activity, increases in independent election spending, and increasing consumption of time by federal office-holder/candidates in raising campaign funds. Though expenses paid from contributions illegal under FECA had to be allocated to federal and nonfederal party accounts, because there were always more state candidates on the ballot than federal, this enabled the greater share of, for example, voter registration drives to be paid for with state funds that were banned by federal law.

The national party committees applied this ruling to their own activities, so that portions of their administrative costs and other expenses were also allocated among federal and nonfederal accounts. The use of soft money, raised free of federal restrictions such as limits on amounts or source, to pay portions of national party expenses also had the effect of freeing up hard money that could be directly given to federal candidates or spent on their behalf (Corrado et al., 1997).

Between 1984 and 1996, soft-money expenses by both major parties grew from $21 million to $271 million. In 2000, soft money represented over $487 million for both major parties out of $1.2 billion raised from all sources (Federal Election Commission, 2001).

Much soft money is raised in amounts and from sources that would be illegal if the strictures of FECA were applied. For example, in the 1992 elec-

tion cycle both parties obtained about 11,000 contributions from corporations and, in the case of the Democrats, from labor unions that would have
been illegal under FECA because of the federal prohibition against corporate and union contributions. The size of many of these contributions also
exceeds federal limits. In the 1992 election cycle, the national parties obtained at least 381 contributions in excess of $20,000, the federal limit on
contributions to political parties. About 30% of the soft money raised came
from contributors of $100,000 or more (Committee for Economic Develop-
ment, 1999). In the 1996 cycle, nearly 1,000 contributions in excess of $20,000
were obtained, and about 27,000 contributions were received from sources
prohibited from giving under FECA. In 1998, at least 218 corporations donated over $100,000, and 16 donated $500,000 or more in soft money (Committee for Economic Development, 1999).

Such donations are legally raised under the applicable state election
laws, even though there are substantial discrepancies between state law
and FECA. For example, Virginia was a popular state for PACs connected
with aspiring candidates for the presidency in the year 2000 because it permits unlimited contributions from both individuals and corporations. However, Virginia is not unique. State political parties may accept corporate
and union donations in 29 states, unlimited individual contributions in 33
states, and unlimited PAC contributions in 33 states (Common Cause, 1998).

The explosion in the use of soft money in the 1996 election was memora-
ble for the direct links to President Clinton's personal campaign and fund-
raising activities, involving "White House coffees and endless advertising,
mysterious gardeners and munificent nuns, Indonesian bankers and Arkan-
sas restaurateurs" (J. Bennett, 1998, p. 1). The innovation in 1996 (continued
in 2000 and 2002) was that the party committees used soft money to fund issue ads that lacked the express advocacy language required by the Supreme Court in *Buckley* (1976) as discussed earlier.

Numerous published accounts by former White House officials have described President Clinton's personal role in authorizing the issue advertising campaign, editing and approving the ads, selecting the locations for
their broadcast, and raising the funds needed to pay for the advertisements
(Corrado et al., 1997). President Clinton's own "White House coffee" videotapes showed him explaining the soft-money gambit to donors. He boasted
that "We realized we could run these ads through the Democratic Party,
which meant we could raise money in $20,000 and $50,000 and $100,000
wads" (J. Bennett, 1998, p. 1). The Republican party followed suit, and the
FEC upheld the practice, overruling its own auditors 6–0, on grounds that
there was no existing legal standard to determine when such ads could be
attributed to candidates rather than parties.

According to Corrado, "What we saw in this election cycle was nothing
less than the breakdown of the campaign finance system. The system we

created in the 1970s essentially collapsed. It's the Wild West out there. It's anything goes" (quoted in Marcus & Babcock, 1997, p. 1). The result was that the expenditure limitations in the presidential race and the contribution limitations in all federal races were essentially evaded, if not outright violated. The repetition of this result in 2000 contributed to the enactment of the BCRA (2002), which purports to ban soft money. The manner in which it does so is controversial and perhaps unconstitutional.

BCRA (2002) Sec. 101 prohibits national political parties from receiving or spending contributions from individuals or PACs (corporate and union contributions are already illegal) that do not comply with the FECA source and contribution limits and prohibits parties from making contributions to other nonprofit organizations. The most controversial provisions are those that prohibit federal candidates from raising money for state get-out-the-vote drives, voter registration, and other federal election activities, that prohibit state candidates from funding communications supporting (but not expressly advocating) federal candidates for office, and that require state parties to comply with the requirements for any activities in a federal (even-numbered) election year. This may possibly require states to move their elections to not coincide with federal election years or change their laws to comply with FECA limits—which may be the purpose of this provision.

The effect is arguably to limit the organizational, administrative, and advocacy activities of state parties and to impose federal contribution limits on state parties. Though Congress clearly has plenary power to regulate Federal elections, BCRA reaches beyond the elections themselves to regulate the fundamental structure of state election processes. Whether it reaches too far so that it impinges upon the reserved powers of the states of the United States in violation of the 10th Amendment to the U.S. Constitution is an issue that will be confronted in the pending lawsuits challenging the BCRA.

EDITORIAL COVERAGE: RESPONSIBILITIES OF JOURNALISTS

Journalism in the United States is considered a professional occupation but is not a licensed or regulated profession in the conventional sense. Journalism programs at universities and colleges are accredited by the Association for Education in Journalism and Mass Communication, but journalists are not required to graduate from an accredited program or possess any other specific credential in order to practice their craft.

However, many voluntary associations of mass-communication specialists have adopted codes of ethics or standards of practice that govern the conduct of their members. The Society of Professional Journalists (SPJ) includes in its mission the promotion of the "flow of information" and the maintenance of "freedom of speech and of the press" (Society of Professional Journalists, 1996). The SPJ Code of Ethics is divided into four categories of standards. The first standard, to "seek the truth and report it" encompasses statements about honesty, fairness, tests of accuracy, identity of sources, misrepresentation, distortion of visual images, avoidance of stereotypes, and other similar processes. The second standard, to "minimize harm," calls for journalists to be compassionate and sensitive to news subjects and victims. The third group of standards demands that journalists "act independently," avoiding conflicts of interest, refusing compromising gifts or treatment, disclosing potential conflicts, and remaining free of compromising associations. A final group of standards asks journalists to "be accountable" by providing explanations of media conduct, encouraging dialogue about the media and its actions, and exposing unethical conduct of colleagues when necessary. The complete list of the standards in the SPJ Code of Ethics is included on the organization's Web site (http://www.spj. org/ethics_code.asp) and is available in English, Spanish, French, Portuguese, Slovene, Russian, and Arabic.

Electronic journalists subscribe to an additional code, the Code of Ethics and Professional Conduct of the Radio–Television News Directors Association. In existence since the late 1940s, this code calls for news professionals to conduct themselves according to specific standards in six areas (public trust, truth, fairness, integrity, independence, and accountability). The most recent version of the code was adopted in September 2000, and is available on the association's Web site (http://www.rtnda.org/ethics/coe.shtml).

The creators of political messages for candidates and parties also subscribe to voluntary codes of ethics. The American Association of Advertising Agencies (AAAA) has a Standards of Practice code through which its members pledge to hold to high ethical standards and to avoid knowingly creating advertising that contains "(a) false or misleading statements or exaggerations, visual or verbal, (b) testimonials that do not reflect the real opinion of the individual(s) involved, (c) price claims that are misleading, (d) claims insufficiently supported or that distort the true meaning of practicable application of statements made by professional or scientific authority, and (e) statements, suggestions, or pictures offensive to public decency or minority segments of the population." The most recent version of these standards—displayed on the organization's Web site at http://www.aaaa. org/inside/standards.pdf—were adopted in 1990 and apply to advertisers who work in the political advertising as well as the commercial advertising arenas.

The professional organization most directly concerned with the preparation and management of candidate and party messages in the United States is the American Association of Political Consultants (AAPC). The AAPC requires all its members to subscribe to a Code of Ethics that includes the agreement that they "will use no appeal to voters which is based on racism, sexism, religious intolerance or any form of discrimination . . ." and "will refrain from false or misleading attacks on an opponent or member of his or her family and will do everything in my power to prevent others from using such tactics." The full code can be found at http://www.theaapc.org/ethics.html.

It is worth reiterating that all of these codes of ethics, those for journalists and those for advertisers and consultants, are completely voluntary. Penalties for abuse are rarely imposed. The AAPC, for instance, has never sanctioned or punished a member for violation of its code. No government agency has the power to enforce these standards.

CURRENT CONTROVERSIES AND ISSUES IN RECENT ELECTIONS

The greatest controversy concerning the elections themselves arose in the November 2000 presidential election contest between George W. Bush and then Vice President Al Gore. It was not resolved until the U.S. Supreme Court ruled on December 12, 2000, that recounts in Florida must be halted (*Bush v. Gore,* 2000). The behavior of the broadcast media in coverage of election results and the making of premature and erroneous predictions was widely criticized and led to congressional hearings.

There were major broadcast network blunders on election night, November 7. The networks CBS, NBC, ABC, and CNN among others predicted initially that Gore had won Florida's 25 electoral votes, then changed their predictions in favor of Bush at 2:00 A.M., and then for no one at 4:00 A.M. (Martin & Ballingrud, 2000). This was symptomatic of the closeness of the election and may have contributed to the multifaceted legal-challenge strategies followed by both major candidates and others. The election limbo in Florida and the nation persisted for 36 days, from November 7 until December 12, 2000.

After the event, it seems that the television networks had all used the same data service, which bungled the job, and all based their varying projections on the same incorrect data. The closeness of the presidential vote in Florida led to automatic machine recounts under Florida state election law and numerous instances of litigation in state and federal court. At the conclusion of the machine recount, Bush had a lead of 930 votes statewide out of nearly 6 million ballots cast in the presidential election.

Many Florida counties used punch-card balloting systems where the voter uses a stylus to punch out a cardboard (prescored) piece (the now infamous "chad"). If a voter did not properly execute the punching exercise, the chad piece might remain attached at one or more corners, causing the automatic counting machine not to count the vote. The Gore team believed that if manual recounts could be had in select heavily Democratic counties where the vote had favored their candidates by large margins, they would recover sufficient "undervotes" (ballots that were read by the machines as no-votes for president, but where the ballot contained indications of the voter's intent to vote though less than fully punched) to overcome Bush's vote total. Accordingly, they requested manual recounts in four Florida counties that used punch-card ballots.

Ironically, a postelection study by the *Miami Herald* and other newspapers in conjunction with an accounting firm undertook full manual recounts under varying criteria and concluded that this was in error: Gore lost under all but one of numerous different scenarios of counting standards (Merzer, 2001). Nonetheless, this belief by the Gore team was the motivation for the entire postelection campaign to secure manual recounts and resolve the election in the courts. Numerous books and articles describe the details of the activities and the litigation (e.g., Correspondents, 2001; Dershowitz, 2001; Dionne & Kristol, 2001; Jones, 2003; Lowenstein & Hasen, 2001; Merzer, 2001; Political Staff, 2001; Posner, 2001).

Though several legal theories were advanced in the litigation in the U.S. Supreme Court, the determinative issue was that the system of statewide manual recounts ordered by the Florida Supreme Court was unconstitutional because it allowed different counties to use varying and inconsistent standards for determining when a partially detached or bulging ("pregnant") chad would be counted as evidence of a voter's intent. Similarly situated voters had their ballots counted or not counted differently according to where they lived, and a majority of the Supreme Court considered this unacceptable and unconstitutional. This was consistent with long-standing Supreme Court precedent, contrary to the remarks of frequently partisan critics of the judgment.

In its decision of December 12 in *Bush v. Gore* (2000), the Supreme Court vacated the opinion of the Florida Supreme Court and ruled that the equal protection clause of the U.S. Constitution had been violated. Seven justices found equal-protection problems, and two justices did not. Five justices concluded that the remedy was to halt manual recounts because it was not possible to carry them out in a constitutional manner by the conceded December 12 federal deadline to submit electoral votes. Two justices thought the state should be entitled to try and differed as to the possible remedy. Critics of the decision paint it as a narrow 5–4 decision while supporters describe it as a 7–2 decision. In any case, it overruled the Florida Supreme Court and brought the contests, recounts, and postelection litigation to an end.

The problems with the vote-counting equipment in Florida were hopefully resolved by a new state law that eliminated punch-card balloting systems. They were replaced for the 2002 and following elections by less easily mishandled optical-scan systems and electronic data-recording systems using touch screens.

The other major controversy has to do with the BCRA of 2002, reviewed earlier. The BCRA did not become effective until after the 2002 elections, and which provisions will be valid under the Constitution will not be determined finally until 2003 or more likely 2004. A meaningful assessment of the new legislation cannot yet be carried out.

EVALUATION OF OVERALL SYSTEM

No country's media system works to perfection, and that of the United States is no exception. The United States is perhaps unique in the degree of freedom from governmental control that all forms of print and broadcast media enjoy. This is primarily attributable to the strength of the protection afforded to free speech and freedom of the press under the First Amendment, the strictness with which the courts scrutinize threats to that freedom, and the narrow scope of allowable exceptions compared even to other established democracies. One result is that candidates and political parties for the most part are free to use paid media in quantities primarily limited only by fund-raising skills.

This relative freedom leads in some cases to excesses on the part of the media that are essentially uncontrolled by the government. Embarrassing gaffes such as the premature prediction of the outcome of the 2000 presidential race in Florida likely will not lead to legislation but may for a time result in some increased level of media self-restraint. Two features, one economic and one geographic, make it unlikely that such restraint will persist over time, barring further blunders of the same type. The economic factor is the desire of the broadcast news media to be first with their predictions to enhance their audience share, their ratings, and consequently their appeal to commercial advertisers. The geographic factor is that the United States mainland spans four time zones (not to mention Hawaii), so that it is inevitable that some polls will be open for several hours after the first ones on the East Coast have closed, and the urge to predict may ultimately prove irresistible.

Scrutiny of election and vote-counting processes by the media during the days following the 2000 presidential election has led to reform in some states, most notably in Florida. Other states that continue to use older voting technology such as the troublesome punch cards have not made changes, so it remains possible that in a similarly close election, the nouveau science of "chadology" could be resurrected.

More generally, there is little the government can do within the confines of the First Amendment to impose mandatory codes of conduct on the media. It is up to the media to exercise their freedom responsibly, and barring the commission of actionable torts of libel, slander, or invasion of privacy, the principal external restraints on media conduct are the need to appeal to the public and to advertisers. This is unlikely to change.

REFERENCES

Bennett, J. (1998, December 8). Quick, pay for a campaign before the rules change. *New York Times.* Retrieved from http://www.nytimes.com

Bennett, W. L. (1996). *News: The politics of illusion* (3rd ed.). New York: Longman.

Berelson, B. (1966). Democratic theory and public opinion. In B. Berelson & M. Janowitz (Eds.), *Reader in public opinion and communication* (pp. 489–504). New York: The Free Press.

Bipartisan Campaign Reform Act of 2002, Pub. L. No. 107-155.

Bopp, J., Jr., & Coleson, R. E. (2002, Spring). The First Amendment needs no reform: Protecting liberty from campaign finance "reformers." *Catholic University Law Review, 51,* 785–830.

Broder, D. A. (1989, January 19). Should news media police accuracy of ads? *The Washington Post,* p. A22.

Buckley v. Valeo, 424 U.S. 1 (1976).

Bush v. Gore, 531 U.S. 98 (2000).

Center for Media and Public Affairs. (2000). Campaign 2000 final: How TV news covered the general election campaign. *Media Monitor, XVI*(6), 1–9.

Committee for Economic Development. (1999). *Investing in the people's business: A business proposal for campaign finance reform.* New York: Author.

Common Cause. (1998). Party soft money state issue brief. Retrieved from http://www.commoncause.org/states/softmoney_fed.htm

Corrado, A., Mann, T. E., Ortiz, D. R., Potter, T., & Sorauf, F. J. (Eds.). (1997). *Campaign finance reform: A sourcebook.* Washington, DC: Brookings Institution.

Correspondents of *The New York Times.* (2001). *36 days: The complete chronicle of the 2000 presidential election crisis.* New York: Times Books.

Dershowitz, A. (2001). *Supreme injustice.* New York: Oxford University Press.

Devlin, L. P. (2001). Contrasts in presidential campaign commercials of 2000. *American Behavioral Scientist, 44,* 2238–2369.

Dionne, E. J., Jr., & Kristol, W. (Eds.). (2001). *Bush v. Gore: The court cases and the commentary.* Washington, DC: Brookings Institution.

Faucher v. Federal Election Commission, 928 F.2d 468 (1991), *cert. denied,* 502 U.S. 820.

Federal Communications Act of 1934, 47 U.S.C. § 151 *et seq.,* as amended by the Telecommunications Act of 1996, 47 U.S.C.

Federal Election Campaign Act of 1971, 2 U.S.C. § 431 *et seq.* (As amended 2002).

Federal Election Commission. (2001, January 12). Party funding escalates. Retrieved May 1, 2002 from http://fecweb1.fec.gov/press/011201partyfunds.htm

Federal Election Commission v. Central Long Island Tax Reform Immediately Committee, 616 F.2d 45 (2d Cir. 1980), *(CLITRIM).*

Federal Election Commission v. Christian Action Network, 894 F. Supp. 946 (W.D. Va. 1995), *affirmed,* 92 F.3d 1178 (4th Cir. 1996).

Federal Election Commission v. Furgatch, 807 F.2d 857 (9th Cir. 1987), *cert. denied,* 484 U.S. 850.

Federal Election Commission v. Massachusetts Citizens for Life, Inc., 479 U.S. 238 (1986), *(MCFL).*

Foote, J. S. (1990). *Television access and political power.* New York: Praeger.

Frank, R. S. (1973). *Message dimensions of television news.* Lexington, MA: Heath.

Franklin, M. A., Anderson, D. A., & Cate, F. H. (2000). *Mass media law* (6th ed.). New York: Foundation Press.

Gans, C. (2000, November 10). Battleground state mobilization efforts propel voter turnout slightly upward in historic but disturbing election. Retrieved from http://www.gspm.org/csae/cgans6.html

Goldberg, B. (2001). *Bias.* Washington, DC: Regnery.

Hallin, D. C. (1992). Sound bite news: Television coverage of elections, 1968–1988. *Journal of Communication, 42,* 5–24.

Hanson, C. (1992). Media bashing: The media's alleged political bias. *Columbia Journalism Review, 31*(4), 52–55.

Hofstetter, C. R. (1976). *Bias in the news. Network TV coverage in the '72 election campaigns.* Columbus: Ohio State University Press.

Holtz-Bacha, C. (1999). The American presidential election in international perspective. In L. L. Kaid & D. G. Bystrom (Eds.), *The electronic election: Perspectives on the 1996 campaign communication* (pp. 349–361). Mahwah, NJ: Lawrence Erlbaum Associates.

Imagine a presidential campaign that made people want to go out and vote. (1996, October 1). *The New York Times,* p. A9.

Iyengar, S., & Kinder, D. R. (1987). *News that matters: Television and American opinion.* Chicago: University of Chicago Press.

Jackson, B. (1990). *Broken promise: Why the Federal Election Commission failed.* New York: Priority Press Publications.

Jones, C. A. (1998). Digital television and media concentration regulation in the US. *Atlantische Texte, 10,* 25–29.

Jones, C. A. (2000). Soft money and hard choices: The influence of finance rules on campaign communication strategy. In R. Denton (Ed.), *Political communication ethics* (pp. 179–201). Westport, CT: Praeger.

Jones, C. A. (2003). Voting from the bench: Media analysis of legal issues in the 2000 post-election campaign. *American Behavioral Scientist, 46,* 642–657.

Jones, C. A., & Kaid, L. L. (1976). Political campaign regulation and the Constitution: Oklahoma's Campaign Contributions and Expenditures Act. *Oklahoma Law Review, 29,* 684–711.

Just, M., Crigler, A., & Wallach, L. (1990). Thirty seconds or thirty minutes: What viewers learn from spot advertisements and candidate debates. *Journal of Communication, 40,* 120–133.

Kaid, L. L. (1999a). Political advertising: A summary of research findings. In B. Newman (Ed.), *The handbook of political marketing* (pp. 423–438). Thousand Oaks, CA: Sage.

Kaid, L. L. (Ed.). (1999b). *Television and politics in evolving European democracies.* Commack, NY: NovaScience Publishers.

Kaid, L. L., Gobetz, R. H., Garner, J., Leland, C. M., & Scott, D. K. (1993). Television news and presidential campaigns: The legitimization of television political advertising. *Social Science Quarterly, 74*(2), 274–285.

Kaid, L. L., & Johnston, A. (2001). *Videostyle in presidential campaigns: Style and content of televised political advertising.* Westport, CT: Praeger/Greenwood.

Kaid, L. L., McKinney, M. S., & Tedesco, J. C. (2000). *Civic dialogue in the 1996 presidential campaign: Candidate, media, and public voices.* Cresskill, NJ: Hampton Press.

Kaid, L. L., Tedesco, J. C., & McKinnon, L. M. (1996). Presidential ads as nightly news: A content analysis of 1988 and 1992 televised adwatches. *Journal of Broadcasting and Electronic Media, 40,* 297–308.

Kelley, S., Jr. (1960). *Political campaigning: Problems in creating an informed electorate.* Washington, DC: Brookings Institution.

Lichter, R. S., & Noyes, R. E. (1995). *Good intentions make bad news.* Lanham, MD: Rowman & Littlefield.

Lichter, R. S., Noyes, R. E., & Kaid, L. L. (1998). Negative news or no news: How the networks nixed the '96 campaign. In L. L. Kaid & D. G. Bystrom (Eds.), *The electronic election: Perspectives on the 1996 campaign communication* (pp. 3–13). Mahwah, NJ: Lawrence Erlbaum Associates.

Lipset, S. M., & Schneider, W. (1987). *The confidence gap* (Rev. ed.). Baltimore: Johns Hopkins University Press.

Lowenstein, D. H., & Hasen, R. L. (2001). *Election law cases and materials* (2nd ed.). Durham, NC: Carolina Academic Press.

Maine Right to Life Committee, Inc. v. Federal Election Com'n, 914 F.Supp. 8 (D.Me. 1996), aff'd., 98 F.3d 1 (1st Cir. 1996).

Marcus, R., & Babcock, C. R. (1997, February 9). System cracks under weight of cash. *Washington Post.* Retrieved April 30, 2003 from http://www.washingtonpost.com

Martin, S., & Ballingrud, D. (2000, December 14). Long run to the White House. *St. Petersburg Times,* p. 3X.

Merzer, M. (2001). *The Miami Herald report: Democracy held hostage.* New York: St. Martin's Press.

Miami Herald Publishing Co. v. Tornillo. (1974). 418 U.S. 241.

Mifflin, L. (1996, November 3). Free TV-time experiment wins support, if not viewers. *The New York Times,* p. 38.

Miller, A. H. (1974). Political issues and trust in government: 1964–1970. *American Political Science Review, 68,* 951–972.

National Association of Broadcasters. (1988). *Political broadcast handbook* (3rd ed.). Washington, DC: Author.

National Association of Broadcasters. (2000). *Political broadcast catechism* (15th ed.). Washington, DC: Author.

New York Times v. Sullivan, 376 US 254 (1964).

Owen, D. (2001). Media mayhem: Performance of the press in Election 2000. In L. J. Sabato (Ed.), *Overtime: The Election 2000 thriller* (pp. 123–156). New York: Longman.

Patterson, T. (1993). *Out of order.* New York: Knopf.

Patterson, T. (1994). Legitimate beef—The presidency and a carnivorous press. *Media Studies Journal, 8*(2), 21–27.

Patterson, T. E., & McClure, R. D. (1976). *The unseeing eye: Myth of television power in politics.* New York: Putnam.

Perry v. Bartlett, 231 F.3d 155 (4th Cir., 2000).

PEW Research Center for the People and the Press. (1996, May 13). TV viewership declines: Fall off greater for young adults and computer users. Washington, DC: Author.

Planned Parenthood Affiliates of Michigan, Inc. v. Miller, 21 F. Supp. 2d 740 (E.D. Mich., 1998).

Political Staff of *The Washington Post.* (2001). *Deadlock: The inside story of America's closest election.* New York: Public Affairs Press.

Posner, R. A. (2001). *Breaking the deadlock: The 2000 election, the Constitution, and the courts.* Princeton, NJ: Princeton University Press.

PROMAX. (1997, April 22). Paid political advertising does not result in more informed voters [press release]. Los Angeles: PROMAX International.

Putnam, R. D. (1995). Bowling alone: America's declining social capital. *Journal of Democracy, 6*(1), 65–78.

Right to Life of Michigan, Inc. v. Miller, 23 F. Supp. 2d 766 (W.D. Mich., 1998).

Robinson, M., & Sheehan, M. (1983). *Over the wire and on TV.* New York: Russell Sage Foundation.

Sabato, L. (1991). *Feeding frenzy: Attack journalism and American politics.* New York: The Free Press.

Sander, T. H., & Putnam, R. D. (2002, February 19). Walking the civic talk after September 11. *Christian Science Monitor.* Retrieved May 1, 2002 from http://www.csmonitor.com/

Skiba, K. M. (1996, November 7). State voter turnout of 57% is lowest since 1920, records show. *Journal Sentinel,* p. 1.

Society of Professional Journalists. (1996). Code of Ethics. Retrieved April 30, 2003 from http://spj.org/ethics_code.asp

Vermont Right to Life v. Sorrell, 221 F.3d 376 (2d Cir., 2000).

The Washington Post/Kaiser Family Foundation/Harvard University Survey Project. (1997). *Why don't Americans trust the government?* Menlo Park, CA: Henry Kaiser Family Foundation.

West, D. (1993). *Air wars: Television advertising in election campaigns, 1952–1992.* Washington, DC: Congressional Quarterly.

WMUR-TV, Inc. 11 FCC Rcd. 12728, (1996).

3

Germany

Helmut Drück

Germany has been a relative latecomer to the world of the democratic system of government. It was not until 1919 in the aftermath of the First World War and with the disintegration of the German and Austrian/Hungarian monarchies that the "Constitution of Weimar" established a truly parliamentary system in Germany, which suffered from serious political weaknesses that were to lead to the rapid demise of early 20th-century democracy in Germany.

An election system based on pure proportionality led to more than 20 political parties in the national parliament, the Reichstag, some with three or even less Members of Parliament, which meant that governments could only be assembled through coalitions between the different party factions. As a result, the Chancellor was in a permanently weak position because a minority coalition partner in the government could upset the balance of power and undermine the position of the Chancellor by leaving the coalition on an issue that had little relevance to the government in general, but was understood to be particularly important to an individual party who were a part of the coalition government. In such an unstable political environment, the life span of governments was usually short and the people, suffering from declining economic conditions and unemployment, lost faith in the capabilities of the democratic institutions.

Such a fragile system of government could not survive once a determined leader exploited the possibilities of the Constitution, coupled with the civil disobedience on the streets, to come to power and to introduce an autocratic system in 1933, which soon turned into a totalitarian order. In this respect the contemporary context of democratic institutions and the democratic process needs to be understood in the context of the failure of the original attempt in Germany to sustain a democratic and parliamentary process and the rise to power of the National Socialist Party and their leader Adolf Hitler, who was elected to power, according to the then constitutional laws of Germany.

THE CONSTITUTIONAL SYSTEM OF GERMANY

In response to the upheavals in German history, the authors of the Constitution of 1949 during the reconstitution of German democracy, after the Second World War, ensured that legislation was in place that guaranteed a number of freedoms that militated against the abuse of the Constitution and a concentration of power. To this end the main features of the 1949 Constitution as they related to the political and public spheres are:

- Parliament and government should be fair and stable and therefore should consist of a system of representation in parliament based on a mixed system of majoritarian and proportional representation. This clause stipulates that a threshold of 5% of the valid ballots is required for parties to gain seats in the parliament (unless a party wins three direct mandates). This 5% barrier prevents minority parties or groups from active participation in political decision making or government, and is considered a contributing factor to political stability in the Federal Republic. The system usually results in between four and six parties being represented in parliament and at the time of writing there are five parties (Christian Democrats, Social Democrats, Liberals, Greens, Post-Communists).
- Political parties should be entitled by law to take part in the political process and that they therefore should enjoy certain privileges, including financial ones.
- Political parties can only be forbidden or made illegal by judgment of the Federal Constitutional Court if it is proven that their aims and performance are against the Constitution.
- Germany should have strong and stable governments, the chancellors of which can be removed from office during their term only by electing a new chancellor by a majority of the federal parliament.
- Citizens should have and enjoy a system of free press and broadcasting as a constitutional right.

All these features have become law, and following the reunification of Germany in 1999 the "new" federal states opted for the existing constitution and only modified some minor articles. These principles are continuously upheld by the jurisdiction of the Federal Constitutional Court, which plays a pivotal role in German democratic society.

MEDIA SYSTEM

Germany regulates its media system according to federal and state laws. The same applies to the executive bodies responsible for media, which to some extent lie within the federal administration, but to a greater extent within the administrations of the 16 regional Länder states or with their specific regulatory authorities.

Article 5 of the constitution guarantees the traditional free-speech privileges: free expression for everybody, freedom of information, and freedom of the media. The freedom of the press and the freedom of broadcasting are interpreted not only as constitutional rights, against undue interference by the state, but also as institutional guarantees for their existence and performance. In many respects media freedom is understood to be the basic precondition for democracy in Germany.

The Federal Constitutional Court has guaranteed this independence from state influence and market concentration in several landmark decisions. In 1958 the constitutional court ruled that freedom of speech ranked higher than commercial interests of a specific film producer (Menzel, 2000). The concept that the media should be free of constraints was also further supported in 1961 when the court rejected the ambitions of Chancellor Konrad Adenauer to establish a state-controlled nationwide television station and held that the principles of public-service broadcasting should be implemented by the federal states. In 1981 the court expressed the view that broadcasting in contrast to the press could not be governed by market competition alone in order to achieve complete information and the forming of public opinion by the citizen (Menzel, 2000).

THE PRESS

The German newspaper landscape is rather diverse: 386 dailies (6 nationals, 7 tabloids) and 23 weeklies have a combined circulation of 30.3 million copies. One can observe a certain degree of economic and financial concentration but the existence of 136 independent "journalistic entities"—entities with full editorial staffs—is evidence that newspaper production is viable, decentralized, and on the national level, pluralistic. From 1954 to 2001 (now including the new federal states) the number of newspapers nationwide has declined from 225 to 136, of which 16 belong to the Axel Springer Verlag AG Berlin, the biggest newspaper publisher in Germany with a total market share of 23.4% (Media Perspektiven, Basisdaten, 2002, p. 52). In more than half of all Länder or smaller cities there exists only one daily newspaper reporting local or regional news.

The press is regulated by the Acts of the Parliament of the 16 Länder, which have no explicit provisions with regard to election coverage. The general principles apply—namely, that the press fulfills a public function when publishing material of public interest and thereby participates in the process of civic opinion building. It therefore has to apply due care with regard to accuracy of content and sources of the material that it publishes. The right of reply, which is guaranteed in all press laws, is of specific importance in election times, but it is, of course, limited to falsely reported facts, not on opinion.

There is no right to free space for parties or candidates in a newspaper. Nor is there a basic right of access to papers, because a paper is as free to deny paid space to political parties or candidates as it is to accept material for publication without charge. An exception to this principle is, however, possible in monopolized markets: If, for instance, a party or candidate in a local election is denied paid access by the only outlet in the electoral district in question, they may go to court to seek an injunction on the grounds of abuse of discretion and monopoly position.

Newspapers will normally accept paid advertisements from parties or candidates on a nondiscriminatory basis. Statements, even those veering toward falsehood, have been judged admissible in the past by the Federal Constitutional Court, and are not generally considered grounds for refusal. The Court regards free speech during an election period as one of the most fundamental human rights and holds that because of its importance, printed and broadcast matter that would ordinarily be unacceptable and therefore challenged, are permitted at election times.

Nevertheless, papers do reserve the right to reject advertisements, and can therefore exclude party statements of racist content or extremist views. Party advertisements have to be paid for by the party itself, the candidate, or a sponsor. Advertisements in favor of a political party or ideology or a specific candidate are often placed by a so-called voters' initiative, which raises funds for that purpose from their members. There have been cases when papers have given advertising space free of charge, but usually only if the majority of the text is generally a nonpartisan plea for participation in the election by the electorate. Discount advertising rates are also sometimes applied for election advertising.

A newspaper might accept the campaign manifesto of the main government party and of the leading opposition party for publication free of charge, either unabridged or in an edited version. The paper would justify the inclusion of this material as a reference point for the reader and voter. It would then lie within the discretion of the editor-in-chief as to whether such reference material should include the manifestos of smaller parties as well, or whether their agendas should only be commented upon.

There are no written rules whatsoever on the amount of election coverage or on the space to be given to advertising. Some newspapers will not place an electoral advertisement for a party on the same page as a profile of politicians from the same party or an article on its campaign convention. These papers want to avoid the impression that they are not independent and have retained the basic notion of independence and impartiality in journalism for professional reasons.

There are almost no political party dailies, and the few weeklies, monthlies, and other periodicals of the political parties have small circulations and marginal influence outside their membership. There is even an ongoing debate as to whether or not papers should publish editorial recommendations with regard to voting. Yet, the financially and politically independent newspapers in Germany can take political positions. For example, the nationwide dailies *Frankfurter Allgemeine Zeitung* and *Die Welt* have a conservative tendency, whereas *Süddeutsche Zeitung* and *Frankfurter Rundschau* regard themselves as progressive liberal or left of center in outlook. Papers can and do support certain ideological streams and there is political diversity within the national press.

The press gives broad coverage of elections for the Bundestag (federal parliament) or state parliaments. There is extensive reporting, critical analysis, and evaluation of the campaign, the issues under discussion, and the candidates; the press also carries extensive interviews with ministers, leading candidates, and other relevant personalities. The importance of the print media's analysis is increased by the frequent inability of electronic media journalism to extract clear and concise answers to their questions from politicians. Comprehensive coverage is, however, focused on the established parties. Extremist groups on both sides of the political spectrum receive much less attention from the press. Their campaign performance and platform is of limited interest and is usually covered by a single report, which includes a short profile of their main candidates. However, the activities of these groups in daily life attract extensive, according to some perhaps too much, attention and coverage, yet the context of violence, racism, xenophobia, or anti-Semitism is, unfortunately, topical.

The self-regulatory body of the German press, the Press Council (Presserat), is seldom called into action regarding election coverage. Those who consider themselves to have been unfairly treated tend to write to the particular editor directly, or to use their formal right of reply. The German press performs its role prior to elections adequately: Coverage is broad, and provides much background and analysis, often with a human touch. Bias or partiality within individual outlets is counterbalanced by the diversity of papers on the market as a whole, though as the trend toward consolidation continues, this may shift the balance.

PRIVATE BROADCASTING

Private radio and television broadcasting was introduced in 1984 and it took several years before private national television channels like RTL, SAT 1, and PRO 7 developed a significant presence in the German television ecology. Today many additional channels are broadcasting successfully (RTL 2, Super RTL, Kabel 1, DFS, MTV, VIVA, ntv, N24) and a surprising number of smaller channels continue to compete.

Competition in the German television markets is intense and only RTL and PRO 7 make a profit and have paid back the deficits they accrued in their initial years. Private radio remains local or regionalized, even though some stations have frequencies in several Länder. The number of private radio stations is enormous and still rising. Radio reaches daily 80% of the population, 55% of which listen to private radio stations.

Private broadcasting has none of the obligations that are placed upon the public channels to provide a variety of programming, but it is not outside regulatory instruments. Paragraphs 20 and 23 of the State Treaty on Broadcasting (Staatsvertrag über den Rundfunk) of 1991/2002 stipulate that the private channels should reflect the plurality of opinion in society, and that recognized professional standards of journalism have to be met.

Political parties are eligible to receive airtime before elections. National channels have to provide appropriate time before federal and European elections if a party is running in at least one state in its entirety (and not merely in certain electoral districts within it). However, such broadcasts are not transmitted free of charge and the stations are entitled to charge for space to cover their costs. Cost should be lower than normal advertising rates, because the profit margin is excluded, but can still be substantial.

The Conference of the Directors of the State Media Boards (Landesmedienanstalten) has issued legal directions with regard to charges and has made it clear that claims can only be made for the technical costs of transmission. They regard a maximum of 35% of the normal advertising price as justified. The Association of Private Broadcasters, however, believes that 55% of the normal rate is appropriate.

It is impossible to purchase additional airtime beyond the allocation of spots to each party. This allocation is meticulously structured and considerably limits any possible discrimination by channels. The same rules are applied for private and public broadcasters and are explained in the next section because they were first introduced by the public broadcasters ARD and ZDF. The legal responsibility for the content of the political advertising lies with the party and not with the channel. The channel can, however, refuse a spot if it does not refer to the election or if the content evidently violates the law.

In the past, the private channels have covered election campaigns and the goals of the competing parties and candidates fairly in news and information-based programs. However, with regard to the selection of interviewees and commentaries, a bias toward conservative positions (both politically and socioeconomically) can be observed; given that the profit motive underlies the operation of, and investment in, these broadcasters, this is perhaps unsurprising. Still, they observe and demonstrate their distance to government and opposition and receive special attention in cases of rigid criticism of conservative positions.

PUBLIC-SERVICE BROADCASTING

Germany has long been a stronghold of public-service broadcasting and it still enjoys one of the strongest and best financed systems. In 1991 the Court confirmed its strong support for public-service broadcasting in formulating a constitutional guarantee for its existence and further development in relation to technological and social change. The Court argued that there are structural shortcomings of commercial broadcasting as a result of its financing by advertising and therefore its orientation toward mass audiences. Freedom of broadcasting is characterized as a freedom to serve the independent formation of public opinion in society and this is also the case in electoral campaigns and elections themselves.

Insofar as the criteria of balanced reporting and of presenting the plurality of opinions apply for public broadcasting and for commercial broadcasters, the latter enjoy a far more liberal regime. Qualifications of this freedom of communication are only permitted via general Acts of Parliament, which at the same time safeguard the principle of equality in a nondiscriminatory way.

The philosophy of equality of opportunity in all sectors of public life, including political, economic, and cultural spheres, that lies behind the constitutional provisions is given its most practical expression in the guaranteed existence and development of public-service broadcasting mostly financed by public revenues. The public-service broadcasters are required by law of the federal states to provide information, education, and entertainment. This means news, background information, documentaries and variety of service programming, quizzes, feature films, and sports, in an unbiased and nondiscriminatory way, at high technical standards, throughout the whole country and at reasonable costs to the citizen. All of these elements serve as preconditions for the active participation of the citizens in public life.

There are 11 independent public broadcasting stations, all founded by Acts of state Parliaments or by treaties between two or more states. These stations operate two national television channels, ARD and ZDF, the European cultural channel 3 Sat and the Franco-German cultural channel ARTE, the documentary channel Phoenix, a children's channel KiKa as well as the two national radio stations of Deutschland Radio. At the regional level, ARD maintains eight regional television channels and more than 50 radio programs.

The public-service channels enjoy the right of self-administration via independent boards, which oversee their programming and operations. The stations are financed by license fees with a supplementary income from advertising, which is strictly regulated and is limited to a maximum of 20 minutes per day but not on Sundays and holidays and not after 8 P.M. In some respects the regulation has become far more flexible as the broadcasters are allowed to draw upon sponsorship revenues and there are no restrictions placed on broadcasters regarding using sponsorship in prime time. The system of limited mixed revenues is seen to allow the public stations to be independent from the state and market and they enjoy numerous relations with both systems.

Public broadcasters are expected to cover the whole range of an election campaign including the smaller parties, by critically engaging with the election, while at the same time observing overall objectivity, which is neither detrimental nor favorable to any candidate. They should observe professional distance and attempt to prevent the impression of partisanship. They therefore have rules for certain abstentions in election times including: (a) nonappearance of politicians in variety shows, and (b) nonappearance of journalists who are candidates or are campaigning for a party or generally known as being a prominent party member or whose spouse, partner, or close relative is a candidate.

The stations will see to it that no unfair advantage takes place and therefore they do not accept invitations or other privileges from parties, apart from their reporters getting close access to candidates. The public broadcasters traditionally provide free airtime to parties and candidates prior to elections, as a service to political parties and to the electorate rather than through constitutional obligation. Many state broadcasting laws do, however, explicitly require the public stations to grant airtime before general elections to political parties or other groups participating in the elections. The principles that govern these broadcasts are as follows:

- Beneficiaries can only be parties or groups participating in the election.
- All participating parties/groups are entitled to access, and it is not within the discretion of the station to select those who are to gain access.
- Airtime has to be appropriate.
- Responsibility for content lies with the party/group.
- The station can refuse access on two grounds: (a) if the broadcast is not related to the election, or (b) if there is a clear and gross violation of general law, and in particular, criminal law.
- Transmission costs are borne by the station, and production costs by the party/group.
- All decisions of the station in this context are formal legal actions and are open to judicial review in a Court of Administration.
- No other programs—in particular, advertising—can be granted to parties or groups participating in the elections, but editorial programs remain possible and are widely used for nonpartisan information and analysis.

On the issue of access, the following two questions have been and remain controversial. They have provoked substantial litigation and prompted many decisions from the Federal Constitutional Court and various High Administrative Courts:

- How many spots of what length can a party or group demand?
- When can a station refuse transmission due to the content of the spot?

QUANTITY AND LENGTH OF SPOTS

The rules are usually ambiguous regarding this question and simply state that the airtime should be appropriate. The granting of arithmetically equal airtime is considered inappropriate because small parties would benefit disproportionately to the detriment of the established parties. Moreover, equal allocation could confuse instead of enlighten the audience about the political significance of minor participants in the election. The allocation of airtime is now governed by the Law on Political Parties and is based on two separate measures:

TABLE 3.1
Allocation of Slots for Political Parties in Germany

Party/Parties	1990 Slots Each Party	1990 Slots Total	1994 Slots Each Party	1994 Slots Total	1998 Slots Each Party	1998 Slots Total
CDU, SPD	8	16	8	16	8	16
FDP, CSU, PDS	4	12	4	12	4	12
Green West	4	4	–	–	–	–
Green East	4	4	–	–	–	–
Green (after unification)	–	–	4	4	4	4
DSU	4	4	–	–	–	–
Republikaner	3	3	3	3	2	2
Others	2	12	2	30	2	
		55 = 110		65 = 130		

Note. Data provided by ARD and ZDF.

- Each party/group receives a minimum of two broadcasts at 2.5 or 1.5 minutes each and 60 seconds in regional elections.
- Each party/group gets additional slots in accordance with the percentage of parliamentary seats gained in the previous election.

The Law on Political Parties grants each party represented in the federal parliament at least half as much time as any other party. In the campaign for the federal elections of December 1990, October 1994, and September 1998, free-access slots were distributed as shown in Table 3.1 on both ARD and ZDF.

In the elections of 1994 no less than 41 parties/groups intended to run. Up to 105 slots were anticipated for transmission by both ARD and ZDF; much less of course on the private channels because of the costs. Finally only 23 contenders demanded airtime from the public stations. Still, an enormous amount of party information is communicated to the audience and it is questionable as to whether this serves the interest of participation in the election or discourages it.

CONTROL OF CONTENT AND DENIAL OF SPOT ALLOCATION

The parties are responsible for the content of the broadcasts. Yet if the content violates criminal law, the broadcasters become de facto an accessory to the violation. The stations have therefore reserved the right to control the content in the event of obvious violations of the constitution or the general laws. Following the refusal of airtime in the past, some political parties have gone to court, and have usually succeeded in obliging the broadcasters to transmit their message on air. Jurisdiction has developed from such cases to the effect that:

> It is not within the power of a broadcasting station to deny an election slot with the argument that its content appears unconstitutional, since the competence to decide upon the unconstitutionality of a party and its announcements lies only with the Federal Constitutional Court. The station has however the right to expect that the party uses its airtime only for legal campaigning, and in particular that no relevant and evident breach of criminal law will take place. The station is therefore entitled to control the content of the slot and—in the case of such a breach of law—to refuse transmission. (Federal Constitutional Court, vol. 47, 1978, p. 198)

This basic decision of the Federal Constitutional Court of 1978 led to the dissemination of many spots of questionable content. Minority parties of the far right or far left claim to have a legal basis for extremist propaganda, which might be unconstitutional, but does not usually violate criminal law. The broadcasts of right-wing groups, of messages of a racist or even neo-Nazi or anti-Semitic nature, enrage many people and there is some support for the abolition of obligatory spot transmissions. However, until the Länder parliaments change their respective broadcasting laws, the stations have no option of turning down demands for election spots, even if the content is dubious. There is a counterargument that the abolition of obligatory airtime for political parties would be to capitulate the democratic majority to an extremist, undemocratic minority. Moreover, because the established democratic parties are disinclined to forsake their own campaigning opportunities via radio and television, a change of the laws is not imminent.

The political campaign material is also signposted to avoid misunderstandings and misinterpretations by the audience: The stations transmit a message before and after the slots that states clearly the fact that the program is a party political broadcast and it states which party is responsible for the broadcast.

FAIRNESS AND IMPARTIALITY

The aim of editorial programming in public-service broadcasting during election periods is the fair representation of parties and candidates. The journalistic rules and professional codes of ethics are implied in the working contracts of each member of staff. The broadcasting boards, which exist in each station, have the final word on the admissibility of a given program, but only of course in the second instance after the editor-in-chief, program director, and director general has decided upon the case.

In some cases, formal program regulations, which describe the duties and responsibilities of writers and editors, form part of the working contracts. Each program, whether produced by a staff member or a freelance journalist, recorded or live, needs to be approved by a responsible editor, who must be a permanent staff member and who is required to guarantee that the program does not violate a law and matches professional standards. As a result of this practice, very few complaints are submitted about programs and even fewer—if any at all—are sustained by the broadcasting boards or the courts. In summary, the political parties and candidates are fairly treated in news and information programs of the public broadcasters.

AREAS OF CONTROVERSY

Although public broadcasting generally works well, there remain some areas of controversy that every now and then are discussed in public or dealt with before the courts. It is unusual for parties and candidates to levy legitimate complaints about the unwillingness of media or journalists to cover their campaign. If there is criticism that can lead to formal cases, it centers around the following four areas:

- The general right of parties to receive airtime.
- Arithmetically equal or weighted allocation of airtime.
- The binding effects of party agreements on airtime.
- The right of access of parties to editorial programs.

The General Right of Parties to Receive Airtime

As mentioned previously, the liberal approach of the courts has provoked criticism especially in the case of extremist views. The ARD has raised the issue in two separate initiatives in 1989 and 1993, asking the prime ministers of the Länder to change the statutes, which force the channels to provide airtime for transmissions. These initiatives have been rejected, mainly on the grounds that the present situation should continue unless there is reason to believe that individual electoral broadcasts will cause lasting damage to the democratic order of the Federal Republic of Germany. Some prominent voices have requested the abolition of obligatory airtime for political parties altogether, but others object to giving up a well-established democratic means of communication just because it can be abused by extremists.

Personally, the author is in favor of maintaining the present arrangement on the grounds that extremists should not be allowed to determine the form of the democratic process. They should be fought with political argumentation—in election spots, for example, in which extremist rhetoric is challenged and undermined. One should in any case be aware that abolishing broadcasting spots will not completely stop the dissemination of right-wing or other extremist propaganda.

Equal or Weighted Allocation of Airtime

There is criticism that parties do not receive equal time slots and that the established parties are on the air for longer than the smaller or new parties. It is argued that the principle of equality of opportunity should negate this arrangement, and it is asked how new parties are ever to gain strength and come to power if they are not treated equally. However, the demand for equal treatment is satisfied if a small party is treated like other small parties; one cannot ignore the fact that these groups differ substantially from parties already represented in parliament and do not therefore merit the same treatment.

The Binding Effects of Party Agreements on Airtime

Radio Bremen is not obliged by statute to grant free airtime but used to do so by tradition. In 1990, the four parties represented in the Land parliament agreed to abstain from using free airtime in a Land election. A minor left-wing party did claim its airtime, but was refused on the grounds that the other parties were abstaining. The Federal High Court of Administration eventually ruled that airtime should be granted because the agreement between major parties should not affect other parties that are eligible for airtime. Because the station was in principle prepared to offer airtime, it had to do so if requested.

The Right of Access of Parties to Editorial Programs

Do political parties or specific candidates have a right to participate in journalistic programs about the campaign, in election debates, or in roundtables? This problem is relevant for public broadcasters alone, because private broadcasters and newspapers can use their editorial discretion freely, as long as they adhere to the professional ethics of journalism.

In two cases, certain parties demanded that their candidates be allowed to take part in an election program, to which only spokespersons of parties represented in the outgoing parliament had been invited. In both cases, the courts, the High Court of Administration in Hamburg and the Federal Constitutional Court, held that the stations are free to decide in what way they wish to inform the voters about the electoral issues and the positions of the parties. They can, for instance, let their journalists make informative, analytical, and commentary programs, within the parameters of correct and unbiased reporting.

If, however, the station decides to invite representatives of campaigning parties to debates or roundtables, and expose them to the questions of journalists, the audience, or rival candidates, then the station voluntarily has limited its editorial discretion. These types of programs are apt to give a general overview of the position of the parties on election issues and to present leading candidates, and therefore have to include all parties. Only fringe groups and parties that, as shown by membership, results in previous elections, and other similar criteria have no relevance whatsoever, can be left out. A station is considered to violate the principle of equality and objectivity if only those parties that represent the power structures and the established opposition are invited.

This judgment has been criticized, particularly by the political establishment, for placing the main parties on the same footing as extremist parties. In the Hamburg case, and in yet another case in Lower Saxony in March 1994, the victories of small right-wing parties in court cases, which upheld their right to participate in election broadcasts, proved to be hollow. The established parties simply withdrew from the programs and the transmissions were eventually canceled.

A review of relevant court cases indicates a legal system that works well. The decisions demonstrate the courts' desire to equalize chances for the individual party or candidate and their willingness to act in the little time that is usually left before transmission or election day. From the courts that undertake the first hearings to the Federal Constitutional Court, all are prepared to take decisions, sometimes within hours, on media election cases. It remains necessary for parties, candidates, and politicians to be aware of possible infringements of their rights by a program or a journalist; but if protests do not help, the courts are an accessible avenue of redress and injunctions are not impossible to obtain.

EDITORIAL COVERAGE OF POLITICAL CAMPAIGNS AND ELECTIONS

Coverage of election campaigning is not qualitatively different from normal political journalism. The amount of reportage and the intensity of focus may increase, but the basic rules of political journalism apply. There is no distinction between the precampaign period, the campaign, and a reflection period before voting day.

Editorial decisions are taken in meetings of the news and political staff, in which the editor-in-chief has the final say and decides who will write editorials and commentaries. It is the general rule that the news section will include "all the news that is fit to print." The political positions of all parties are reported, but it is left to the discretion of the editors to decide the emphasis given to the various parties and groupings. Reporting from conventions is compulsory, and is usually divided into three segments: (a) reporting on the election platform, (b) reports on the atmosphere at the convention and among delegates, and (c) personality piece/interview/biographical feature on the leader/main candidate.

The manner in which such an event will be commented upon varies according to the general political orientation of the media outlet in the case of papers or private television and radio channels. Public broadcasters are obliged to reflect the whole political spectrum, and will therefore ensure that commentaries from more than one journalist are provided. This is not arranged too rigidly, so that commentary A is counterbalanced immediately by commentary B, and the stations seek rather to achieve a balance within the overall program.

There cannot be equal coverage of all parties and candidates. One should be aware that about 40 parties and groups took part in the federal election in September 2002; of these, only 7 really mattered and only 6 could expect to cross the 5% hurdle which finally 5 only did. The natural shape of election coverage will be for the bulk of attention to be paid to these seven parties, with special emphasis on the three borderline parties whose showing will decide the composition of the governing coalition. The many smaller or minority parties can only expect cursory coverage, in the form of one or more articles or broadcasts on the "little parties" as a genre, which summarize views and appraisals.

Although a media organization can expect a certain loyalty from its staff, no journalist can be forced to write an article or commentary against their own convictions. This strengthens the independence of the journalist in specific instances, but in the long run, he or she is likely either to comply with the general ideological line of the employer or to change to a job where there is greater harmony between employer and employee on basic professional questions. If a journalist chooses to work for a tabloid or certain private radio stations, they know what is expected from them and should not complain if a sensationalist or populist presentation of serious political issues is demanded. If, on the other hand, a journalist works for a public broadcaster or certain national or regional papers they can reasonably expect to enjoy the traditional freedom of work and expression that is part of the professional culture of such papers and stations. A few broadcasting laws and public broadcasting regulations have instituted specific procedures in the case of conflict between management and journalists on questions of journalistic independence.

Ultimately, the vigilance of journalists and their professional representation toward encroachment upon their rights is a powerful and effective weapon in the protection of journalistic independence. Yet two examples illustrate the way in which external forces and decisions can thwart the attempts of journalists to do their work independently.

First, the private television channel SAT 1 (in which two financial groups, Springer Publishers and Kirch Media, were shareholders) started a new series in the "super election year" of 1994. Titled *Back to Business Chancellor,* the program featured well-known journalists appearing to ask challenging questions of Chancellor Helmut Kohl; in fact, they were simply giving cues upon which Chancellor Kohl could elaborate unquestioned. The close ties between the Springer and Kirch management, and between Kohl and Kirch personally, were relevant in this context.

Second, it might occur that the incumbent candidate is not interested in participating in a television debate, because it may aid his opponents. Since 1985, whenever Chancellor Kohl has been challenged by the Social Democratic Party's candidates to take part in such a debate, his standard reply to journalists had been that he could not participate in a debate with his opponent because he was the leader of a coalition and would therefore have to bring along the two chairmen of his coalition partner parties. The Social Democrats were not interested in participating in a debate on a three-against-one basis, and it has therefore never taken place.

In 2002, for the first time on television there have been two such debates or "duel of the candidates," one on the public, the other on the private national television channels. The duel included the two central candidates for the chancellorship. The decision to include only two candidates was challenged in the courts by the leader of the liberal party (FDP), who are, according to opinion polls, expected to gain about 9% of the vote. As the public broadcasters did not include the candidate, the administrative court were asked to make a ruling and it supported the decision of the public service broadcasters based on the fact that the FDP candidate did not have a realistic chance to be elected as chancellor. There are also duels in the press as well. In both cases elaborate procedural rules are negotiated between the parties and the media to safeguard balance and fairness.

As in the United States, the process of forming public opinion and of electoral decisions in German democracy is more and more influenced by the performance of the media and mainly by television. The term coined for this trend is *mediacracy:* Politics by events and politics by polishing personal images of politicians rather than debates on different party programs and past achievements of politicians dominate the campaigns (Meyer, 2002). So the presentation of the candidates for chancellor in the "media duels" seems to be of utmost importance for the party managers rather than a serious concern with the real election issues.

Generally the public service broadcasters do inform the public about the positions of the candidates toward different central issues and this information is appreciated by the public (Brettschneider, 2002). These examples show how sensitive the editorial coverage of elections are and to what extent quantitative and qualitative aspects have to be taken into account. The responsibility of journalists is remarkable; only a few programs of the public broadcasters have been challenged in court due to their high prestige and credibility in news and politics. ARD has issued recommendations for editors that are based on the principle of equality of treatment and chances, stipulated in Article 5 of the Federal Law on Political Parties of 1976/1994, which states:

(1) Where a public authority provides facilities or other public services for use by a party, it must accord equal treatment to all other parties. The scale of such facilities and services may be graduated to conform with the importance of the parties to the minimum extent needed for the achievement of their aims. The importance of a party is judged in particular from the results of previous elections for central or regional government. In the case of a party represented in the Bundestag by a Parliamentary Party, the significance accorded to it must amount to at least half that granted to any other party;

(2) As regards the granting of public services in connection with an election Para. (1) applies only for the duration of the election campaign to parties which have submitted election proposals;

(3) The public services referred to in Para. 1 may be made dependent upon certain preconditions which all parties have to fulfil.

The ARD reminds their editors that programs during the campaign period or in close vicinity to election day have to be scrupulously balanced and that two forms were always accepted by the courts, namely the "duel" of the top candidates, that is, incumbent chancellor versus contender, or a so-called "election hearing" with representatives of all parties.

CONCLUSION

Controversies regarding election coverage will stay on the agenda as long as we have a democracy. Rules and regulations can help to keep a balance between the individual interests of a party or candidate and the public interest, but of greater importance are the professional standards and the ethical beliefs of the active political journalists. They will occasionally be exposed to new situations for which no precedent exists, which will occasion debate, and with which they should be able to deal correctly if they:

- Consider themselves as servants of the electorate.
- Are aware of the importance of the position of gatekeeper.

- Act in as independent, balanced, and unbiased manner as far as possible.

- Be prepared to oppose their superiors and have the courage not to give in to external pressure from interested parties, whatever their prominence.

The application of these norms and guidelines should be supported always by an adequate institutional framework for broadcasters. Only then in the interplay of guaranteeing freedom of broadcasting by organizational means in a legal framework on the one side and observing the personal rights and responsibilities of journalists on the other side democracy can prosper.

REFERENCES

Brettschneider, F. (2002). Kanzlerkanditaten im Fernsehen: Häufigkeit—Tendenz—Schwerpunkte [Chancellor candidates on television: Frequency—tendency—key aspects]. *Media Perspektiven, 6,* 263–276.

Media Perspektiven, Basisdaten 2002, Frankfurt, 2002.

Menzel, J. (2000). Verfassungsrechtsprechung [Constitutional jurisprudence]. Tübingen, Germany: Mohr (Siebeck).

Meyer, T. (2002). Mediokratie: Auf dem Weg in eine andere Demokratie? [Mediocracy: On the way to a different democracy?]. *Aus Politik und Zeitgeschehen, B 15/16,* 7–14.

Staatsvertrag über den Rundfunk im vereinten Deutschland in der Fassung des Sechsten Rundfunkänderungsstaatsvertrags in Kraft seit 1 Juli 2002 [The agreement between federal states on broadcasting incorporating the sixth amendment, into force since 1 July 2002] (2002). *Media Perspektiven Dokumentation, I,* 2–50.

4

South Africa*

Arnold S. de Beer

HISTORICAL BACKGROUND

The situation of the media vis-à-vis elections in South Africa is linked to its history, and present and future position within the context of sub-Saharan Africa. Even more so, new endeavors to link the countries of Africa into a larger unit, namely the African Union, based on the example of the European Union, makes the relationship between South Africa and its neighbors on the continent even more crucial. One reason for starting the chapter from this point of departure is that there is a perception that South Africa with its liberal constitution is a "beacon of light" in Africa to be evaluated not against the realities of postcolonial Africa, but rather within the context of the liberal-democratic societies of Europe and North America. This said, South Africa has a unique position in terms of the topic of this book.

The aforementioned departure point is highlighted by the vast difference between the way the first and second democratic elections in 1994 and 1999 were conducted in South Africa when viewed against the extremely controversial way in which the 2002 election in its neighboring country Zimbabwe was held; for example, according to the British Foreign Secretary, Jack Straw, it was "a tragedy for the people of Southern Africa as a whole" (The Electoral Institute of Southern Africa, 2002), whereas another report branded it as "fraud, repression and arrests in Zimbabwe" (Frontline, 2002).

There is a general view that societies that have the postcolonial history and racist characteristics and legacy like South Africa's experience the transition to a democratic dispensation as a difficult process, yet the formal election-based transition in this country since 1994 and then again in 1999 has been relatively painless. The transition itself was managed as a top-down operation by both the old as well as the new political elite (Friedman, 1993; Kotzé, 1998; Sisk, 1995). Prior to 1994 both sides (the ruling National Party, and after 1994, the African National Congress [ANC]) had to learn how to negotiate and to make compromises in the process of regime change. It is this process of hope that lies behind the gradual transformation of South African society since 1994, after the initial fears among the old elite that it would not have been possible to prevent constitutional change by means of a violent revolution.

Yet, accepting a liberal democracy entailed the necessity of the new order as well as the old having to adapt. It is clear that the supporters of the old order—especially the privileged classes such as the Whites—did not fully appreciate the value of liberal democracy as the normative paradigm for governance. For the ANC government, the adaptation entailed a shift from the idea of socialist centralism. As in all ideological shifts, important remaining elements of an old ideology can still be observed in the views of certain government policymakers. However, these views are coming under increasing pressure as a consequence of the impact of globalization, not least from reports and comments in the national and international media. These trends ensure that Western Europe and North America also exert a stronger influence on the policy positions of the government and hence systematically and increasingly displacing the earlier ideological affinity with its communist and even Stalinist socialism (Lodge, 1987).

Against the background of the weak performance of the opposition in South Africa's democratic elections thus far, these international patterns of influence, as well as media pressure, may even prove to have a greater impact on policy decisions than that of opposition parties.

Following the June 1999 election, South Africans were entering an era in which the ANC government no longer instilled the same fears in minorities (especially Whites and so-called coloreds), nor awakened the same high expectations among the Black majority. The massive victories achieved by the ANC and its alliance partners, the South African Communist Party (SACP) and the Confederation of South African Trade Unions (Cosatu), the major allegiance of labor movements, in 1994 and 1999 may also herald the beginning of a one-party dominant system with all of its innate shortcomings.

Whereas it is often said that "the electoral process lies at the heart of democratic government" (Butler, 1980, p. 1), elections can also point to a watershed in a country's political history. In the second democratic election of 1999, the citizens of South Africa clearly expressed their choice. Almost two thirds of the voting population placed their future in the hands of the ANC–SACP–Cosatu alliance. With this big majority and the absence of the "sunset clauses" or protective measures that were built into the Constitution for the first 5 years of democratic rule under the Government of National Unity (GNU), South Africans were now entering a new dispensation.

The result of the election came as no surprise. What was surprising was the fact that such a large number of voters arrived at the polls in spite of the ANC not having a single mainstream daily or weekend newspaper supporting it outright as its own mouthpiece like the National Party used to have in certain Afrikaans dailies (such as *The Transvaler*).

In contrast to the other post-*uhuru* elections in Africa, South Africa's voting percentage of 89% of registered voters was exceptionally high (about 71% of the potential voters voted). This figure could also be put in context, when one considers that South African voters would queue for hours, also through hail and rain to vote, whereas only 28% of French voters went to the first-round polls of the presidential election in 2002 (Letter in *Time,* June 3, 2002, p. 5).

A total number of 16.25 million voters went to the polls in 1999. This figure was nearly 3.5 million (or 18%) less than the number of voters who voted in the first democratic election of 1994. There was also some dispute as to the number of potential voters, with the Independent Election Commission (IEC) putting this figure at 22.8 million and Idasa giving a figure of 23.9 million (*Business Day,* June 10, 1999).

Against this background the following questions could be posed: Do the results of 1994 and 1999 mean that the voters are satisfied with what the ANC has achieved, and promises to achieve in the coming years? What do the results tell us about the voting behavior in South Africa? Does this mean that a one-party dominant system has now been irrevocably established with dire consequences for the media, especially during election time? (See de Beer, 2002.) Taking these questions as guidelines, the broad aims of this chapter are to give an overview of the socioeconomic and political context against which the 1999 election took place, and to describe the role of the media in this process.

THE SOUTH AFRICAN SOCIOECONOMIC
AND POLITICAL CONTEXT

In 2002, after 9 years of democratic rule, South Africa was still in the consolidation process of democracy, although the broad process was still on course. However, what was clear was that liberal democracy, a model exported from North America and Western Europe, was going to make particularly high demands of rulers of an African state such as South Africa. In addition to the fact that the South African Constitution has created a culture of rights with freedoms such as a general franchise, freedom of movement, association, and speech, language, and especially as far as elections are concerned, freedom of the press, the Western world (and other capitalist states) also expects that the principles of "good governance" find expression in the political, economic, and social fields.

Given the particular historical background of South Africa and that of the previous governing party, it is understandable that so much attention has been devoted to the restitution of the rights of the country's inhabitants. It sometimes appears as if management of the various commissions that have been called into being—such as those for truth and reconciliation, human rights, land restitution, and gender equality—has a higher priority over matters that have to do with good governance, especially in the economic field.

In contrast with other democratic states, based on the same principles found in the South African Constitution, there is almost no possibility that the ANC governing party can be voted out of power in the foreseeable future. Under such circumstances, and given the past history of racial discrimination, it becomes very important to consider the progress made with reconciliation and what the socioeconomic and political context is against which the ruling party's leadership and policies should be evaluated when the outcome of the 1999 election is assessed.

One of the major tasks of a society long under the rule of an oligarchy and especially a racist one such as South Africa, is how, after a democratic transition through fair and free elections, a democratic transition can transpire and how a democratic opposition and media can help to consolidate and deepen democracy. In what is effectively a one-party majority democracy, this is obviously an enormously important brick in building the future democratic South Africa. Contemporary efforts to consolidate democracy were faced by a long history of racial inequality and cleavage. This was skewed in favor of a White minority, which lost its monopolistic hold on political power in 1994, yet remained overwhelmingly in control of the economy, and to a large extent of the printed media (at least until 1999, with the exception of the public broadcaster, the SABC). This has led to what Southall (2001) described as a question where politics is not only about the struggle for power, but also under the hegemony of the ANC, a struggle for wealth (as well as influence through the media) in a drive to attain its "historic mission" (p. 17).

Going hand-in-hand with the issue of building not only a strong democracy but an economy as well, is the question of the role of the media and just as important, the role of the opposition. Since coming into power in 1994, and especially after the election of 1999, more and more pressure was put by the ANC on both the media (discussed later) and the opposition parties to act in a responsible way in the interest of building a viable and economically strong nation.

Much in line with the position elsewhere in Africa, the idea of the promotion of national reconciliation and coexistence between the country's potentially warring racial and ethnic communities, it seemed that the opposition and the media should not only be responsible, but that they could also be rewarded for acting responsibly (see, e.g., the inclusion of opposition leaders into governmental structures whereby the opposition is "brought and bought" into the government, and the need for government to have met formally with the press in 2001 to find ways in which they could help the process of nation building—discussed later).

The result of the ANC's hegemony is therefore a cause for fundamental tension between dominant one-party rule and the ideas of democracy. Such dominant parties are able to manage and to establish electoral dominance for an almost uninterrupted and prolonged period. They are also in a position of dominance in determining the public agenda and to pursue "historic ideals." The consequence is that in the long run, even though the society might be described as a democracy, one-party dominance under the facade of democracy could turn out to be a concealed authoritarian regime (Southall, 2001).

One of the "miracles" that developed out of South Africa's first two general elections was the almost unbelievable movement in ANC thinking away from communist-socialist-controlled economic policies to embrace the idea of a free-market economy. This was evident in the efforts to attract foreign investment to the country, and also through the process of privatization of the large number of parastatals (e.g., transport and steel production) inherited from the previous National Party government. This miracle is even more astounding when one considers that the ANC actually governs through a tripartite with the Communist Party and Cosatu. As can be expected, there is continuous strife between the members of the tripartite in terms of deciding on economic policies. As Southall (2001) showed, as a result of its superior political weight, the ANC is becoming an "alliance of a black middle class and—unionised—labour aristocracy, whose interests increasingly take preference over the non-unionised and unemployed blacks" (p. 18).

Contrary to the gloomy perceptions of some observers for South Africa, there are those who argue that South Africa could follow Malaysia, which operates as a so-called "syncretic state." Such a society "operates multi-dimensionally, including mixing coercive with democratic procedures, engaging in ethnic mobilization while cultivating a national following, and pursuing a combination of economic practices, ranging from liberal capitalism and state intervention into the economy, of special arrangements" (Southall, 2001, p. 18). Syncretism has therefore allowed the ANC to mix nonracialism with Africanism, acceptance of the free market with regulation of the labor market, and state patronage of African contractors with continued near monopolies for White-controlled operations.

CONCEPT OF THE ROLE OF THE MEDIA

In order to understand the relationship between the nature of democracy and one of its primary elements, namely regular elections, and that of the media, it is necessary to conceptualize the situation in contemporary South Africa. Like all democracies, South Africa should be considered democratic not only in a technical way, for example, holding regular elections and counting votes accurately, but also in that the spirit of a democratic society should be maintained such that a free media system can operate. Schrire (2001) summarized this in the following way:

- Opposition parties are free to compete for electoral support and established and accepted procedures, including periodic free and fair elections, are in place.
- Groups within civil society, such as trade unions and business organizations, are free to interact with government to further their sectional interests.
- Civil liberties are recognized and protected, and the population has access to an independent mass media.
- There is some form of separation of powers—at least at a minimum between the executive and the judiciary.
- All parties—the ruling and the opposition—agree to play the political game by the rules. This implies that the losing parties accept the legitimacy of the winners who in turn accept the legitimacy of constitutional opposition. (p. 28)

Though South Africa under National Party rule never had a press censorship law as such, the media was restricted in many ways. According to some researchers (e.g., Hachten & Giffard, 1984) more than a hundred laws were in place that could adversely affect the freedom of the press and the free flow of information, especially during elections. Like all institutions of society, the legal system of South Africa underwent some profound changes after the democratic 1994 election. For the first time there was a liberal democratic constitution recognizing human rights, which previously White regimes had suppressed. Basic human rights were now enshrined in the Constitution's Bill of Rights. These include freedom of expression, freedom for the press and other media, as well as freedom to receive and impart information.

Section 16 of the Bill of Rights of the Constitution (Act No. 108 of 1996) states:

16(1) Everyone has the right to freedom of expression, which includes
    (a) freedom of the press and other media;
    (b) freedom to receive or impart information or ideas;
    (c) freedom of artistic creativity; and
    (d) academic freedom and freedom of scientific research.
  (2) The right in subsection (1) does not extend to
    (a) propaganda for war;
    (b) incitement to criminal violence; or
    (c) advocacy of hatred that is based on race, ethnicity, gender or religion, and that which constitutes incitement to cause harm.

With the introduction of the Bill of Rights, there was criticism against article 16(2)(c) in the sense that this might be construed as a form of censorship especially during election time. This criticism was offset by the argument that the freedom of expression also includes the right to equality (S-9), the right to human dignity (S-10), the right to freedom and security of the person (S-12), the right to privacy (S-14), and the right to freedom of religion (S-15).

There is no hierarchy of rights. Even given the liberal nature of the Constitution there may, especially during election time, also be legitimate considerations other than competing fundamental rights that would justify the limitation of the right of freedom of expression of the media. Apart from the limitation contained within Section 16 itself, freedom of expression may be limited in terms of law of general application to the extent that the limitation is reasonable and justifiable in an open democratic society based on human dignity, equality, and freedom (S-36). A typical example would be political parties using, as a platform, the violent overthrow of the government, which would require state security measures to be put in place. On such occasions, the right to freedom of expression will have to give way to other rights. During election time, as in all other circumstances, in deciding such conflicts between freedoms, the Constitution holds that courts must promote values that underlie an open democratic society based on human dignity, equality, and freedom (S-39).

Consequently, it follows that the freedom of media expression during elections cannot be absolute. In fact, no legal system in the world allows absolute freedom, although the limits might be drawn more tightly in some countries than in others. As such, the degree of freedom is closely associated with political, cultural, and historical factors present in each society. In some countries, and during certain periods, one finds the media severely restricted by laws passed specifically to deal with the media in circumstances such as elections. In other societies, the press finds itself facing no greater limitations than the person in the street does. This is essentially the situation in South Africa, also as it relates to the elections. The media and everyone else may express him or herself freely, but where a right of free speech contravenes some criminal provision, the offender will be prosecuted by the state. It thus becomes a matter of criminal law.

Where a right of free expression infringes upon the right of another individual, the law grants the injured party a claim for damages. This is a matter for civil (or private) law. In South Africa the arena of free media expression is limited by competing rights of others and by the proscriptions of criminal law. These limitations must be conceptualized within the framework of the Bill of Rights.

Finally, the fact that a particular statute negatively impacts on the freedom of the media is found to be unconstitutional, does not necessarily mean that it is instantly invalid. Rather than create a vacuum by striking down the statute, the Constitutional Court may allow parliament time to correct the defect.

Since 1994, the Bill of Rights has been interpreted quite widely and courts have made it clear that during election time a certain amount of leeway must be allowed, for instance in political cartoons and in reporting on opposing political speakers, or reporting about or commenting on their published political material.

Since 1994 one of the main areas of conflict between the government and the press was the issue of exposés of official corruption and the abuse of power. Laws dating back to the era before 1994 made it quite easy for the state to place all kinds of acts under a broad blanket of "security," which made it almost impossible to legally report on a wide range of issues, such as taking people during election time into custody under the Suppression of Communism Act, or prohibiting the media to report on such persons under coverage of the Prison Law.

Now complaints of official corruption or other forms of illegality reported in the media before, during, or after elections may be lodged with an official Public Protector. The practical implementation of this law is still doubtful in terms of the Constitution. Such matters may, however, be debated in parliament and the media can lawfully report on such debates.

However, a vigorous press wanting to report on irregularities of corruption and other evil doings during elections, being under investigation by the Public Protector, could find itself hit by Section 7(2) of the Public Protector Act, which provides that no person or the media shall disclose the contents of documents under investigation by the Public Protector.

The task of the media of probing official corruption and abuse of power during the elections was simplified by the inclusion in the Constitution of the right of access to information. As mentioned, Section 32 provides that everyone has the right to access information held by the state. During election time, for the press to justify reporting on injustices or evil-doing during elections on the basis of truth and public interest, it is not necessary to prove that the statement is true; it is sufficient if the gist of the allegation is true.

However, the publication of the information must be in the public interest. Interest does not merely refer to information, which might satisfy the curiosity of the public (e.g., private scandals about politicians participating in the election). Interest implies that the public should be able to derive some meaningful benefit from the information being published. Most information concerning politicians falls in this category, whether in election time or not. Thus, a newspaper report, raking up the murky past of a parliamentary candidate, could probably be justified.

Post-1994 restrictions on the media to track down shady politicians and political dealings, especially in the heat of elections, have now been changed considerably. For instance, the horror stories surrounding politicians during the apartheid period that emerged before the Truth and Reconciliation Commission, would pre-1994 have led to huge damages awarded by the courts simply because the press would not have been in the position to establish whether these accusations were true. Post-1994 these overrestrictive requirements have been set aside in ground-breaking cases such as that of *Holomisa v. Argus Newspapers Limited* in 1996. In this specific case, the court held that an inflammatory statement, which relates to "free and fair political activity" is justified, even if false, unless the plaintiff can show that the publisher acted unreasonably. Steps should therefore still be taken to establish the truthfulness of allegations before publishing. Provided this is done, liability is unlikely to arise.

Politicians are constantly, and especially during elections, targeted for comment by the media. Provided such comment is fair, it is justified. Post-1994 four requirements must be met for the defense of "fair comment" by the media to be upheld:

- The statement at issue must be a comment.
- The comment must be fair.
- The facts commented on must be true (here the exception relating to statements concerning free and fair political activity would be applicable).
- The comment must be on a matter of public interest.

Pre-1994 it was difficult to determine where forceful media comment ends and defamatory imputations begin. A political party, for instance, published a pamphlet claiming that an opponent had a "corrupt image" and that he was about to bring "shame and disgrace" on the constituency. A lower court held the pamphlet to be acceptable during the election time, though on appeal the Supreme Court held that even in an election context, political comment has its limits, and reversed the decision (Barker, 1998).

It is quite clear that as a growing democracy it will take some time before the legacy of old apartheid laws affecting the media have been amended in such a fashion as to comply with the Constitution. For instance, the possibility for the media to escape the liability for defamation on the grounds that a mistake occurred (following from the fact that intention is one of the basic ingredients of defamation) was made more difficult for the media. In the case of the media an exception is made—liability is quite strict. The reason for this is that false news reports can cause immense harm. The law thus holds everyone connected with a publication to be strictly liable. This includes the reporter, the editor, the printer, and the publisher. It is likely that the ruling on strict liability regarding the media, especially during election time, would not withstand a constitutional challenge based on freedom of expression.

A last example regarding the free flow of information during election time is that a liberal constitution and a guarantee for press freedom would always have to be weighed against other interests, such as South Africa's legacy of racism. In this regard a controversial law, which impacts on the ability of the media to report fully on the political and election scene, is the Films and Publications Act (Act 65 of 1996), which makes it a crime to "distribute a publication which advocated hatred that is based on race, ethnicity, gender or religion and which constitutes incitement to cause harm." Because the freedom of expression provision of the Bill of Rights caters to such a statute, there could be no question of this restriction eventually being declared unconstitutional. On the one hand, given South Africa's past, it is not surprising that this law (the Films and Publications Act) has been passed post-1994. It is nevertheless controversial, because its effect is to hide from the public the anger and bitterness that might flow from racist attitudes and intentions during elections that could give rise to vitriolic utterances.

Again, given the liberal democratic nature of media freedom in South Africa and apart from the restrictions in the Bill of Rights, the media still has to be on the look-out during election times for matters that might be construed as being related to state security. Some of these laws are in the process of being changed or might have been changed by the time of the publication date of this chapter, but are still part of the apartheid legacy being carried over to the post-1994 years. Election candidates transgressing these laws, and the media reporting on them, might find themselves on the wrong side of the law:

- The Internal Security Act (Act 74 of 1982) makes it possible to declare a political organization unlawful if there is reason to believe that it intends to bring change to society through violence.
- There are also a number of laws relating to the protection of official secrets, strategic supplies, nuclear energy, and armaments, which fall broadly under the rubric of state security issues.

In the final analysis, what is important to realize is that as far as elections are concerned, the post-1994 era has brought significant developments in terms of media freedom, which have meant that:

- Newspapers need no longer be registered.
- The powers of the minister of law and order to prohibit the printing, publication, or dissemination of a publication has been abolished.
- Stifling provisions preventing adequate coverage have been lifted (e.g., where political parties would want to expose corruption in the police force or detrimental circumstances in prisons).
- The outdated Publications Act, which restricted the publication and distribution of films, videos, and magazines, has been replaced.
- Public and commercial broadcasting have been put on a sound footing.

MEDIA AND SOCIETY

Unlike many other countries of the world, the issue of race is one that is integrally linking not only parts of South African society as a whole, but its media system as well. As Bird (2000) contended, although there is no clear link between media freedom and race, it is imperative to realize that the building of democracy and its institutions, such as elections, are dealt with not only in terms of society as a whole, but very specifically also taking into account the important role of the media. Nowhere was this clearer than during the public hearings that the Truth and Reconciliation Commission held in 1997 on the media (see de Beer & Fouché, 2001), and again in November 1999 when the South African Human Rights Commission (SAHRC) conducted a full-scale inquiry into racism in the media (Steenveld, 2002; Tomaselli, 2000). These hearings illustrated how firmly some of the media, its management, and reporting staff were still rooted in the past. (However, see also Van Niekerk, 2000.) Although the hearings themselves and their outcomes were greatly criticized, especially as contained in the so-called Braude Report (Tomaselli, 2000), there was a general feeling that the media was inevitably still very much affected by the decades of apartheid's legacy (for a full discussion of these issues, see de Beer, 2002).

One of the positive spin-offs of the hearings was that the South African National Editors' Forum (Sanef) took the lead in reassessing the nature, role, and operation of the media in South Africa in 2001, to breach racial divides and to make a clear and a conscious effort by the media to overcome issues relating to race and racism that would negatively impact on the growth of democracy. After a special meeting with the government in 2001 at Sun City, a number of resolutions were taken in which Sanef members would look at their own position. One was a national workshop on media ethics (including reporting on elections) and the other a national audit on journalism skills, including on political issues (see de Beer & Steyn, 2002).

Other significant developments for media reporting on elections, following the SAHRC inquiry, was the eventual Promotion of Access to Information Act, which came into being in 2002. This act allows everyone to have the right of access to information held by government. This right was applicable to any information held by the government (and later) by other organizations in the exercise or protection of the individual's rights.

Another further important development was the founding of the Media Development and Diversity Agency (MDDA), which would make it possible for the government and other institutions to finance small community newspapers and local radio stations in order to broaden the scope of the media outside the mainstream set-up and to make information, also about the elections and democracy, more widely available to the country as a whole, and especially in the rural areas (see Bird, 2000). The MDDA became law in 2002.

As in many developing countries, there are continuous clashes, or at least debates, between government and the media over the purpose of national news reporting on political and governmental issues. Media scholars such as McQuail (1983) have shown that there is a wide difference in opinion between the role of the media in liberal democratic societies (where the press is seen as an adversarial watchdog of government), and so-called development societies where the role of the press, during and in between elections, are seen to be directed at the following:

- The press should promote positive developmental tasks in line with nationally (governmentally) established policy (e.g., nation-building efforts).
- Freedom of the press should be open to restriction according to the political, social, cultural, economic, and developmental needs of the country.
- The press should give priority in its news reporting and comment to common binding socioeconomic political and cultural factors.

- Journalists and other media workers, as well as media organizations, would enjoy individual freedom in their information-gathering and -dissemination tasks, but only within the context of their societal responsibility.
- In the interest of meeting developmental needs, the state has the right to intervene or restrict media operations. Censorship, subsidies, and direct control over the media could therefore be justified.
- The overriding implications of the developmental media system is that the media should first and foremost show a basic devotion to economic, political, cultural, and social development of society as their primary national task. All institutions in the country (including the national media system) should be committed to this end.

It is in the context just described that the polemical debate between the government and the media on the issue of national and public interest is haunting the South African journalistic community (de Beer & Schreiner, 2001).

Resurfacing during a climactic meeting in June 2001 between the South African Editor's Forum and the government, the latter once again voiced its concern about the media's reluctance to embrace the concept of national interest. Its position was that the press should make national interest its main objective, whereas the press emphasized its role in serving the public interest.

> In its emphasis on the national interest, the Government apparently revealed a lack of understanding of the public interest principle which drives the media. For instance, the Government might regard proposed new legislation as being in the national interest, while the media might regard rejection and vocal opposition to the legislation as being in the public interest. (Louw, 2001, p. 8)

This quotation highlights the basic problem: the difference in opinion about the essence of democracy, the role of the press, the concepts of national and public interest, and the function of news reporting. In a free-press system, a relatively peaceful, homogenous society with a highly developed social, economic, and technical infrastructure can afford a pluralist adversarial press. Such a press can criticize at will the president and his government's policy in the public interest as defined by the press. In a developmental system, freedom of the press is restricted according to the cultural, political, and socioeconomic priorities and developmental needs of society; that is, serving the national interest should be the media's paramount task (see McQuail, 1983). This schism underlies the present rift between the government and the press, especially as it relates the image of the president and his government during election time.

How do newspapers see their role in fulfilling the mandate of national and/or public interest?

South African newspapers constitute a wide spectrum of opinion. The *Sowetan* (aimed at Black readers), for instance, shows great affinity toward *national interest.* The subtitle of the newspaper's name is *Building the Nation,* and the paper is perhaps best known for its nation-building initiatives. The paper also endeavors to create a positive, committed national state of mind that will make South Africa the leader of a redeveloping Africa. Media Tenor (South Africa)'s 2001 research (www.mediatenor.co.za), shows for the *Sowetan* a negative rating of the government of 30% as well as an approval of 35%, with 35% of reports being neutral.

In contrast, the weekly *Mail & Guardian* claims its role as a defender of the *public interest,* and recently stated its policy beneath a banner headline reading: "Remember the last time people said: *We didn't know what was happening.* Think. Again."

The *Mail & Guardian* sees its task as being "independent, fearless, provocative, truthful, offering in-depth journalism and the watchdog of the people in power" (*M&G* 2001 advertisement in *Rhodes Journalism Review,* vol. 20, p. 2). Media Tenor (South Africa)'s 2001 (www.mediatenor.co.za) analysis shows that the government is rated about 75% negative, only 15% positive, and 10% neutral.

The discrepancy between the positions of these two newspapers indicates that for the South African press, the dilemma is how to perceive and act upon its mandate. Does its prime allegiance lie with the government and the latter's perception of the national interest, or should it follow its own adversarial notion of the public interest? Or is the answer somewhere in between? Whichever way, there seems to be a broad consensus in both government and press circles that the press in South Africa has to rethink its mandate and attitude toward news reporting. Needless to say, this would have had an impact on the general election planned for 2004.

MEDIA COVERAGE OF ELECTIONS

South Africa's media has a long history of covering elections. During the apartheid years, there was a continuous struggle between those media supporting the National Party and those supporting the ANC and other liberation movements in their effort to democratize the country (see, e.g., Beukes, 1992; Dommisse, 1980; Froneman & de Beer, 1993; Hachten & Giffard, 1984; Mervis, 1989; Van Niekerk, 2000).

Almost all mainstream newspapers in South Africa belong to the South African National Editors' Forum, which is the parent body of the office of the Press Ombudsman of South Africa. By accepting the ethical code of the Ombudsman, the newspapers are obliged to follow the code in terms of its spirit and wording in its reporting on all matters, including elections (Ombudsman, 2001). This spirit includes accuracy, balance, fairness, and decency and a belief that vigilant self-regulation is the hallmark of a free and independent press. The code states the following:

- In reporting the news, the press shall be obliged to report truthfully, accurately, and fairly. In addition, the news shall be presented in context and in a balanced manner without an intentional or negligent departure of the facts (e.g., distortion, exaggeration, misinterpretation, material omissions, or summarizations).

- Only what may be reasonably true, and having regard to sources of the news, may be presented as facts and such facts shall be published fairly with due regard to context and importance. Where a report is not based on facts or is founded on opinions, allegations, rumor, or supposition, it shall be presented in such a manner as to indicate this clearly.

- Where there is reason to doubt the accuracy of the report and it is practicable to verify the accuracy thereof, it shall be verified. Where not, it should be mentioned in the report.

A newspaper should usually seek the views of the subject of serious critical reportage, for example, a story about corruption during elections in advance of publication, provided that this need not to be done where the newspaper has reasonable grounds for believing that by doing so, it would be prevented from publishing the report, or where evidence might be destroyed or witnesses intimidated.

The code also states clearly that exceptional care and consideration should be taken involving the private lives and concerns of individuals (also during elections in terms of public figures and those involved in the election process). It should also be borne in mind that any right to privacy might be overridden by legitimate public interest. Newspapers have a wide discretion in matters of taste, but should not bring the freedom of the press into disrepute or be extremely offensive to the public.

In terms of discrimination, a special section of the code addresses this issue, clearly indicating that discriminatory or denigrating references to people's race, color, religion, sexual preference, physical or mental disability, or illness or age are not allowed. The press should not refer to any of these items unless they are strictly relevant to the matter reported or add significantly to the reader's understanding of the matter. (This is a matter under consideration. Critics argue that the press should under no circumstances refer to the aforementioned groups of people.)

Although the press has the right and indeed the duty to report and comment on all matters of public interest during election and other times, this should be balanced against the obligation not to promote racial hatred or discord in such a way as to create the likelihood of imminent violence.

Of particular importance during election times, a newspaper has the obligation to protect confidential sources of information, and not to pay for articles to persons engaged in crime or other notorious misbehavior.

Lastly, a newspaper is justified in strongly advocating its own views on controversial topics such as politicians and their actions, political party policies, and elections, but that comment and opinion should be made clearly distinguishable from facts; also relevant facts should not be misapprehended or suppressed in order to advocate a certain policy and facts and texts in headlines should also not be utilized for this purpose.

Within the South African context there is *free access* to all the media in the form of interviews being given, media releases being sent to all relevant media, and media conferences being held. As in any other democracy, at times there are the usual political skirmishes on the fringes of media coverage, but this is no different than what one would expect in any election held in Europe or the United States (e.g., the extreme right-wing political parties are known not to give access to Black journalists to their meetings; e.g., see the far-right-wing newspaper *Die Afrikaner* [May 30, 2002, p. 01] on the exclusion of a *colored* reporter from a political meeting).

Should access be denied to a political meeting, redress is possible through the Independent Election Commission, the Press Ombudsman, or the Broadcast Complaints Commission, or eventually through the courts. One of the main forums of free access to the press is that of letters-to-the-editor columns, which can become quite heated during election time, though some leeway is given here. The Electoral Act stipulates that after an election date has been set, all published material relating to the election must by identifiable by naming the author(s), the person(s) responsible for the headlines, and the editor.

Paid direct access is possible in some newspapers in the form of advertisements, but not all accept this. Those who do often distinguish between advertisements, giving only information about a meeting to be held vis-à-vis political propaganda. Journalists being paid to write certain stories at the behest of politicians (which is quite common in certain African countries and in the East, where it is seen as an extra source of income) is not allowed in terms of the ethical rules of the Press Ombudsman. In the period between elections, the media is actively involved in monitoring the political scene as was demonstrated earlier in the case of the role of the media in South African society regarding the issue of national interest vis-à-vis public interest.

THE ROLE OF BROADCASTING IN ELECTIONS

Television played no role in political elections until 1975 when it was first introduced. The then Minister of Post and Telegraphs, Dr Albert Hertzog, for many years refused to allow TV transmissions through what he called the "evil black box," which would bring "anti-apartheid propaganda" to the country. The SABC's monopoly public TV and radio channels have been used by the National Party to "advance self-development of all its peoples and to foster their pride in their own identity and culture" (Mersham, 1998, p. 212). This era came to an end with the first democratic elections in 1994 and the opening of the airwaves. Apart from a large number of commercial and community radio stations, a pay TV channel (M-Net) and a free over-the-air TV channel (e-tv) were introduced.

The SABC as public broadcaster, like the other radio and TV broadcasters, is allowed to carry news and commentary during election time, set within the parameters described elsewhere in this chapter, and in terms of special acts, such as the Broadcast Act of 1999, as well as regulations stipulated by the Independent Communication Authority of South Africa (Icasa) and the Broadcast Complaints Commission.

ADVERTISING

Political advertising is not allowed on television, but the SABC's radio stations (national and regional) are obliged to broadcast so-called PEBs (party election broadcasts) as set out in a number of rules and regulations by the acts and bodies mentioned previously. Only the SABC radio services are required to transmit election advertising. Icasa (www.icasa.org.za) has developed a broad formula to allocate PEB time slots.

The general factors determining allocation are as follows:

- The need for all parties to be heard by potential voters. (This factor serves as a numerical filter to ensure that the electorate is afforded an opportunity to hear all parties potentially exercising influence in policy decisions affecting their lives. It also limits the time differential between parties occupying and contesting a large number of seats and those contesting fewer seats.)
- In line with international practice, political parties most likely to contribute to policy decisions affecting South Africans are afforded more PEB time than smaller, marginal parties. It is argued that the voting public would want to hear more about their policy statements than those of

marginal parties who might not make the 5% cut-off number of delegates to the national assembly.

- Historical record: The current number of seats in national parliament and provincial legislatures, and a strong performance in the previous election.
- PEB points are also allocated in direct proportion to the number of national and provincial seats contested.

With regard to the fairness factor:

- As a general rule, fairness requires that the differential between new, untested parties and established parties should be relatively low. Recent public opinion polls could be used to determine PEB time-slot allocations.

EQUITABILITY

The Broadcast Act directs Icasa to ensure that contesting parties are treated equitably. Equitable treatment is defined in South African law and by means of international precedent as being fair. Equitability must be based on the following principles:

- No political advertisement shall contain anything that might lead to or lend support to acts of violence or criminal or illegal activities, or appear to condone such acts, nor contain alarming or inflammatory statements. Political advertisements should be of an informative nature and should be truthful statements and claims.
- A PEB shall not contain any material that may reasonably be anticipated to expose the broadcasting licensee to legal liability.
- In making advertising time available to political parties, no broadcaster shall discriminate against any political party or make or give any preference to any political party or subject any political party to any prejudice.

No radio broadcaster to whom a PEB advertisement has been submitted shall in any way edit or alter the advertisement. There will be four time slots of 1 minute each during election periods for political advertisements clearly identified as PEBs.

EDITORIAL MATTERS

As a matter of principle, ICASA does not intervene in the content of news and programming operations of broadcasters. Broadcasters' role during elections does not differ from their normal journalistic role during nonelection periods. Normal ethical considerations will continue to apply. A distinguishing feature of the election period is the obligation to achieve equitable coverage of political parties without abdicating news value judgments. Consequently, broadcasters shall afford reasonable opportunities for the discussion of conflicting views and shall treat all political parties equitably, and afford parties a reasonable opportunity to respond to criticism. All editorial content should adhere to the basic element of fairness. This will include:

- All news coverage should be fair to all interests concerned and avoid any expression of the broadcaster's own views.
- Care should be taken to balance the exposure given to the nonpolitical activities of candidates (such as attendance at functions, sporting events, etc.) that may be covered in non-news programs.
- All parties should receive equitable treatment on current-affairs programs. If the programs intend to feature party representatives, all parties must be invited, with reasonable notice, to participate either in the same programs or in a series of programs.
- The requirement that broadcasters give an opportunity for conflicting views to be heard should not be interpreted as a requirement that all parties must be heard on any subject, only that all views be heard. Nor is it a requirement that all views be heard on the same program.

INSTITUTIONAL FRAMEWORK
OF MIDTERM MONITORING

One of the typical processes of midterm monitoring was a study done on the 1999 election undertaken by the South African Human Sciences Research Council (HSRC, 1999), with financial assistance from the Department for International Development (DFID) and the European Union through the Conference, Workshop, Cultural Initiatives (CWCI) Fund.

The research team found that the electorate's confidence in the ability of the Independent Electoral Commission (IEC) to deliver a free and fair election in 1999, and its satisfaction with the IEC's administration of the election process itself were at notably high levels. However, the distribution of voters, queuing time, electoral administration, planning, and logistics would have to be attended to before new local and national governmental elections were held.

Dr Yvonne Muthien, executive director at the HSRC and editor of the report, said in a media release (HSRC, 1999) that the 1999 election provided the HSRC with the first major opportunity to test the strength of democratic consolidation since the 1994 election by gauging citizen participation in and voter evaluation of the country's second democratic election, and to set a valid benchmark for the evaluation of future elections. Although the 1999 election was far better organized than the one in 1994, many political parties and voters still believed much could be done to improve the electoral machinery and regulatory framework, she said.

The HSRC evaluation was based on a first South African exit poll on election day, as well as interviews after the election with senior spokespeople of the various political parties, election observers, and groups of voters in selected areas in each province.

Other 1994 election aspects covered included a survey conducted for the IEC in 1998 and HSRC national opinion polls on sociopolitical issues and voting intention.

Nine policy guidelines for future elections emerged from the HSRC's election research. They were:

- *Voter education:* Voter education should be a central objective in the total electoral process, conducted under the broad management of the IEC, funded appropriately and on time, and targeted at rural and illiterate people in particular. Voter education should be continuously presented as part of more general "democracy education," and materials should be translated into the local languages.

- *Registration and maintenance of voters' rolls:* Voters' rolls should be updated continuously by the IEC, the Department of Home Affairs, local authorities, political parties, and voters themselves when listed addresses are changed. Alternatively, temporary officials should be recruited to conduct door-to-door registration shortly before an election. The actual addresses of voting stations should also be provided in time to avoid confusion on election day. The IEC should also consider a special program of registering for the elderly and the disabled.

- *Training of electoral staff:* It is crucial that electoral staff receive thorough, relevant, and timely training to ensure that they have the necessary knowledge and understanding to be effective as election observers or presiding officers. The certification of trained officials would simplify recruitment during subsequent elections.

- *Voting-district demarcation:* It is essential that the number of voters per voting district be limited to manageable numbers. The IEC should therefore bring the demarcation of voting districts in line with the number of registered voters per district.

- *Counting of votes:* Because evidence showed that many officials on duty at voting stations on election day were too exhausted to count votes, a fresh team should be appointed to handle the counting process.

- *Special votes:* Declaration and special votes should only be permitted under the most stringent conditions, otherwise the quality of the voters' roll might be compromised, and the number of votes cast could be suspect. Procedures and requirements for these votes must be communicated to voters and officials well in advance of an election.
- *Collaboration:* The task given to the IEC was generally executed through collaboration between government, the private sector, civil society, and the media. This collaboration should be strengthened to enhance the electoral process in future.
- *Electoral funding:* Political parties with adequate funding were able to reach larger numbers of voters than were small parties with less funding. The existing legislative framework around electoral funding required fundamental review, with due regard being given to international practice and the promotion of multiparty democracy and competition.
- *Independent evaluation of election process:* Apart from the monitoring of media reports on election events by the Independent Broadcasting Authority (IBA), the election process was also monitored by several national and international nongovernmental organizations. However, the degree to which monitors were representative of the spectrum of role players involved in the election differed from place to place, and could be rectified.

CONCLUSION

It seems that democratic elections in South Africa are alive and well and that South Africa is indeed a beacon of hope in this regard for Africa. However, it remains to be seen what the future position of the press would be, given the difference of opinion between the government and the press on the issue of national or public interest, and whether the press should function under a liberal-democratic or developmental model, or something in between.

*ACKNOWLEDGMENTS

The author wishes to thank Dr. Gordon Barker, School of Law, Rhodes University, South Africa, for liberally using his chapter on media law (in de Beer, 1998); Professor Hennie Kotzé, Head, Department of Political Science, Stellenbosch University, for his extensive input in the sections on the historical, political, and economic background to this chapter; Dr Yvonne Muthien, executive director at the HSRC and editor for a monitoring report

on the 1999 election; Wadim N. Schreiner, Managing Director, Media Tenor
(South Africa), for his input in the section on national and public interest;
Dr. Lang Stefaans Jansen van Rensburg, Head, Department of Anthropology,
Potchefstroom University, for critical comments; and Dr Nicolette de Beer
(Imasa) for editorial assistance.

REFERENCES

Barker, G. (1998). *Media law—To tread cautiously with new-found freedom.* In A. S. de Beer (Ed.),
   Mass media towards the millennium—The South African handbook of mass communication (pp.
   267–288). Pretoria, South Africa: Van Schaik.
Beukes, W. D. (Ed.). (1992). *Oor grense heen: Op pad na' n nasionale pers, 1948–1990* [Across borders—On the road to a national press]. Cape Town, South Africa: Nasionale Boekhandel.
Bird, W. (2000). South Africa. In J. Grobler, C. Sasman, & Z. Titus (Eds.), *So, this is democracy?—
   State of the media in Southern Africa* (pp. 82–99). Windhoek, South Africa: The Media Institute
   of Southern Africa.
Butler, D. (1980). *Democracy at the polls.* Washington, DC: American Enterprise Institute for Public Policy.
de Beer, A. S. (Ed.). (1998). *Mass media—Towards the millennium. The South African handbook of
   mass communication.* Pretoria, South Africa: Van Schaik.
de Beer, A. S. (Ed.). (2000). Focus on media and racism. *Ecquid Novi, 21*(2), 151–280.
de Beer, A. S. (2002). The South African press: No strangers to conflict. In E. Gilboa (Ed.), *Media in
   conflict—Framing issues, making policy, shaping opinions* (pp. 263–280). New York: Transna-
   tional Publishers.
de Beer, A. S., & Fouché, J. (2000). In search of truth: The TRC and the Afrikaans press—A case
   study. *Ecquid Novi, 21*(2), 190–206.
de Beer, A. S., & Schreiner, W. N. (2001). National vs public interest: The dilemma of the press.
   South African media and government clash over the purpose of news reporting. *Media Tenor
   South Africa Quarterly, 2*(4), 8.
de Beer, A. S., & Steyn, E. (2002). Sanef's "2002 South African National Journalism Skills Audit": An
   introduction, and the Sanef report regarding the media. *Ecquid Novi, 23*(1), 11–86.
Dommisse, E. (1980). Afrikaans en English press—the case of the goose and the gander. *Ecquid
   Novi, 1*(2), 118–127.
The Electoral Institute of Southern Africa. (2002). Zimbabwe, presidential elections. Retrieved
   October 13, 2002 from http://www.eisa.arg.za/WEP/Zimbabwe.htm
Friedman, S. (Ed.). (1993). *The long journey.* Johannesburg, South Africa: Ravan.
Froneman, J. D., & de Beer, A. S. (1993, August). *The Afrikaans press—Heading for demise, or a con-
   structive role in a plural society?* Paper presented at the meeting of the International Commu-
   nication Division, Association for Education in Journalism and Mass Communication, Kansas
   City, MO.
Frontline. (2002). Fraud, repression and arrests in Zimbabwe. Retrieved October 13, 2002 from
   http://www.frontline.org.za/fraud.htm
Hachten, W. A., & Giffard, C. A. (1984). *Total onslaught: The South African press under attack.* Johan-
   nesburg, South Africa: Macmillan.
Human Sciences Research Council. (1999). All satisfied with IEC's handling of the 1999 election
   [Media release, December 10, 1999]. Pretoria, South Africa: Author.
Kotzé, H. J. (1998). South Africa: From apartheid to democracy. In M. Dogan & J. Higley (Eds.),
   Elites and crises in regimes (pp. 213, 216). New York: Littlefield.

Lodge, T. (1987). The African National Congress after the Kabwe conference. *South African Review, 4,* 1–12.

Louw, R. (2001, April 22). Rift remains between media and government. *The Citizen,* p. 8.

McQuail, D. (1983). *Mass communication theory.* London: Sage.

Mersham, G. (1998). Television—A fascinating window on an unfolding world. In A. S. de Beer (Ed.), *Mass media—Towards the millennium. The South African handbook of mass communication* (pp. 239–266). Pretoria, South Africa: Van Schaik.

Mervis, J. (1989). *The Fourth Estate—A newspaper story.* Johannesburg, South Africa: Jonathan Ball.

Ombudsman. (2001). *Press Ombudsman of South Africa: Constitution, Rules of Procedure, Code of Conduct.* Johannesburg, South Africa: Office of the Press Ombudsman [pressombudsman@ombudsman.org.za].

Schrire, R. (2001). The realities of opposition in South Africa: Legitimacy, strategies and consequences. In R. Southall (Ed.), *Opposition in South Africa's new democracy* (pp. 27–35). Johannesburg, South Africa: Konrad-Adenauer-Stiftung.

Sisk, T. A. D. (1995). *Democratization in South Africa: The elusive social contract.* Princeton, NJ: Princeton University Press.

Southall, R. (2001). Introduction. In R. Southall (Ed.), *Opposition in South Africa's new democracy* (pp. 7–25). Johannesburg, South Africa: Konrad-Adenauer-Stiftung.

Steenveld, L. (Ed.). (2002). *Training for media transformation & democracy.* Grahamstown, South Africa: The South African National Editors' Forum and the Independent Newspaper Chair of Media Transformation, Rhodes University.

Tomaselli, K. (2000). Faulting *Faultlines:* Racism in the South African media. *Ecquid Novi, 21*(2), 157–174.

Van Niekerk, P. (2000). Racist: A most provocative insult leveled at the "Mail and Guardian." *Ecquid Novi, 21*(2), 256–266.

5

France

Elisabeth Mauboussin

Access to the electronic media at election times is crucial for candidates standing for election to the institutions of government, who require the platform that television and radio offers them to communicate to the public. But are the media and elections compatible? The audience that candidates reach through the mass media constitutes an infinitely larger public than the one that they may address at public meetings. A variety of traditional media are still used by candidates at election times to promote their campaigns, such as ballot papers with a "declaration of principles" and traditional meetings, and these remain essential for both prominent and lesser known candidates. However, radio and television constitute the privileged platform for candidates during an election campaign. Moreover, as French law imposes restrictions on election expenses, this platform, which is free to speakers, is enticing.

Radio and television are in the contemporary world the key places for the communication of electoral messages, and the question about the impact of the media on the public is a constant theme in public debate. Within a few years the move from a state television monopoly to a more plural and competitive audiovisual landscape has provided a whole range of new radio and television channels and, given the trends in technology, we are today moving to an age of abundance in the sectors. The fact that there are many more channels does not provide a solution to the problem of ensuring plural access to radio and television for the various political views held by the political parties. As a result, the role of the state and regulation in this domain remains crucial, as according to French law, it must guarantee access to, and diversity of, the broadcast media.

The task of ensuring diversity of opinion and thought during an election campaign is achieved in two complementary ways. On the one hand, the CSA (Conseil supérieur de l'audiovisuel), which is the audiovisual regulator in France, provides recommendations on the principles that broadcasters have to guarantee, in respect of the right of the candidates and political organizations taking part in the poll, access to broadcast media. As a consequence a broad array of political opinions are delivered to the audience through the electronic media and citizens are therefore allowed to vote for whatever party they wish to, based on, among other things, the information they receive through television and radio. On the other hand, the CSA organizes the production and transmission of official election campaign programs on public radio and television channels. This guarantee of democratic access to airtime is all the more important as it is part of the legislative context, which includes a ban on paid political advertising on broadcast media. As a result, the role of the media during election periods is crucial and the regulatory authority has a vital role to play in guaranteeing that certain standards are maintained. Audiovisual media therefore play a key role in the communication of the candidates during campaign periods and even more so because restrictions on electoral expenditure impose budget ceilings. This is why access for candidates to various broadcast media must be organized during the election campaigns and extra vigilance is required during these periods. Indeed the democratic process is built upon the guarantee of complete and plural information being available to the electorate.

REGULATORY AUTHORITY

Independence for broadcasters from state dominance was guaranteed by the formation in 1982 of an independent regulatory body to regulate the audiovisual industry. In severing the ties of dependency, the legislature empowered the regulatory authority to ensure respect for pluralism within the programming of the radio and television stations during election campaign periods.

Today the CSA regulates the audiovisual media and it is an independent administrative authority, set up by the Law of January 17, 1989, to ensure the freedom of audiovisual communications, according to the conditions specified by the modified Law of September 30, 1986. It is made up of a college of nine members, who are appointed by decree of the President of the Republic for a 6-year term of office. Three of these members, one of whom is the chairman, are appointed by the President of the Republic, three members are appointed by the chairman of the Sénat, and three by the chairman of the Assemblée nationale.

THE CONTEXT OF FRENCH REGULATION

From the end of the Fourth Republic, the resources and principles necessary for candidates to access the audiovisual media have been guaranteed according to principles that were laid out in 1956. Drouot (1994) identified the features that were evident right from the beginning of television in France, hence:

> The first broadcast campaign was organised for the general elections on January the 2nd 1956. . . . A decree granted fifteen minutes on radio and five minutes on television to each political party and defined the rules: drawing the order of appearance of each candidate, the same shooting conditions and the possibility to have thirty minutes for preparation.

As of 1956 the principle of equality among the candidates was set forth in official campaigns on radio and television. However, during this period access to the airwaves and to programming seems to have been reserved for the representatives who held the seat of power, and it is not until the presidential election in 1965 that the French public discovered the opposition parties on television and radio and the rise of more equitable access to the electronic media for political parties and candidates for office was firmly established.

BAN ON PAID POLITICAL ADVERTISING
ON BROADCAST MEDIA

Contrary to some other countries, the regulation dealing with access for political parties to audiovisual media was established in France based on the exclusion of paid for political advertising, which is banned on radio and television channels pursuant to Article 14 of the modified Law of September 30, 1986, relating to the freedom of communication. A permanent ban results from the Law of January 15, 1990, relating to the limits of election expenses and a clarification of political financing, which modified Article 14 of the Law of September 30, 1986. Before establishing this ban, the question of political advertising on radio and television was, nevertheless, the subject of certain legislative debate.

Prior to the Law of December 13, 1985, political advertising on electronic mass media was not subject to any legal provision whatsoever, and if one takes the principle that what is not banned is allowed, then technically paid political advertising was allowed. The flexibility in the law, however, has never been employed and the twists and turns of the legislation that provides for the election law first imposed a ban on political advertising during the elections in 1985. The Law No. 85-1317 of December 13, 1985, restricted this principle of authorization, including in the first paragraph of Article L52-1 of the Electoral Code, a provision that forbids, during the election campaign, "the use of any advertising through the press or by means of audiovisual communication for an electoral propaganda aim." The restriction on political advertising was subsequently established by the Law of September 30, 1986, relating to the freedom of communication. The Law has granted the right for the predecessor of the CSA, the Commission Nationale de la Communication et des libertés (CNCL), to control, by any appropriate means this ban, as well as the content and production methods of the programming of both commercial and political advertising that is aired on radio and television.

The ban was imposed until the Law of July 30, 1987, which established a complete ban on paid political advertising until a law aiming to guarantee the openness of the financing of political movements in France came into force. On March 11, 1988, this second law came into being and confirmed the temporary ban lasting 4 years from the promulgation date. Before the 4-year period of the ban expired, however, the principle of a permanent ban on paid political advertising on radio and television was already set forth in the Law of January 15, 1990, and the instruments provide a coherent body of law for the rules on the ban of paid for party political advertising.

One of the reasons that paid political advertising is banned is because of the unequal resources enjoyed by the different candidates and parties, which was established by the Constitution of October 4, 1958. As a result of this inequality, paid for party political advertising would favor some parties and candidates and disadvantage others. Such a situation would undermine the principle of fair and equal treatment of the candidates and would act to distort the balance in debate and diversity of opinion and hence adversely affect the democratic process.

ACCESS FOR CANDIDATES

Access for candidates to radio and television channels is specified by the CSA pursuant to the measures contained in the Electoral Code. The first paragraph of the modified Law of September 30, 1986, relating to the freedom of communication sets down the general principle of pluralism and free expression of opinion on both radio stations and television channels. To this end the CSA is empowered to ensure the enforcement of the principle, which is set out in a Directive *(principe de référence)* that establishes the overall guarantees for independence and balance, and the requirements that broadcasters have to fulfill with regard to pluralism in their coverage of the elections.

The CSA's overall mission is therefore particularly important at election times and the Law specifies the CSA's role; it is entrusted with the task of addressing special recommendations to broadcast media for the duration of the campaign. Thus, with each election, regardless of the nature of the election, the CSA enacts recommendations that it addresses to radio and television channels, which are published in the *Official Journal.* In this text, the CSA defines the principles that serve as an analysis grid in order to estimate how far pluralism has been reached and the extent to which broadcasters have respected the principle of media pluralism during the election period.

ENSURING PLURALISM DURING CAMPAIGN PERIODS

To evaluate pluralism the CSA makes a distinction between what is related to the election campaign and what is understood to be unrelated. There is, in this sense, a distinction made between coverage of political issues within traditional formats such as current affairs and news bulletins that are understood to be unrelated to the actual election campaign itself, and programming that is directly related to the elections. This enables the broadcasters to make precise calculations as to the access granted to candidates during the campaign period and a precise calculation as to the balance in access as a percentage of airtime allocated to the candidates together with the topics covered.

The two categories are as follows:

- Comments related to current affairs and unrelated to the election. This includes all political commentary about topics other than programming directly related to the election campaign, which do not have a clear connection to the elections. This category includes national and international television and radio news and broadcasters have to ensure balance between the amount of airtime allocated to members of the government, representatives of the majority in Parliament, and representatives of the Parliament opposition and to grant the same programming conditions. In addition, broadcasters have to ensure a fair amount of airtime among the representatives of political organizations who are not represented in Parliament.

- Airtime directly related to the elections and the time allocated to election affairs with a classification by political organizations or candidates according to the nature of the election. The CSA requests that broadcasters ensure that each candidate taking part in the poll enjoys fair treatment as regards access. This category is based on a number of crucial principles set down by the CSA.

The first principle provides a useful guide to manage news and current affairs programs, but it is insufficient during election periods when the second category, that related directly to elections, is introduced.

REGULATORY PRINCIPLES AT ELECTION TIMES

Fairness

The doctrine of fairness obliges broadcasters to grant airtime to candidates whatever their prominence, their responsibility, and the weight of the political organizations that support them on a nondiscriminatory basis. However, given the large number of parties and candidates the idea that all parties can be treated equally in terms of coverage is extremely complex. In the 2002 elections a record number of 16 candidates contested the presidential elections.

Although equal access is a key criteria employed by the CSA, it is not a rigid category and the allocation of airtime to the candidates is also based on their presumed influence, their representation, and their level of activity during the election campaign. To account for this principle of equal access, the broadcasters enjoy a degree of flexibility and therefore they can take the importance of each candidate list into account in their coverage. Fairness therefore does not mean absolute equal airtime and it is possible that more airtime is allocated to a more prominent candidate as long as inequality does not cross a certain threshold that can be judged as unfair. A special case is made for the presidential elections, where the allocation of the same time to every candidate during the official campaign is required by law. This is not established by the CSA, but by legal provision.

From Balance to Fairness

For specific elections, the CSA has established two rules for two distinct periods. The first period is before the official campaign begins, which the CSA calls the precampaign time. During this period the broadcasters are asked to ensure a balance between the potential candidates. In the second stage, after the launch of the campaign, the CSA requires broadcasters to ensure fair access among the candidates. So once the official candidates have been announced and the official campaign period begins, the requirement of pluralism becomes even more important for the broadcasters to take into consideration.

The CSA is empowered by the modified Law of September 30, 1986, related to the freedom of communication to make recommendations for the "duration of the campaign." However, it makes its recommendations before the campaign as the broadcasters do not wait for the start of the campaign to report on the pending elections, and the recommendations are enforced months prior to the official election campaign period.

Editorial Freedom and Monitoring by the CSA

The principle of editorial freedom is also an important part of the overall regulation that guarantees fairness and independence. It is left to the discretion of the broadcasters as to how to apply the principle of fairness defined by the CSA. Indeed, in matters of audiovisual communication, the principle of editorial freedom applies. Although this principle is required by the CSA, the audiovisual media define and implement their editorial policies and, subsequently, it is the right of the broadcasters to decide how they cover the election campaign and the candidates. As a consequence the broadcasters are free to select the format of programs and to choose between interviews, reports, and debates. The principle of editorial freedom, however, does not exclude the CSA from having an important role in the question of balance and editorial freedom. Quite the reverse is true, as it measures and monitors pluralism in two ways to ensure that the recommendations are complied with by broadcasters. The CSA can also intervene before a broadcast, which may infringe on the rules on balance, if it believes that there is a case to suggest that the rules will be violated in some way.

Whereas the broadcasters are free to determine their own editorial policies, the CSA retains an important role in guaranteeing that the rules and guidelines are abided by and ensuring that breaches of the fairness doctrine are identified. If the principle is judged to have been breached by a broadcaster, the CSA has certain powers to demand compensation from the offending broadcaster.

The CSA requested such measures in the local elections of March 2001, asking Canal+ to add additional comments and responses from the other candidates to a debate between two of the candidates, in order to ensure fair conditions for each candidate's appearance. In this instance, although the CSA was not empowered to force Canal+ to organize a debate between all the candidates standing for the local election, the CSA had to ensure that the main rivals of two of the candidates enjoyed the same programming airtime, ensuring fair access to airtime among the candidates. It should be noted that the judge in chambers, presiding on a submission by one of the challenging candidates who was excluded from the debate, had dismissed the claim for canceling the debate on the condition that the CSA continued to look for solutions appropriate to the principle of equality between the candidates (Conseil d'Etat, Ordonnance of February 24, 2001, M. 'Jean Tiberi).

Such an approach leads to a reduction of diversity in political coverage offered to the electorate in the first ballot. Hence, it is necessary to offer another form of access to airtime for the candidates excluded from the debate to guarantee that complete and plural information is accessible for the electorate. Regardless of the nature of the election, compensatory measures are all the more important as the broadcasters tend to anticipate what is at stake in the second ballot as the number of candidates is narrowed down to contest the second and final stage of the election. In anticipating the runoff between the candidates in the second stage, there is a reduction of diversity of political coverage broadcast to the electorate in the first ballot, as the media tend to focus on the main running candidates.

Calculating and Monitoring Access. The CSA is responsible for monitoring and evaluating compliance to the measures for the terrestrial national channels. This enables efficient and speedy calculations to be made and, subsequently, any broadcaster that breaches the balance and fairness rules can be notified and the imbalance can be addressed as soon as possible. The closer the election gets, the more often these evaluations are carried out to enable any possible rebalancing of the coverage.

For each candidate the CSA calculates the speaking time granted to him or her on the terrestrial national channels, together with the total airtime that is allocated to the candidates (the speaking time of the candidate together with the commentary and analysis of the candidate). The CSA therefore measures speaking time and the amount of airtime allocated that is related to various topics devoted to the candidates. This enables the CSA to check if airtime is equal among the various candidates.

Other broadcast media are required to submit details to the CSA about the speaking time on their channels to allow the CSA to monitor compliance to the rules and regulations, although the CSA does not have a role in collecting the information directly.

Processing Claims. During campaign periods candidates or political organizations frequently write to the CSA to call its attention to what they deem to be unfair treatment of their candidates. The CSA has a role in acting as an arbiter in such cases to bring the broadcasters and candidates or political parties together, to resolve any access or fairness issues that arise. For each claim, it carries out an investigation, which includes a review of the program in question, and if necessary it requests further information from the relevant broadcaster. On the occasion of the local elections in March 2001, the CSA processed hundreds of claims. The procedure for the evaluation of the claims is set out clearly:

> For each one, the CSA carried out checks, viewing the sequences in question and asking the broadcasters for further details if necessary. In many cases, in the research that the CSA has carried out, it has been noted that the equality principle had been respected, either because the claimant had enjoyed access to airtime, contrary to what was said, or because their appearance had been programmed one hour after the airing of one of the other candidates, or finally because the viewing of the offending sequences revealed that the complainant did not enjoy any discriminatory treatment. In fewer cases, the CSA intervened and stressed to the broadcasters that they had to ensure fair treatment between of all the candidates in a given district. (Letter to the CSA, No. 139, April 2001, 10 et seq.)

Requirement of the CSA for Addressing Imbalances. Fairness must be attained in a global sense in relation to the entire coverage of candidates for the election during the period when the recommendations are in force. The CSA regularly makes an evaluation to enable the broadcasters to restore any possible imbalance. If the CSA identifies persistent imbalance in coverage, it requires the offending broadcaster to restore fairness. It should be stressed, however, that the CSA cannot force a broadcaster, who breaks the rules, to grant access to a candidate. The CSA can penalize broadcasters who breach the requirement of pluralism after a formal demand without effect, which has not been fulfilled. But, such an action cannot require that offended candidates obtain speaking time or airtime.

Reports, Comments, and Presentations Made by Journalists

The CSA recommendations to broadcasters also provide guidelines relating to journalists, who should ensure that reports, commentary, and presentations relating to the elections are balanced and accurate. The editorial staff must ensure that the selection of the declaration extracts, manifestos and written speeches of the candidates, lists of political organizations' representatives, and the comments published, are not distorted and are accurate.

Individuals associated with certain radio and television channels may also stand as a candidate for election before the start of the campaign. If such a case arises, the CSA requests the relevant candidate to ensure that their appearances on radio and television have no impact on the ballot, which would be to the detriment of equality between the candidates and therefore undermine the fairness doctrine. The CSA also requests that candidates who are related to particular media outlets refrain from appearing on the radio or television programs for which they work during the official campaign and until polling closes.

THE ROLE OF THE JUDICIARY

The candidates for election regularly submit cases to the electoral judge, who can intervene twice, either before polling, or more often when the results of the election have been published. The majority of cases related to the media during election periods that are submitted to the judiciary relate to unequal treatment between the candidates and access to airtime. More commonly cases are submitted by less well known candidates who have requested the judge to force the broadcasters to grant them equal airtime. All of the cases submitted to the civil judge have ended with the judge declining jurisdiction and refusing to pass judgment.

The administrative judge of the summary proceedings, who in 2001 received a complaint submitted by a candidate excluded from a televised debate during the local and cantonal elections of March 2001, did not, however, decline jurisdiction. Pursuant to the ruling of February 24, 2001, the judge dismissed the claim, provided that the CSA looked for appropriate solutions to the requirement of equal treatment between the candidates in cooperation with broadcasters.

The judiciary more often intervenes after the poll results have been announced. Each candidate can make an appeal against the ballot and each candidate can invoke, in support of their appeal against the ballot, the speaking time allocated to the candidates. In such cases the judge has to check if the imbalance questions the authenticity of the election results. Two conditions must be fulfilled to make a complaint about unfair balance in airtime allocated to each candidate. The first is that inequality must be established on the basis that unequal treatment must go beyond objective differences in public standing.

The second condition is that the difference between the results of the candidates must be small enough so that the effects of the unequal treatment may influence the authenticity of the results of the ballot. The irregularity alone is insufficient to cancel the results of the ballot and there is a causal link between perceived irregularities in balance and the cancellation of the poll. It will only be declared invalid if the violation distorts the poll results, to an extent where the results of the election are likely to be undermined.

The usual procedural approach consists of the election judge assessing the nature of the violations to the election rules and subsequently evaluating the impact of the violations on the final result of the polls. In its assessment of the issues, the judge considers if the irregularity is due to an act, some particular event, or some last-minute pressure likely to break the balance between the candidates to the extent that the results of the poll may be prejudiced. In this case, the judge will take into account a number of criteria, the most important of which is the degree of difference in the amount of votes for the candidates in the final result.

As far as access to airtime on radio and television channels is concerned, the judge can estimate that the treatment is fair and dismiss the appeal. A second option is to adjudge unfair treatment with the infringement having no impact on the authenticity of the poll. Finally, the court can judge the treatment is unfair and the irregularity has influenced the reliability of the poll. In this last case the judge holds the right to cancel the poll.

Fair Treatment Regarding Access to Airtime

The judge acknowledges that the CSA's recommendation about "fair access to airtime between the various candidates and parties" allows the broadcasters a margin for interpretation as it would be unrealistic to force absolute equality on the broadcasters "organising debates between the representatives of the 15 various lists, even though what is essentially at stake is hardly concentrated on half of these lists" (Conseil d'Etat, Ruling Horblin et al. of October 20, 1989, on the occasion of the European Parliament elections of June 18, 1989). Although there were 15 candidates for the poll, only some of these were invited to debate during peak viewing time on television. The excluded parties, complaining about unequal treatment in access to airtime, lodged an appeal against the poll results. The judge ruled that the different treatment of several candidates or parties is not necessarily unfair.

Unfair Treatment With No Impact on the Poll Results

In one case the ratio between the two lists in terms of the access to airtime was 1 to 20. The judge ruled that the broadcaster had flouted the fair-treatment doctrine that they were required to respect. However, considering the difference in votes dividing the lists for the seat allocation, the judge considered that it had no impact on the consistency of the poll (Conseil d'Etat, Ruling M. Malardé of December 30, 1998, regional elections of March 1998, in the department of Morbihan).

Unfair Treatment and Impact on the Reliability of the Poll

In other cases the unfair treatment of a candidate in regard to access to airtime has had far-reaching consequences for the election. In March 1992, on the occasion of the poll of the Conseil Régional in La Réunion, a candidate appealed to the judge against the poll results by submitting a claim of unfair access to airtime granted to a candidate. The complaint was against the winner of the poll who, through his control of a number of radio stations, was granted, according to the complainant, excessive access to the airwaves, which distorted the election process and subsequently the results of the poll.

The judge relied on several factors to evaluate the case. The first consideration was the number of programs dedicated to the candidate. The second consisted of the schedule of their broadcasts between November 1991 and March 1992 and the content of the broadcasts, which could not be understood as information-based programs, but as political-campaign material. Finally, the results of the ballot were taken into consideration, which showed only a small difference between the numbers of votes for the candidates. The judge therefore considered the difference in airtime allocated to the candidates as questioning the authenticity of the poll, and therefore moved to cancel the entire poll results.

In addition, the judge considered that the programs transmitted covering the winning candidate should be considered as campaign programs and therefore the candidate should incur the costs of such programs. They should therefore have been accounted for in his electoral expenses. As a result, with the additional expenses that should have been recorded in the electoral expense account taken into consideration, the candidate was adjudged to have surpassed the expenditure ceiling and the account was therefore refused. Hence, the candidate was declared ineligible for the regional election (Conseil d'Etat, Ruling M. Lallemand et al., National Commission of the campaign accounts and the political financing of May 7, 1993, cancellation of Camille Sudre's election at the regional Council in La Réunion that took place on March 22, 1992). In a similar way, and based on a similar principle, the local elections in Vitrolles were canceled on December 18, 1996.

END OF ACCESS TO AIRTIME

The Electoral Code provides for a short period before polling when political commentary and broadcasts are not allowed. The second paragraph of Article L49 of the Electoral Code states: "From the day before the election poll day at midnight, it is forbidden to broadcast or to get any message of (or related to) election propaganda broadcast by any means of audiovisual communication" (L49 of the Electoral Code). This legal provision aims to avoid political commentary or campaign messages being transmitted immediately prior to polling within a time framework, which could result in other candidates having insufficient time to reply effectively, and it may therefore influence and prejudice the results of the election.

In the same way, the Law of July 19, 1977, bans any publication, reporting, and commentary on any opinion poll having a direct or indirect relationship with the ballot during the week before each ballot and during polling (Modified Law No. 77-808 of July 19, 1977). Enforcement of this law is limited, which poses further problems, but if a change in the situation leads the judiciary to reconsider the rules of the Law of 1977, such a circumstance could not have an effect on the impact of the Law, or on the task of the regulatory body, which has to ensure its enforcement, as the administrative court has recently reiterated (Conseil d'Etat, Ruling Alain Meyet of June 2, 1999). The Law of July 19, 1977 was modified in 2002. See p. 119, this chapter.

ARTICLE L49 OF THE ELECTORAL CODE

The legal provisions pursuant to Article L49 ban political broadcasts from the day before polling at midnight. There have, however, been a number of occasions when this rule has been breached and a similar procedure is followed as in the cases discussed previously, where television and radio coverage and the results of the election are considered.

Regardless of the nature of the material, if it is transmitted within the period when the ban is imposed, and it is judged to be related to the political campaign, it violates the requirements of Article L49 of the Electoral Code. There have been a number of cases where breaches have been adjudged to occur.

In 1998 the Constitutional Court (Conseil Constitutionnel) canceled a partial general election because of a 15-second sequence, which was transmitted as part of a satire on polling day. The content of the clip clearly incited people to vote against the National Front party. The judge did not consider the format or genre of the program, and the fact that the comments were not made by politicians or journalists, but by actors, was deemed irrelevant in the context of the law. In the evaluation of the case, the comments were considered to be political in nature and they therefore represented a breach of Article L49. Not only was the principle of fairness broken, because of the large audience for the program and the possible influence that the program may have had on voters' intentions, but that coupled with the small difference between the numbers of votes for the two candidates (there were 33 votes between the two candidates), which was crucial to evaluating the case, caused the legitimacy of the ballot to be put into question.

Similarly, comments made at an election meeting were broadcast the day before the second ballot in a news bulletin on national television channels. The Constitutional Court canceled the election because the candidate referred to in the newscast could not respond to the comments made within the remaining time before the final poll and would ensure that the response would reach the same audience. As a result the radio and television channels are not allowed to broadcast debate in favor of, or to the detriment of, a candidate without having an impact on the election results, particularly on the last day of the election campaign (Decision No. 81-955 of December 3, 1981, AN Seine et Marne, 4th district).

GUARANTEED MINIMUM ACCESS TO AIRTIME FOR CANDIDATES ON PUBLIC TELEVISION AND RADIO

All candidates and parties have the right to have free access allocated to them during the election campaign on public radio and television channels. The CSA is responsible for organizing these broadcasts and they have wide discretion in this area, even though the Courts retain a watchful eye on the whole process. In reality, the election campaign begins in the media long before the official election campaign period. The broadcast media discuss what is at stake in the election and the various manifestos are outlined and debated in the news and current-affairs programs on the channels where the political representatives are invited to express their views. Thus, the central candidates enjoy wide coverage on the channels even before the broadcasting of the official campaign programs.

Allocation

As the CSA is responsible for organizing the official campaign on radio and television, it lays down several rules to this effect. Initially, the CSA sets forth the production, broadcasting, and scheduling conditions for the programs. Once the number of candidates is officially known, the CSA establishes the number and length of the program slots to be allocated to each candidate, according to the amount of time allocated to each one by the Electoral Code. Finally, the CSA determines the scheduling time for these programs, and draws the order for the appearance of each of the candidates. The CSA monitors the whole process of production, programming, and broadcasting operations with the help of an executive producer of Télédiffusion de France (the public body responsible for broadcast transmissions) and the public service broadcasters (France Télévision, Radio France, RFO, RFI).

Predetermined Amount of Airtime

Each candidate is allocated a certain amount of airtime on national channels for the duration of the official campaign, which, depending on the type of election, can vary from 2 to 3 weeks. The amount of airtime varies ac-

TABLE 5.1
Provisions of the Electoral Code Regarding
the Official Campaign on Radio and Television

	Beneficiaries	Time Allocated on Each Public Channel
Presidential elections	Candidates	For the first ballot, the CSA established a time of no less than 15 minutes per candidate.
		For the second ballot, 1 hour for each candidate can be reduced by the CSA according to the candidates.
General elections	1. Parties represented by a group in the Assemblée nationale.	For the first ballot, a total of 3 hours; parties in the majority sharing 1.5 hours airtime and parties in the opposition sharing 1.5 hours of airtime.
		For the second ballot, 1.5 hours instead of 3; same split between majority and opposition parties.
	2. Other parties with at least 75 candidates.	For the first ballot, 7 minutes for each of these parties.
		For the second ballot, 5 minutes for each of these parties.
European elections	1. Lists from parties represented by a group in parliament.	2 hours split evenly between the lists.
	2. Other lists.	30 minutes split evenly between the lists.

cording to the election (general elections, European elections) and is allocated based on the relative position of a particular party in parliament (Article 16 of the modified Law of September 30, 1986). The rules are not set by the CSA but are established either through legal provision or by the government (see Table 5.1).

In terms of the organization of each official radio and television campaign, two dominating principles underpin all of the CSA's requirements.

One Requirement: Equality of Treatment. The most determining requirement bearing on the CSA is to ensure strict equality of treatment of the various candidates. Each candidate has to be allocated the same means and conditions of production, equal access to time for recording, the same number of cameras, and an equal number of studios and editing resources to produce their programs. In this respect, the programs are recorded and produced in studios and facilities, which are specially fitted for this purpose, that all candidates have access to. Throughout the campaign, the CSA sees to it that the recording, production, and broadcasting conditions for the programs are of good quality and consistent for all of the candidates.

Requirement for the Viewing of Programs. The official radio and television campaign has come in for sharp criticism with many observers pointing to its outdated nature and cost. Many people are of the opinion that the majority of political campaign broadcasts turn viewers off. However, it is important to note that since the end of the monopoly of the public radio and television channels, the viewers can choose, if they wish, to listen or watch the campaign broadcasts on the national radio and television channels, or alternatively they are free to switch to the other channels if they do not wish to watch the campaign programs. Due to the increasing disengagement of viewers with the political campaigns the CSA, since 1993, has attempted to combat the problem by encouraging that the production and programming conditions of the programs create renewed interest and make the party political broadcasts more attractive.

RECENT REFORMS OF THE CSA

To modernize party political broadcasts the CSA has developed initiatives in three domains: production, formatting, and the scheduling of campaign programming. The production instruments have been improved to make the programs more attractive (more cameras, use of graphics and video effects, etc.). In addition to putting production studios at the political organizations' disposal, the CSA has granted the parties the resources to shoot coverage from outside the studios and they can also collect material from a broader range of sources. Program clips and recordings can also be inserted into the programs at their own expense, pursuant to the Law of January 15, 1990, relating to the limitation of election expenses and the clarification of political financing.

The program formats have also been modified. Past experience has shown that programs lasting more than 5–10 minutes pose certain problems for engaging with the audience, and the candidates have had difficulties in delivering high-quality performances over such a long slot. In this context, the CSA divides the amount of airtime that each candidate enjoys between longer programs, which enables the candidates to develop more in-depth programs that elaborate on their manifestos, and shorter programming. The latter allows the candidates to emphasize or reiterate the main points of their message. Because of their limited duration they can be aired at peak viewing times, and as a result of their limited nature they are able to engage with the audience, although it should be stressed that the second kind of programs are very limited in the amount of information the format can communicate from the candidate to the viewer. In the ruling Horblin et al. of October 20, 1989 (request No. 108 130), the Court supported the CSA's discretion to distinguish between short and longer programs on the public channels. It considered that the division enabled the lesser known parties to appear on television at the beginning and the end of the campaign, and it provided them with a peak time slot for their broadcasts, as well other times in the schedule.

In dividing the election programs into two types, the CSA has increased the number of programs produced in an extremely short period of time and it has further allowed repeat airings of some of the shorter political broadcasts. The aforementioned measures are widely seen to have improved the attractiveness of the programs and have subsequently supported greater audience engagement with the political broadcasts by the parties. At the same time, the broadcasting of campaign programs on all public channels will always be challenged by the more attractive programming of the commercial audiovisual sector. For this reason, with the exception of the general elections, for which the law requires the simultaneous broadcasting of the programs on public television channels, the CSA spreads out the official campaign broadcasts over the daily schedule and at different times according to the channels, to ensure that there is a broad opportunity to reach viewers. The Electoral Code provides during general elections for "simultaneous broadcasting on the public television channels" of party political broadcasts during a general election. This is a clearly defined rule, which excludes party political broadcasts being aired on France 2 and France 3 at different times in the schedule. During the 1997 election the CSA accepted different programming times for the election broadcasts. However, the court ruled that although the programming on the private television channels limited the impact of this provision, imposing simultaneous transmission across channels was still necessary and the CSA does not hold the legal right to change this arrangement (Conseil d'Etat, Ruling Meyet of May 23, 1997). The Law was modified in July 2001 and simultaneous transmission is not now a rule.

CONTENT OF THE OFFICIAL ELECTION CAMPAIGN BROADCASTS

The candidates and political parties are allowed to express themselves freely in their party political broadcasts. The CSA does, however, require certain standards to be maintained by the candidates and these requirements include respect for public order, a ban on using national symbols such as the national anthem and national colors, as well as respect for the rights and honor of other members of the community. The CSA has established a number of rules in this respect, which relate to production, programming, and broadcasting conditions for programs, and the CSA has the role of ensuring that these recommendations are respected.

In the same procedure as that employed in the treatment of access to airtime, in the coverage of radio and television the judge can intervene twice, either to judge the legality of the preliminary acts and before polling, or alternatively as election judge; in other words, once the ballot results have been announced. The CSA's decisions are also open to judicial review, as in the case of the other areas discussed previously, and again the Court can intervene at two crucial times: either before election polling begins or after the election results have been announced. In the former case the legality of the preliminary acts for an election, such as the one concerning production, programming, and broadcasting conditions of the official campaign programs that the CSA sets forth, can be disputed before polling. Indeed, penalizing the irregularities has more impact before the end of the official campaign rather than after the poll when the effects of the violations are difficult to assess.

NEW MEDIA AND THE INTERNET

The Internet has provided some interesting challenges to regulation as it relates to the election campaign and the audiovisual media. The difficulties arise due to the fact that the Internet belongs to the audiovisual communications landscape and it subsequently comes under a certain number of the provisions of the Electoral Code. However, unlike the radio and television sectors, these provisions must be considered in the context of the reality and the appropriateness of rules that were designed for the audiovisual media and their applicability to the Internet. There are a certain number of characteristics raising obvious practical difficulties for existing regulation.

Article L52-1, first paragraph, of the Electoral Code bans the practice of political advertising through the press or by means of audiovisual communication for an electoral campaign broadcast during the 3 months before polling. Thus, it has to be determined if the Web site of a political party or candidate constitutes political advertising used for electoral purposes (Article L52-1) and if it must be closed down during this period. Article L49 of the Electoral Code forbids the distribution of bulletins, circulars, and other documents on the day of voting. From the day before polling at midnight, it is forbidden to broadcast or get a message promoting a candidate communicated by means of audiovisual communication.

Finally, the Law of July 19, 1977 bans the publication and the dissemination of certain opinion polls, which are directly or indirectly related to an election. The ban is imposed a week before the ballot and during polling. In 2001, a director of a Parisian weekly was sentenced because he posted an opinion poll on the Web site of the magazine within the banned period of time (Tribunal de grande instance de Paris, April 6, 2001, Paris Match). On February 19, 2002, the matter was clarified by the legislature and Article 11 of the Law of July 19, 1977 was modified, restricting the publication of opinion polls during the week preceding the election ballot to the day before the ballot and the day of voting.

It is therefore obvious that the Internet raises some significant challenges that the courts will clarify in the course of future elections. The legislator is responsible for intervening to modify the texts if it is considered necessary, and new media clearly raise a number of important issues to be resolved in order to ensure that the principles of the election law are effective and successful in the context of the areas and sector where they are applicable.

CONCLUSION

In the spring of 2002 both the election of the president of the republic and the elections for parliament took place. As with all elections the events provided a test for the existing regulation and an opportunity to evaluate how well the system works to ensure fair and equal media coverage and access for the various candidates.

During the period of the precampaign of the presidential election, which took place between January 1 and April 4, equality of access for the candidates to the relevant broadcast media was satisfactory. However, the CSA stated that there was a lack of total time dedicated to electoral news. In fact it remarked that for several years there has been a tendency to reduce the time dedicated to information and political debates on most public channels. At the occasion of the presidential election, the CSA expressed its concern about this reduction of time dedicated to political debate, in particular during the elections period.

This tendency was proved true during the period of the official campaign of the presidential election, between April 5 and 19 for the first ballot and April 22 and May 3 for the second ballot. The period was characterized by a small amount of debate between the candidates for the first ballot, which did not make it easy for the candidates to publicize the content of their propositions to the voters. This tendency is explained by the great diversity of the political parties standing for the first ballot (16 candidates), and also by a general public dislike of the campaign. The campaign of the second ballot was marked by more dramatic events and by massive demonstrations against one of the candidates leading the right-wing nationalist party, who gained enough votes to go through to the second stage of the ballot and the final run-off. The subsequent protest was unprecedented in recent French election history, and the public, journalists, and political parties all joined together in protest.

The CSA had to deal with the situation in the context of the large amount of coverage on radio and television of this hostile response across France to Le Pen. If the equality of speaking time and broadcasting time of the two candidates and their supporters was respected, the editorial treatment of the two candidates was not marked by what could be considered total neutrality.

During the first ballot of the presidential election, the transmissions of the official campaign broadcast on France 2, France 3, and La Cinquième within 2 weeks reached about 22 million viewers during the first week and about 27 million in the second. For the second ballot the programs of the official campaign transmitted in 1 week had a far larger public of 48 million viewers. This increase in the audience is partly due to the length of the daily programming of those programs that brought together two candidates, which increased in comparison with the first ballot of 16 candidates. The greater audience shows a greater interest of the French people during the period of the election campaign.

The system that organizes the transmissions of the official media campaign is generally efficient, responds to the concerns for equality and fairness, and provides the resources for candidates to promote their manifestos. The system, however, is also criticized, especially by the major political parties, which reproach it for heavy constraints; they also point out that the system is unpopular with the public.

In order to try to remedy this criticism, the CSA in October 2001 discussed major reform of the system for the electoral deadlines in spring 2002. The reform debate was based on an idea that the candidates for all of the elections would be permitted to choose their own production team and produce and be responsible for their own broadcasts, within a minimum framework predefined by the CSA. Furthermore, the state would financially fund these programs and reimburse, at the end of the campaign, a fixed maximum limit for expenses incurred. In view of the uncertainties concerning the juridical weakness of passing the reform into law, especially regarding the demand for equality of treatment and in view of doubts about certain political groups, the CSA decided to abandon the project.

REFERENCES

Code électoral—Partie Législative [Electoral code—Legislative part].
Code électoral—Partie Réglementaire—Décrets en Conseil d'Etat [Electoral code—Regulatory part—Decrees of the Conseil d'Etat].
Décret n° 2001-213 du 8 mars 2001 portant application de la loi n° 62-1292 du 6 novembre 1962 relative à l'élection du Président de la République au suffrage universel (Journal Officiel n°

58 du 9 mars 2002) modifié par le décret n° 2002-243 du 21 février 2002 (Journal Officiel n° 46 du 23 février 2002) [Decree nr. 2001-213 of 8 March 2001 implementing the Law nr. 62-1292 of 6 November 1962 on the election of the President of the Republic by universal suffrage (Official Journal nr. 58 of 9 March 2002) modified by the Decree nr. 2002-243 of 21 February 2002 (Official Journal nr. 46 of 23 February 2002)].

Drouot, G. (1994). *La politique sur les ondes: des premières émissions aux campagnes actuelles.* Rapport présenté lors du colloque sur Les campagnes électorales radiotélévisées [Radio policy: From the first transmissions to current campaigns. Report presented at a colloquium on Broadcast Electoral Campaigns]. Université d'Aix-Marseille. Avril 1994.

Les élections municipales et cantonales dans les médias audiovisuels [Municipal and cantonal elections on audiovisual media]. La lettre du CSA, n°139, avril 2001, p. 10 et seq.

Loi n° 77-808 du 19 juillet 1977 modifiée relative à la publication et à la diffusion de certains sondages d'opinion [Law nr. 77-808 of 19 July 1977 as amended on the publication and broadcasting of certain opinion polls].

Loi n° 86-1067 du 30 septembre 1986 relative à la liberté de communication modifiée et complétée [Law nr. 86-1067 of 30 September 1986 on the freedom of communication modified and completed].

LEGAL RULINGS

Conseil d'Etat, Ruling Horblin et al. of October 20, 1989, on the occasion of the European Parliament elections of June 18, 1989.

Conseil d'Etat, Ruling M. Malardé of December 30, 1998, regional elections of March 1998, in the department of Morbihan.

Conseil d'Etat, Ruling M. Lallemand et al., National Commission of the campaign accounts and the political financing of May 7, 1993, cancellation of Camille Sudre's election at the regional Council in La Réunion that took place on March 22, 1992.

Conseil d'Etat, Section 26 March 1993, Party of workers *(Parti des travailleurs).*

Conseil d'Etat, Ruling Meyet of May 23, 1997.

Conseil d'Etat, Ruling Alain Meyet of June 2, 1999.

Conseil d'Etat, Ordonnance of February 24, 2001, M. Jean Tiberi.

Conseil constitutionnel, Decision No. 81-955 of December 3, 1981, AN Seine et Marne, fourth district.

Tribunal de grande instance de Paris, April 6, 2001, Paris Match.

6

Russia

Daphne Skillen

In the last 10 years of transition to democratic reform, the Russian electorate has for the first time experienced real contested elections and peaceful transfers of power through the ballot box. In that time there have been three parliamentary elections, two presidential elections, and in a country as vast as Russia, numerous gubernatorial and local elections in the 89 subjects of the Russian Federation. With an electorate of 109 million voters, at the last count, there does not seem to be a time when people somewhere in the country are not going to the polls. It would appear that Russians have been given an unprecedented opportunity to choose their leaders and influence their future. In practice, however, the situation is not so clear; nor can we make any great claims for the triumph of democracy.

Officially the main institutions of democracy have been established, but the way these institutions work are not necessarily democratic. Although over the 10 years lawmakers have modified, revised, and expanded electoral laws in order to improve the conditions in which free and fair elections can take place, political forces have often subverted or exploited the laws for their own ends. The most recent elections in 1999 and 2000 are cases in point. By right, they should have been an improvement on previous elections if democratic reform had genuinely taken root; instead they were the least equitable of the 10-year period. The question often asked today is the extent to which elections in Russia have become a mere formality. Does the established institutional framework limit foul play or are the institutions merely a form of *pokazukha*—an elaborate "facade" manipulated by ruling elites at will, where appearance belies reality in a way that has so often been a feature of Russia's Byzantine political traditions?

MEDIA LANDSCAPE

Elections are that season of the democratic calendar that test the credentials of the media more than at any other time. As the mainstay of democracy, the media should provide accurate, balanced, and impartial information to enable the electorate to make informed choices. As a rule the Russian mainstream media is a high-quality product: articulate, stimulating, professional. The news is taken seriously in the broadsheets and the electronic media, whose plethora of news bulletins and current-affairs discussions on terrestrial channels outstrips anything in the West. For anyone interested in the frenetic nature of Russian politics, television is compulsive viewing. When it comes to elections, however, the media have tended to kowtow to the Kremlin or other vested interests. More often than not this has taken the form of biased coverage, but the accumulation of dirty tricks during the 1999 campaign, unprecedented in the post-Soviet period, introduced a new aggressive factor and a more dangerous development for future elections. This period coincided with the shifting of power from Boris Yeltsin to Vladimir Putin, first as Yeltsin's prime minister and designated successor 4 months before the 1999 election, then as acting president after Yeltsin's premature resignation on December 31, 1999.

It can largely be said that elections in Russia are won by controlling the media, but in looking over the 10-year period the pattern is not consistent. During the 1996 presidential election the nationwide channels voluntarily worked in cahoots with the Kremlin to reelect Boris Yeltsin and defeat his communist rival. There can be no talk here of pressure from the Kremlin. In the 1999 and 2000 elections, the Kremlin was in full control and relentlessly applied the might at its disposal to promote chosen political candidates, using what came to be known as "killer-journalists" to do their dirty work. In both cases the impact of the media on the electorate had the intended results.

Earlier, however, in the 1993 parliamentary election the conventional wisdom was that those who control TV don't win. The expected landslide for "Democratic Russia" was deflected by that astute "clown" of Russian politics, Vladimir Zhirinovsky. In the 1995 parliamentary election, the failure of the so-called party of power, "Our Home—Russia," also demonstrated a rejection of media impact. Perhaps what distinguishes these two elections is that they were the earliest, the electorate was far more robust, and after decades of totalitarianism they chose to reject overt propaganda. The successful Soviet-style use of the media as a tool of propaganda in the most recent elections may say more about society's disillusionment of what has been perceived as freedom and democracy and the belief of most of its citizens today that a "strong hand" is needed to establish law and order in the country. At any rate past experience shows that the influence of the media on the Russian electorate is not inevitable. The Communist Party with firm support from its members and a disciplined structure has consistently received high gains with a minimal use of the media.

Partially the media have themselves to blame for degrading their profession during elections, seduced by money, political clout, and personal ambition; partially the cards are stacked against them. Economic problems are never conducive to media independence and especially since the 1998 financial crisis the media have been beset by economic difficulties. Russia's main television channels are mostly in debt, even though lavish sums of money may go to presenters, production, or acquisitions. With state-controlled channels the subsidies promised do not always get paid so that, in the end, as with private channels, the primary source of revenue is advertising.

Pressure from state and corporate interests—or that monster of political and criminal connections called the "mafia"—is hard and sometimes dangerous for journalists to withstand. During the last 10 years more than 117 Russian journalists have been killed in the course of their professional work, and many instances of intimidation and abuse can be seen from the lists monitored by the Centre for Journalism in Extreme Situations and the Glasnost Defence Foundation. In the regions the media are far more susceptible and dependent on local authorities for their everyday survival. Pressure from local officials can come in a variety of ways through tax penalties, eviction, libel suits, fire inspections, electricity blackouts, and so on. A study called "Public Expertise," conducted by the Union of Journalists in 1999, showed that not one of Russia's 89 regions promotes a climate favorable to free and pluralistic media. The gap between the regions and the capital cities of Moscow and St. Petersburg is wide. If the regions are easily brought to heel, the capital cities have a flourishing intellectual environment and access to the outside world that help to safeguard their freedoms. All the worse, then, that the mainstream media have allowed their influence to be abused.

An ominous sign is that media outlets now look to the elections as a way of earning money and resolving economic problems. The revenue may come from legitimate paid political advertising or it can come in forms of *zakazukha*—concealed public relations (PR) or articles and news reports commissioned for money. Television is increasingly becoming a market where investments in elections can be more profitable than in production.

MEDIA STRUCTURE AND OWNERSHIP

As in most countries, the major nationwide television channels have the greatest impact during elections. Russia does not have a public service broadcaster. ORT, the largest channel in the country with an audience reach of 98%, is a public broadcaster in name only, which in translation stands for "Public Service Russian Television." The misnomer was recently corrected with the announcement that ORT would be renamed the "first channel" from September 2002. ORT is a hybrid channel with 51% owned by the government and 49% by private shareholders. For a long time the main financier of ORT was one private shareholder, the controversial media magnate and politician, Boris Berezovsky, who used his position in ORT to help Putin to power. Since then he has fallen out of favor and been pressured into handing over his shares to a Kremlin intermediary, although no information has been released about who precisely now owns the shares.

RTR is a fully state-owned company, part of the large VGTRK group. As with ORT, RTR is a transformed legacy of the Soviet period. RTR covers 96% of the country and, if not as popular or financially endowed as ORT, it has improved its new coverage and programming.

TV Centre is one of the smaller channels in the big league, set up in 1997 by the Moscow government and, therefore, largely in the hands of the popular Moscow Mayor, Yuri Luzhkov. Luzhkov, who had pretensions of becoming president, was the main target of vilification by ORT during the 1999 election. TV Centre reaches 40% of the country.

NTV was by world standards a highly professional and creative television channel. The largest and most popular of the private TV networks, reaching 73% of the country, it was owned and founded in 1994 by media magnate, Vladimir Gusinsky, and became part of his Media-Most empire. A channel that opposed Putin and criticized military tactics in Chechnya, NTV and Gusinsky have suffered a grim fate with the demise of the channel in its old form in 2001, the enforced exile abroad of Gusinsky and his director-general, and the imprisonment in Russia of his financial officer. Ostensibly the cause of NTV's downfall has been massive unpaid debts, but the relentless persecution of the channel and the way criminal investigations were conducted suggest that political motives were the cause of its downfall. It was no accident that the takeover was engineered by Media-Most's shareholder, Gazprom, which happens to be the government-dominated gas monopoly now well in tow to the Kremlin. The double-standard approach of Russian politics to the media can be seen from the state Audit Chamber's investigations of VGTRK and ORT. Both companies were found guilty of financial malpractice similar to Media-Most's, but they have gone unpunished, their debts have not been recalled, and criminal investigations have not been opened.

The new NTV is now under the control of Gazprom-Media's appointed managers, thus placing it unofficially in Kremlin hands. Although it has not been entirely emasculated, it has lost its previous punch and sophistication.

The more prominent of the old NTV team of presenters and reporters moved to TV6, which had been a less ambitious national channel directed mainly at young viewers. This channel was part of Boris Berezovsky's remaining media empire. Although previously an archenemy of Gusinsky, who had earlier accused him of putting out a contract to kill him, Berezovsky now placed NTV's main anchorman and executive, Yevgeny Kiselyov, in charge of the TV6 staff. This team, having toned down its critical approach, continued to produce quality current-affairs programs, but not for long.

Neither the old NTV team nor Berezovsky escaped the wrath of the powers that be. Bankruptcy proceedings were instigated against TV6 by a minority shareholder, Lukoil-Garant, partly state-owned, on the grounds that the company had failed to earn a profit. Despite the company's denial and increased popularity ratings since the old NTV team took over, TV6 was put into liquidation. Against a background of general legal confusion and accusations of political intrigue, TV6's screen was simply blacked out at midnight on January 22, 2002. With the closure in highly dubious circumstances of the two main sources of alternative information, excuses about debt and unprofitability cannot disguise what had been a long Kremlin-orchestrated attempt to silence critical voices.

In March 2002 a tender for the TV6 license produced a typically cynical outcome to the whole affair. The winning group, Media-Socium, consisted of Yevgeny Kiselyov, now somewhat compromised in the eyes of former supporters and colleagues in his effort to stay on top at all costs, and a Kremlin-backed consortium of oligarchs, headed by Yevgeny Primakov, a former presidential rival turned ally of Vladimir Putin. In this marriage of convenience the Kremlin can claim media independence with the return of Kiselyov, while ensuring control over the channel through its powerful financial supporters in the consortium. The story, however, is not over yet as legal wrangles continue for control of the channel. Currently TV6 is broadcasting under the name of TVS.

The cases of Gusinsky and Berezovsky starkly demonstrate the close ties between politics and the media. Although undoubtedly neither of them is any more innocent of fraudulent financial dealings than Russia's other oligarchs who made enormous fortunes out of the privatization period, their operations went smoothly so long as they were connected with the Kremlin. Nor are they champions of free speech, although a qualification must be made for Gusinsky, the only Russian media tycoon who has tried to turn his empire into a legitimate business and not simply a tool of political influence. The newspapers and radio station in the Media-Most group all showed high standards of professionalism; even a foolhardy satellite venture made sense within the concept of a modern media business. Less can be said for Berezovsky's multifarious and notorious machinations, but both men had no trouble in receiving massive credits from banks while they were in favor. These credits were considered more in the way of hidden subsidies, as few political allies have expected to pay them back. The crunch only comes when political support is removed from the equation and the vulnerability of business on its own is exposed in a situation where the rule of law does not operate.

The big-league television channels in Russia have always been dominated by politics and not business. Television is a prize to be awarded for political favors. The lack of any regulation of media ownership has meant that such favors can be granted with impunity. Media support may be used for a variety of political purposes, but it is most vital during the elections. The contours of the media landscape as we know it today originated in the 1996 presidential election and the campaign to reelect Yeltsin. As opinion polls showed that Yeltsin's ratings were no more than 3% early in the year, it required media expertise and money in massive doses to turn the tide of events.

The "liberal" media did this willingly, fearful of a communist president and the possibility of losing their freedoms. Financial and banking structures that had profited from the early days of "bandit capitalism" were also willing to fund Yeltsin's campaign in amounts that had no relation to set campaign limits. The ensuing campaign was brilliantly masterminded by NTV's director-general Igor Malashenko. Western-style PR, introduced in full force during these elections with an American PR company working behind the scenes, has since become a dominant part of the election scene. The main violation of the 1996 election was the massive campaign overspending that enabled such a slick campaign to be conducted. The exposé of half a million dollars being carried out of the parliament building in Xerox boxes by two members of Yeltsin's campaign team was only the tip of the iceberg. Although an undoubtedly biased campaign was run, there was also some fine reporting, such as NTV's legitimately probing interview with the communist candidate, Zyuganov. If Zyuganov's image suffered, it was also due to the rigidity of a man set in the old Communist Party's ways. The worst sins of the liberal media were the cover-ups. The incident of "money in Xerox boxes" was hysterically denounced by the liberal media as a plant by conservatives in Yeltsin's entourage bent on staging a coup. But the worst offense was the media's silence over Yeltsin's heart attack, which occurred before the second round of the elections.

Through this campaign a relationship was forged between the media and the men who came to be known as "oligarchs." For services rendered, NTV, which had only been broadcasting in the evenings, received a full channel without bidding in a tender. The oligarchs were rewarded in the scandalous loans-for-shares scheme and began buying up media outlets. At this stage, journalists brought up in the Soviet era to fear primarily control by the state had a fairly rosy picture of the commercial media, which they tended to call "independent," as if in private hands they were safe. The Rupert Murdoch syndrome was not part of their experience.

However, very quickly the newly acquired media outlets became the instruments of corporate interests with different oligarchs fighting for their vested interests on television, as if it were their personal fiefdom. This peaked in what came to be known as the "information wars" and the change from simple biased reporting to scandal mongering, *kompromat* or the use of incriminating material, sensational leaked videotapes, and an attention to sex scandals, which had never previously elicited much concern. A curious "pluralism" operated as the veil was slightly lifted from the goings on of rival financial and political circles. The puzzle was to work out which section of the security forces had provided the leak or whose interests were at stake. It was partial information, but it was more information than had been revealed before about what was happening behind the scenes. The main question was always "who stands behind" an event—a variant of the old Soviet habit of reading between the lines.

The problem of media monopoly and concentration in Russia has had the inevitable consequence of limiting pluralism and diversity, as well as the potential for impartial and balanced coverage. With this background in mind, provisions regulating the media in electoral law were expanded in an attempt to provide a more level playing field for the elections of 1999 and 2000.

MEDIA LAW

The media during elections are regulated by electoral laws, as well as by those laws under which they work permanently—the Constitution and the Law of the Mass Media—which set out their rights and responsibilities. The Russian Constitution enshrines free speech in Article 29, which states:

29.1 Everyone is guaranteed freedom of thought and speech.
29.4 Everyone has the right freely to seek, get, transfer, produce and disseminate information by any lawful means.
29.5 Freedom of the mass media is guaranteed. Censorship is forbidden.

The Law on the Mass Media was passed in 1991 and amended several times. It is one of the most democratic laws in the country. The law confirms the three articles in the Constitution protecting the freedom of the media. It emphasizes editorial freedoms: The editorial staff conducts its work on the basis of its professional independence and journalists have the right to remove their signature from reports that contradict their convictions or have been distorted in the process of editorial preparation—that is, the journalist's freedom is also protected from editorial pressure. The law safeguards the confidentiality of sources. If the media print or broadcast information that is inaccurate or false, the law requires that an apology is printed in the same place or broadcast at the same time as the original information. The activity of a media outlet may only be suspended or ended by a decision of a court of law or by its founders.

Accreditation and access to information is a problem area for journalists. There are enough loopholes in the law for arbitrary decisions to be made on accreditation. On access to information, the law guarantees the right to information if the information does not contravene state or commercial secrets, but access has often been denied without legal justification. This area should improve, however, with the new Code of Administrative Offences, which came into effect on July 1, 2002, as the code puts pressure on public officials to disclose information by applying penalties for obstruction. There has also been an attempt since 1997 to push through a law on freedom of information, but the draft law was recently rejected by parliament for the second time.

The Law on Information, Informatization and the Protection of Information (1995) determines what information cannot be classified as secret, but the absence of a mechanism for applying the law has limited access to journalists. Although the list of secret information is contained in the Law on State Secrets, this list is extremely vague.

Libel and defamation laws have been regularly applied to stifle political opposition and investigative journalism. The Russian Constitution and the Civil Code provide for the defense of a person's honor, dignity, and business reputation. Most often libel cases go against the media as the burden of proof is placed on them as defendants. State officials frequently use this means of muzzling the media, knowing that the smaller outlets do not have the financial resources to pursue cases or pay compensation.

Thus even though the media law stands out as one of the most competent and progressive laws of the land, the lack of a system of legislative acts regulating the media negates much of its force. One of the authors of the media law, Mikhail Fedotov, has described the situation as judicial chaos, whose destructive effects can to some extent be softened by reference to the Constitutional Court.

The Ministry of the Press, TeleRadio-Broadcasting and Mass Communications, which replaces a nonministerial state body, issues licenses to the electronic media. As the Television and Radio Broadcasting Bill has been stalled for the past decade, licensing is regulated by government provisions. Broadcasters also need a second license from the Ministry of Communications to operate on a television or radio frequency.

There seems to be an obvious conflict of interest in the appointment of Kremlin-insider, Mikhail Lesin, as Press Minister. His position as cofounder of the powerful advertising monopoly, Video International, is at odds with his role as minister, invested as he is with powers to decide between competitors for licenses. Although Lesin claims to have pulled out as shareholder of the company, this is largely disbelieved. For his lack of support of the media, he has been declared Enemy No. 1 by the Union of Journalists. The media law contains several conditions whereby licenses can be revoked: if the license is obtained under false pretenses, if it has been secretly transferred to or used by another broadcaster, and if violations of law continue after written warnings. The last condition was used during the recent elections to intimidate media not supportive of the Kremlin position, as the law states vaguely that "more than one" warning can involve a license being revoked.

ELECTORAL LAWS REGULATING THE MEDIA

The latest parliamentary and presidential electoral laws impose extensive new duties and restrictions on the media to guarantee equal terms and conditions to all candidates and parties. Specificity and greater transparency have been added, but the expanded texts have also led to a lack of precision, variance in terms used with presumably the same meaning, contradictions, and so on. In purely mechanical terms, such as setting up free and paid access to the media, they have been a great improvement. In more complex matters, the laws are a mystifying phenomenon for ordinary journalists trying to go about their work.

Russia has a federal system of government. Federal elections are conducted for the State Duma (the Russian parliament) and the presidency. The State Duma is the lower house of the Federal Assembly, elected for a 4-year term, and is made up of 450 members elected through two types of mandates. One half of the members (225) are elected on a single-mandate majoritarian system. The other half of Duma members are elected by proportional representation where citizens vote for a political party (known as electoral associations and electoral blocs) that has successfully registered its candidates on federal lists. The seats won by a party or bloc are awarded to their candidates in the same sequential order as they were ranked on their respective federal lists.

The president is elected by direct, popular vote for a 4-year term. The Constitution gives the presidency extraordinary powers. The president can propose draft laws to parliament, as well as issue decrees in areas not regulated by formal laws—a practice extensively used by Boris Yeltsin.

The key federal law governing elections is the law "On Basic Guarantees of Electoral Rights and the Right of Citizens of the Russian Federation to Participate in a Referendum," amended in 1999 and undergoing revision again, which contains the fundamental principles establishing the basis for equal campaign opportunities. This framework law has priority over all other electoral laws.

Elections to the State Duma are governed by the federal law "On the Election of Deputies of the State Duma of the Federal Assembly of the Russian Federation," 1999, which replaced the law that governed the Duma election in 1995. The presidential election of 2000 was governed by the federal law "On the Election of the President of the Russian Federation," adopted in December 1999, as the last act of legislation passed by Yeltsin before he resigned.

The Central Electoral Commission is the permanent, independent body charged with overseeing elections. It is authorized to issue instructions on questions regarding the application of laws. The Commission's functions include formalizing provisions governing the granting of airtime and print space by the media and allocating funds to registered candidates for use in their campaigns.

FREE AND PAID POLITICAL ADVERTISING

There are two key areas of media regulation in the Duma and presidential laws: the allocation of free and paid airtime and print space to candidates and parties to promote their campaigns and the editorial coverage of the elections.

For the first time, access to free and paid time and space was regulated by law with due precision. Previously, access had been issued only through instructions from the Central Electoral Commission. A distinction in responsibilities is made between state- or semi-state-controlled media and commercial media. The former category is defined as media founded or co-founded by government institutions and/or those that receive at least 15% of their funding from government institutions. The state-run media are obliged to provide free time and space on equal terms and conditions, with expenses covered from their budget.

Apart from variations in the Duma and presidential laws relating to municipal, small, and specialized outlets, as well as in the conduct of reruns and early elections (campaigning in the early 2000 election was reduced by one fourth), the basic provisions governing the media in the electoral laws are as follows.

Election campaigning starts on the day when a candidate or party is registered and ends at midnight, local time, 24 hours prior to voting day. Campaigning starts on television and radio 30 days prior—for the press 40 days prior—to voting day, and ends 1 day prior to voting day.

State national TV and radio must provide at least 1 hour daily of free airtime on working days in prime time for campaigning purposes, whereas regional TV and radio at least 30 minutes. In the Duma election the state national media is reserved for parties with registered federal lists of candidates only; regional media for regional groups of candidates and candidates registered in single-seat constituencies. Free airtime is distributed by drawing lots for dates and times, organized as a rule by election commissions in the presence of relevant participants. Candidates and parties can determine the form and nature of their political advertising campaign, but a certain time is also allotted for debates, roundtables, and other joint events.

The most prominent leaders do not usually take part in joint activities and there has never been a debate between leading candidates in presidential elections. Campaign advisers feel that incumbents would be diminished by appearing with lesser, aspiring, candidates. Yeltsin's stated reason in 1996 was that in the 30 years he had spent in the Communist Party he had heard enough "demagogy" not to want to listen to Zyuganov. Putin also declined to be engaged in competitive events. The debates and other joint activities that do take place in free airtime tend to be bland and uninspiring. Usually, campaigning focuses on personalities, rather than party platforms—other than general ideological stereotypes of right and left. Issues close to everyday life such as health, education, transport, or the environment are rarely defined in party programs. This lack of specificity can work to the advantage of candidates, as in Putin's case, by playing on the electorate's hopes and wishful thinking allowed for by an indistinct context.

Both state and commercial media may allocate paid time for political advertising if requested by candidates and parties, but the procedures differ. State broadcasters are required to reserve paid airtime. The total length of time reserved must not be less than the total length of free airtime, but must not exceed free airtime more than twice. All registered candidates and parties are entitled to equal shares of the reserved paid airtime, which are determined by drawing lots. State broadcasters must make their rates public in advance, and they must be the same and available to everyone.

Commercial television and radio must also publish information in advance about the length of airtime at their disposal and the terms of payment, which must be the same for all candidates and parties. A commercial channel may refuse to provide airtime to a candidate or party, but in that case it cannot provide paid airtime to any other candidate or party on the principle of access to all or to none. Lot drawing is not required, with time slots being concluded on the basis of contracts.

For newspapers and magazines the same basic procedures apply. State newspapers are obliged to provide free print space, giving over a specific percentage of the volume of their paper, and the allocation of space is determined by drawing lots. Both state and commercial newspapers must provide equal rates, terms, and conditions.

CAMPAIGN FINANCING

The Duma and presidential laws also significantly tightened the regulation of campaign financing and expenditure. New disclosure requirements have provided more information in an area where fraudulent behavior is widespread. Assets for the purpose of campaigning must now be allocated to electoral funds. All payments for airtime or print space must only be made through electoral funds, irrespective of whether the broadcaster or newspaper is state controlled or commercial, with due amounts paid in full before any political advertising is provided. This safeguards the media in cases where candidates in the past received political advertising for future payment, which never eventuated. For the first time, candidates and parties have had to file campaign finance reports before the election, as well as during and after the election. The electoral commission is obliged to provide the media with data on the receipt and expenditure of campaign funds, which state newspapers are obliged to publish within 3 days.

Some of these improvements on campaign finance were negated by the unrealistic limits set on campaign expenditure. By comparison with Western countries, the ceilings are very low: The limit for the presidential election, for example, was under a million dollars. Although most participants in the Duma and presidential elections considered these limits too low, there was scant debate or interest in the issue, presumably because few felt that there would be compliance with the law in this area anyway. Reporting on financial violations is a crucial part of the journalist's duty to voters, but such investigations are difficult, expensive, and time consuming at the best of times. The amounts revealed by PR firms working for candidates in the elections suggest, however, that financial limits are ignored.

Regulation also covers publicizing the results of public-opinion polls by the media during elections. The results of polls must be accompanied by specific information about the organization that conducted the poll, the sample studied, the statistical margin of error, and so on. No media outlets are permitted to broadcast or publish public-opinion findings or election forecasts in the 3 days prior to and on voting day.

For adjudicating grievances, the Central Electoral Commission may refer cases of violation of campaign activities in the media to law enforcement bodies, to a court of law, or to the Press Ministry for the purpose of exacting penalties and sanctions. Increased fines were introduced under the

Code of Administrative Offences in Elections, which can be applied by the Commission. Another body with the right to adjudicate grievances was the Judicial Chamber of Information Disputes under the President. An advisory body without judicial force, its success at arbitration in the first 1993 election prompted an extension of its functions. It could review cases either at the request of any party concerned or on its own initiative, and recommend penalties and sanctions, most often on questions of journalistic ethics. Although attached to the president's office, its specialists in media and law were known for their independence and their decisions were treated with respect. It was therefore regarded with some concern when after the 2000 election Putin disbanded the Judicial Chamber.

The Duma and presidential laws largely represent a progressive step in regulating the media and ensuring accountability. In some areas there was little to complain about. The specific legislation governing campaign access to the media, the obligations of state-controlled and commercial media, and equal terms and conditions for candidates and parties were adequately enforced and showed improvement on previous elections. In other areas there were obvious flaws. At present, for example, if candidates commit a violation of the law while using free or paid access to the media, the editor is liable for the violation. Thus, candidates have the right to determine the format, nature, and content of their campaign, which the editor is obliged to disseminate, but for which he becomes liable. If the editor rejects libelous material he breaks the electoral laws, and if he accepts it he breaks Article 57 of the media law. Greater clarity in such instances has been recommended to the Commission.

Another problem was the contradiction between electoral laws and the media law in questions regarding the honor and dignity of candidates. The Duma law states that the media are prohibited from making public any information that may cause damage to a candidate's honor and dignity if the media cannot provide the candidate with a right of reply before the end of the campaign period (Article 60:40). While the media law makes clear that the right to reply depends on the imparting of inaccurate information (Article 43), the electoral law does not distinguish between factual information and unsubstantiated slander. Under this article, a candidate can demand equal time in either circumstance, which only acts to stifle the journalistic coverage.

The worst dilemma of the 1999–2000 elections lay, however, in identifying who may or may not participate in campaign activities.

EDITORIAL COVERAGE OF ELECTIONS

The most problematic area of the recent elections regarding the media was the interpretation of preelectoral campaigning (*agitatsiya*). The problem was not so much in the law as in the Central Electoral Commission's interpretation of the law.

In the Commission's Clarification of August 13, 1999 (No. 8/52-3), Article 9 states that "campaigning through the media (via the channels of television and radio organisations and through the print media) can only be conducted by registered candidates, electoral associations and electoral blocs that have registered federal lists of candidates; and exclusively at the expense of their electoral fund." The document stresses that "no other participants" have the right to engage in campaigning. This entails that journalists do not have the right to engage in campaigning that, according to the definition of campaigning in electoral law, means that they cannot "encourage or aim to encourage voters to participate in the elections" or "to vote for or against any registered candidate" or party (Article 8:2 of both the Duma and presidential laws). In this way the electoral commission's interpretation managed in one fell swoop to contradict the Constitution, the media law, and electoral laws as both the Constitution and the media law guarantee the media the right of free speech and free expression; though electoral laws specify those groups disqualified from taking part in electoral campaigning, journalists are not among them.

It turns out that if a journalist cannot say anything for or against a candidate or party, he can do nothing other than paraphrase their words. Given that candidates are naturally prone to exaggerating their virtues, the journalist becomes simply a mouthpiece for their political ambitions, which in itself is reporting "for" candidates. This precludes all probing and investigative journalism, and denies journalists the right to conduct their professional duty and act as watchdogs of the public interest. The basic confusion lies in the Commission's misunderstanding of two important but totally different activities—political advertising and editorial coverage. The former is a campaigning activity, regulated through free and paid access to the media; the latter involves journalism and the provision of information and analysis, which rightly has no relation to campaigning. Journalistic commentary, for or against, so long as it is fair and accurate, is a prerequisite of the voter's right to know.

The Commission went further than the law as well in restricting coverage on television news bulletins. The laws state that the round-up of electoral news should be set out in a "separate bloc, as a rule at the beginning of the programme, without commentary." This is sensible enough as a guarantee of providing unbiased information in the main body of the news, but the Commission interpreted the article as prohibiting commentaries not only within the bloc but after it and, by implication, commentary in any other current-affairs program.

Although the Commission's aim can be seen as well intentioned, directed at curbing a partisan and biased media from manipulating voters, these draconian measures did nothing to prevent the excesses of the media campaign in the 1999 parliamentary election. All stops were removed to discredit the opposition Fatherland-All Russia bloc and its leaders, Primakov and Luzhkov, as future presidential candidates. A correspondingly persistent propaganda campaign was run to promote the Putin-backed Unity bloc, thus opening the way for Putin to win the presidential election. With the assistance of the media, Unity, a movement that had not existed 2 months earlier and lacked a party platform, managed to achieve resounding success.

The main offender in the negative campaign was ORT. The character assassination of both Primakov and Luzhkov was relentlessly conducted in a continuous stream of scurrilous and anecdotal invective mainly by ORT's clever, but unscrupulous presenters, Sergei Dorenko and Mikhail Leontyev. Luzhkov in particular came in for ridicule every Sunday on Dorenko's program "Vremya," his face contorted by computer graphics to resemble either Mussolini or Monica Lewinsky. Reports made claims of his excessive wealth, his gigantic security service, his support for allegedly evil Scientologists, and his part in the murder of an American businessman. Primakov was accused of being incriminated in the attempted assassination of Georgian President Eduard Shevardnadze and was made out to be too old and feeble to run as future president after hip surgery. One such operation was shown in long and bloody detail on "Vremya" to imply that nobody could come out of such excruciating surgery with the stamina to become president. NTV and TVTs opposed Unity and Putin, but tended to steer away from scandal mongering. NTV justified its position by claiming that it rectified the imbalance in the total coverage.

Spin has its own spin in Russia. In a country known for its Potyomkin village syndrome, as well as a Soviet past in which the most implausible lies were maintained in the face of incredulous disbelief, black PR has taken off with a vengeance. Gogolian "dead souls" appear on voting registers; three candidates campaign under the same name; groups of scrofulous down-and-outs or, in a country still mainly homophobic, alleged gays are paid to support a candidate to his detriment. The common lie is proffered with a garish dressing. Not only the tabloids but any willing media, either due to payment or pressure, will find room for such coverage. At the best of times, however, the coverage is lively and stimulating. In Moscow the propaganda mill can never completely stifle the cacophony of voices; nor are affiliated newspapers rigidly disciplined or wholly predictable—occasional outbursts from rogue journalists will contradict their master's prescriptions. Some of the more interesting debates of the 1999 campaign took place on NTV's studio program, "Glas Naroda," where differing views, particularly among the democrats, were instructive and often trenchant. These debates however were marginalized by the fact that pro-Unity candidates refused to take up NTV's invitations and be subject to critical scrutiny, preferring to be interviewed within the safe walls of state television. Without true debate among political rivals, the thrust of propaganda was overwhelming.

Despite the Commission's restrictive understanding of campaigning, the media did not suffer unduly from sanctions, nor were the main culprits appropriately penalized. The Press Ministry rightly condemned the Commission's interpretation of campaigning as placing a "moratorium" on free speech, but used this argument to refuse the Commission's request on one occasion to issue a well-deserved warning to ORT. In all, the Press Ministry issued three warnings. Only one warning was issued against the worst offender, ORT, whereas two were issued against TVTs, Luzkov's channel. As the second warning could have involved revoking TVTs' license, it can be seen as a threat to keep the channel in line. The curious nature of the alleged second offense, that TVTs had not notified the ministry of a change of address, makes this obvious.

Under the Press Ministry's direction, Primakov was offered the right of reply on Dorenko's program, but refused claiming his reply would be distorted. Luzhkov chose to pursue a case against ORT and Dorenko through the Supreme Court and won. However, under Russian law the fine imposed in such cases is financially insignificant and provides virtually no deterrent. Thus, ORT's systematic smears and RTR's less stark violations went unpunished, whereas channels that were not part of the Putin support campaign suffered. NTV was under legal and psychological pressure throughout the campaigns. Overall, the Commission's interpretation of the laws had the effect of baffling journalists and scaring off more vulnerable media outlets, while doing nothing to regulate those with Kremlin ties.

By comparison, the presidential campaign was subdued, given that the field had been cleared by the Duma election to ensure Putin's success. In many ways it was a nonevent. The passions were spent and the result a foregone conclusion. In fact, Putin did not need to campaign at all and refused to take part in the contest. Claiming that it was fair to give other candidates a chance, he was nevertheless rarely off the screen in his position as acting president. Using what is known in Russia as "administrative resources," he made the most of the powers inherent to incumbency. Consequently, there was no need for fraudulent financial expenditure, as witnessed in the Duma or the 1996 presidential elections.

Putin won because the political infrastructure was relentlessly applied in his favor. As Yeltsin's heir he inherited his political administration, the support of most of the oligarchs, and their pliant media. That is not to say that he did not demonstrate qualities attractive to the electorate. He was young, "normal," and dynamic. His macho image only helped to boost his popularity—such as in his notorious remark about Chechen fighters that "we will waste them in the lavatory." Nevertheless he was a figure plucked out by the political elite, with no publicly known past political record and no explicit campaign program. The little that was known of his political views showed him to be an advocate of strong central government with a determination to "manage" democracy, bring about law and order, and come to grips with the war in Chechnya. These views could be gleaned from a timely book of interviews and from what passed as a political manifesto in his "Open Letter to the Electorate," printed in the newspaper *Kommersant* on February 25, 2000. This letter actually broke the electoral law with its publication before the start of the campaign: something the Central Electoral Commission "noted," but issued no warning to an obvious presidential winner. Had Putin been a less presentable candidate, his success would still have been inevitable. His attitude was sublimely confident; his remarks to the press often flippant: His comment that he would not sell himself like a product—"Tampax or Snickers"—made a mockery of any true contest. His behavior during the campaign was that of a person above the fray: a president before the results were out.

A serious piece of investigative journalism into vote fraud in the presidential election was published 6 months later by the respected English-language newspaper, *The Moscow Times,* which turned up evidence that 2.2 million stolen or falsified votes in regions with questionable electoral reputations, such as Dagestan and Tatarstan, were decisive in preventing a second round. It is unlikely that Putin would have lost the race, but it would have dented his unassailable image. Interestingly, the eight-page report received no immediate response from the electoral commission and nothing substantial from the Russian press, except for *Izvestiya*'s attack on foreign interference.

SELF-REGULATION

Many of the cases of improper journalistic practice are matters of ethics and conduct, which rightly should come under self-regulation. In most Western countries, it is usually the threat of a tarnished reputation that make quality newspapers and national channels abide by codes of conduct, as losing the moral high ground tends to go with financial losses. This is not the case in Russia, where political influence counts more than business. Nor are pariah journalists ostracized from the profession, by either their colleagues or public opinion.

Nevertheless there has been an attempt at self-regulation. There are a number of well-formulated and principled journalistic codes, drafted and approved by journalists themselves. The Union of Journalists has its own code of ethics and a Grand Jury, which presides over particularly notorious violations. It issued a public reprimand to Sergey Dorenko and declared he could no longer call himself a journalist, but as the Union lacks general support its decisions have little effect. Another document is the Charter of Television and Radio Broadcasters, signed by most of the top stations, but its signatories did not once invoke the charter during the parliamentary campaign's massive violations of taste and decency. There is also the Russian National Association of Telebroadcasters' Memorandum on Elections, and NTV's Instructions to its journalists.

These codes contain fine words, but an unruly community of disparate journalists, tied to various vested interests, struggling to survive or maintain lifestyles in unstable economic conditions, often without any clear moral purpose, is unlikely at this stage to come to an agreement on community conduct. The bad atmosphere created by the media takeovers with former allies fighting each other has increased the fragmentation.

CONCLUSION

Given the rapid changes that have taken place in the last few years, we can assume that the political landscape will look somewhat different by the next elections in 2003 and 2004. Since Putin has come to office, centralist forces have strengthened and state structures have exercised considerable influence in all spheres of political life. Hardly anyone opposes the president anymore, and those behind-the-scenes struggles that have prompted such apparent unanimity are not the subject of public discussion, as they were during the Yeltsin years. Under Putin, Russia has enjoyed greater economic prosperity; although largely due to the increase of oil revenues on the world market, he has also pushed through important legislation on taxation, land reform, and in other spheres. His popularity ratings remain at a regular 70%, although when asked specifically about his policies, such as the war in Chechnya, his approval ratings tend to be more in the range of 35%. He has no rivals to compare with, as they were mostly eliminated in the previous elections. The party structure will have also changed by the next Duma elections. The strong grip of Kremlin influence has succeed in merging the two fierce rival parties of the 1999 Duma election, Unity and Fatherland-All Russia, into one strictly disciplined bloc called Unified Russia.

The draft law on the "multiparty" system, conceived within the presidential administration, is directed at reducing the number of parties and placing them more firmly under state control, as parties will now receive state funding. In accordance with the approved draft law, only those parties or blocs that garner not less than 10,000 people and have member organizations in a majority of Russian regions can have the right to participate in elections. This will cause serious problems for such liberal-right parties as Yabloko and the Union of Right Forces. It can be assumed, then, that the major contenders in the next Duma election will be United Russia, the party of power, and the Communist Party, which has been severely weakened by splits within its midst. The democratic parties talk of uniting into one group, but serious rivalries make this unlikely.

One of Yeltsin's main virtues was that he did not interfere with the media. If the media have not always taken their responsibilities seriously, there has been a learning curve of self-awareness and the potential to grow into a valuable democratic institution. State imposition, or what Putin calls "managed democracy," Russia's endemic method of enforcing change from above, will produce passivity in the media and not the critical participation necessary to an open society. Putin has claimed commitment to the free media, but there is little evidence to substantiate this claim. Asked about the disintegration of NTV, he disingenuously replied, "Leave it to the courts"—a laughable comment given the judicial system's notorious lack of independence. It is not surprising that Putin, as a former KGB man, sees the media as a propaganda tool in the service of the state. His purpose may well be to build a strong Russia and improve the economy, but all the signs indicate that he plans to do this by less than democratic means. If Russia has incorporated the capitalist market, albeit in its more ruthless form, democracy has always been Russia's Achilles' heel. Increasingly coercive methods of governance will further distance the goal of democracy. Dubious machinations behind the scenes can continue without touching the institutional trappings of democracy. In this way the political reasons for the closure of Russia's private channels have been suitably disguised as a matter of business litigation.

Media forces have certainly been tipped in the Kremlin's favor. With the change in ownership of ORT, NTV, and TV6, Russia's major nationwide channels will tend to toe the line. Gusinsky's remaining media empire has been sold to Gazprom, but Berezovsky still retains a voice through his national press outlets.

A whole series of moves have already taken place under Putin to gain control of media structures. Some of these are the increasing powers of the Press Ministry; a Kremlin-tied breakaway journalist union; the centralization of state subsidies to the state media previously in the hands of regional and local authorities—with the sums involved labeled in the state budget for the first time as "top secret," usually designated only to parts of the defense budget; censorship laws introduced in the reporting of the Chechen war; the strengthened position of Kremlin-favored oligarchs running the advertising monopoly, Video International; and the disbanding of the Judicial Chamber of Information Disputes. A sinister development is the appointment to senior executive positions in media groups of former FSB and other secret service officers.

The new information policy as set out in the Doctrine for Information Security, which sees media as "strategically important for the national information security of the Russian Federation" could be used as a channel to justify acts of censorship. Certain media outlets continue to produce critical commentary and journalistic investigations, whereas online publications still remain beyond Kremlin control but, as one politician quipped, "We have free speech, but not in prime time." The journalist community lacks both the strength and solidarity to mount any serious protest, as it did in the past. With the return of a "strong hand," the old Soviet mentality of paying lip-service to authority has returned faster than could have been expected. Self-censorship among journalists can already be witnessed without waiting for crude state control.

A seemingly positive, if vague, reform of the media industry has grown out of the Russian-American Media Entrepreneurship Dialogue held at summit meetings between Putin and President Bush in November 2001 and May 2002. Since then Putin has spoken of reducing the state's role in the media in a gradual way: more evolutionary than revolutionary, he has said. Press Minister Lesin even envisaged a future when the state would own only one outlet of each medium with the piecemeal sale of the rest of the state media. Whether we are to take these remarks seriously is a moot point: They may be no more than an attempt by Putin, now on good terms with the West especially since his support of the United States after the September 11 terrorist attack, to rectify the bad coverage he received abroad over his media tactics. If these reforms actually do take place, it would be unlikely to happen before the next elections, whereas the sale of state media can always be managed to fall into safe hands. It would be imprudent as well to forget Putin's statement early on in office when he hinted that he would like to extend the term of president from 4 to 7 years after the 2004 election.

Although a total clampdown on the media is not possible, there is an undoubted slipping back into the behavioral patterns of the past. The lack of tolerance for credible opposition and critical media presents a bleaker picture for the next elections. With a less free media, there can only be less free elections.

ACKNOWLEDGMENTS

The author would like to thank the International Foundation for Election Systems for their permission to use some of the material previously published in the IFES Handbook in this chapter.

REFERENCES

European Institute for the Media. (2000). *Monitoring the media coverage of the 2000 presidential elections in Russia, final report.* Dusseldorf, Germany: Author.

European Institute for the Media. (2000). *Parliamentary elections in Russia, final report.* Dusseldorf, Germany: Author.

International Foundation for Election Systems. (2000). *Monitoring the media coverage of the December 1999 election.* Washington, DC: Author.

International Foundation for Election Systems. (2000). *Parliamentary and presidential elections in Russia 1999–2000, technical assessment.* Washington, DC: Author.

7

United Kingdom

Anthony McNicholas
David Ward

POLITICAL BACKGROUND

The United Kingdom has a long tradition of democratic parliamentary elections and, although it does not have a written constitution, within the legal framework there are numerous rules and regulations relating to how elections should be conducted, as well as to how the media should act during the period when candidates stand for election to parliament.

Unlike most European countries, which use various methods of proportional representation, the UK operates a "first past the post system," divided, at the last election in 2001 into 659 (the number varies) geographical constituencies, each returning a single member of parliament (MP). Only votes for winning candidates count and those cast for losing candidates are discarded. Every system of voting has its own peculiarities, and in the case of the UK, the principal ones are the large number of "wasted" votes, the sometimes distant relation between votes and seats in parliament, and the emergence of a two-party system. Table 7.1, which shows the absolute vote, percentage of votes, and number of seats in elections from 1979 onward, illustrates some of these points. The Labour Party, for example, in its worst recent performance in 1983, managed to obtain 209 seats with a 27.57% share of the vote, whereas the Liberal/Social Democrat Alliance, just over 2% behind, was rewarded with only 23 seats. Not surprisingly, the Liberal Democrats, as they are now constituted, have been calling for electoral reform. Because parties have to compete, constituency by constituency, on a "winner takes all" basis, percentage share of the total vote is no indicator of success and though there are three main parties in UK politics, in terms of seats, the third party trails far behind the other two.

One of the central features of UK elections in recent years has been the failure of the Liberals to reestablish themselves as a "third force." The remainder of seats (included in the Others column in Table 7.1) go to the mainly nationalist parties of Wales, Scotland, and Northern Ireland. Though an occasional independent may win a seat, small parties do not thrive in the UK system; the "Greens" for example have had no domestic electoral success, whatever the level of support they have throughout the country. Though it is admitted that the system is inherently conservative, in its defense it is often argued that it favors clear-cut decisions, prevents government by coalition minorities as elsewhere, and militates against extremist parties.

The maximum period permitted between general elections in the UK is 5 years as determined by the Parliament Act 1911. Only twice since the Act was passed, under exceptional circumstances, has parliament been extended beyond this period. According to constitutional law the Queen is responsible, under the royal prerogative, to formally dissolve parliament. In reality the incumbent prime minister advises the Queen and, when the deci-

TABLE 7.1
UK Elections 1979–2001—Votes, Share (%), and Seats

Year	Conservative	Labour	Liberals[a]	Lib/SDP	Lib Dem	Others
1979	13,697,923	11,532,218	4,313,804			1,677,417
	43.9%	37.0%	13.8%			5.4%
	339	269	11			16
1983	13,012,376	8,456,934		7,780,949		1,120,878
	42.43%	27.57%		25.37%		4.63%
	397	209		23		21
1987	13,760,935	10,029,270		7,341,651		1,398,348
	42.30%	30.83%		22.57%		4.3%
	376	229		22		23
1992	14,093,007	11,560,484		5,999,384		1,961,119
	41.93%	34.39%		17.85%		5.83%
	336	271		20		24
1997	9,600,940	13,517,911			5,243,440	2,925,817
	30.69%	43.20%			16.76%	9.35%
	165	418			46	30
2001	8,357,292	10,740,648			4,816,137	2,454,453
	31.7%	40.7%			18.13%	9.47%
	166	413			52	28

Note. From the Electoral Reform Society (2001).

[a]The Liberals entered into an alliance with the newly formed Social Democratic Party for the 1983 election and merged to form the Liberal Democrats for the 1997 election.

sion to dissolve parliament is taken, the formal period of election campaigning begins with an issue of the commencement of the election campaign. Traditionally the prime minister announces the date of dissolution and explains the reasons for dissolution.

Once the dissolution of parliament has been announced, Writs of Elections are issued by the Clerk of the Crown in Chancery, and the election period officially begins. During this period the government continues in office, but there ceases to be any members of parliament. The period of the election campaign is 1 month from the issue of the writs and royal proclamation.

MEDIA ECOLOGY

Traditionally, the television and press industries have experienced wide variations in how the two sectors are regulated. Broadcasting has been closely regulated by bodies established by the state, with a commitment that they should operate at arms length from the government. Competition has been limited. The press has experienced little regulation from the state and except for ownership restrictions and legal matters such as defamation, the sector is effectively self-regulated by the Press Complaints Commission (PCC). The newspaper sector is a highly competitive one, which is characterized overall by a steady decline in readership.

The British broadcasting system has evolved through a system of duopoly and shared responsibility that has historically supported one of the most stable broadcasting environments in the world. In many respects it can be understood as being part of the postwar compromise, which was first seriously challenged with the advent of Margaret Thatcher's Conservative government in 1979. It was not for at least a decade that the repercussions of the deregulatory agenda of the Conservative government, supported with large majorities in the House of Commons if not of the voting public, started to show in the sphere of broadcasting. Indeed it was not until the 1990 Broadcasting Act that the first sweeping changes were introduced in order to support more competitive structures in television and radio. The New Labour government, today in its second term in office, have done little to change the direction in which television and radio broadcasting appear to be heading.

Recently, broadcasting in Britain has undergone tremendous changes with the increasing diffusion of cable and satellite delivery systems, a less public-service-oriented ITV network, and a wide range of channels available to the public. However, although these changes constitute long-term challenges to the existing structures of television, it is important to put them into context. The vast majority of viewers in the UK largely watch terrestrial television, and although approximately half of British viewers at the time of writing have access to cable, digital terrestrial television, or satellite, the five terrestrial channels collectively remain the most popular. Furthermore, the core public-service broadcaster, the BBC, retains a prominent position in the television landscape.

In terms of the rules and regulations that govern the media's role at election times, surprisingly little has changed over the decades, and although there have been modifications, the guidelines that determine the parameters as to the nature of the election coverage by broadcasters have remained stable throughout.

Despite the growth of television and radio broadcasting, the press is still also central to the electoral process. In contrast to the restrictions and obligations imposed upon broadcasters, the press in the UK has been left very much to its own devices. The high value placed upon freedom of expression has, in the case of the press, caused governments to allow self-regulation in matters of content. A free marketplace of ideas, which in theory, if not in practice, is open to all, has been deemed preferable to what would be considered state interference.

The British press is technically three markets that are distinguished both by content and along class lines. The broadsheets, middle-range titles, and tabloids all to a certain extent package news for their readers in differing ways and there is considerable difference in the style, focus, and depth of news and information that is reported by the different types of newspapers. Although there is a strong regional press in the UK, the central feature of the British press is that it is nationally based and the main newspapers have a national, rather than regional focus. There are 10 main national titles and approximately 50% of the market is commanded by the populist tabloids and a further 27% by the middle-range newspapers, with the final 23% being taken by the broadsheets, although the leading broadsheet *The Telegraph,* is responsible for over a third of the market share of the serious press.

Although the state has adopted a laissez-faire attitude toward the press, the relationship between newspapers and legislators has not been without its difficulties and the threat of statutory regulation has at various times been raised as an alternative, usually in response to tabloid excesses. To date, such threats, however, have proved empty. Most memorably, Conservative Minister David Mellor warned in the early 1990s that the popular press was "drinking in the last chance saloon," only to lose his job following newspaper reports about his private life. More serious engagements with the perceived problem of the behavior of certain sections of the newspaper industry were two reports in the 1990s by Lord Calcutt. The first, in 1991, set the press 18 months to clean up its act or face regulation by parliament. The result was the PCC, established by the proprietors in the same year. In his second report in 1993, Calcutt, dissatisfied with progress, urged statutory regulation, but the government of the day declined to act and in February 2002 the PCC, which enforces a code of practice drawn up by newspaper editors themselves and only has powers of censure, celebrated its 10th anniversary.

ELECTION COVERAGE RULES
FOR THE MASS MEDIA

Newspapers have almost complete freedom in the reporting of elections and those statutes that do apply are technical in nature and are intended to prevent the use of the press to distort results. Once a writ for an election has been issued, it is illegal for anyone to publish a false story about one of the candidates with the intention of affecting the outcome of an election. Such stories or statements covered by the law must concern "personal character and conduct" and are not in themselves political. It is the motivation of those making the statement, advantaging one candidate over another, that is held to be political. Candidates may obtain injunctions preventing publication, if able to provide prima facie evidence of the statement's falsehood. If an editor, on the other hand, can give proof of the truth of the statement, which must be demonstrated as fact, not opinion, no injunction would be permitted (Robinson & Nicol, 1992, pp. 403–404).

Apart from these requirements there are some technical restrictions. However, the main constraints on the press in the UK at election times are the same as those applying generally—the laws of defamation. In the heightened atmosphere of an election, defamation is a potential pitfall. The danger lies in the statements of candidates and their agents about rival candidates, made either in their election literature or at meetings. In order to give them the maximum freedom of speech, statements made by MPs in parliament have parliamentary privilege, meaning they are not subject to the laws of defamation. Journalists are protected by what is known as "qualified privilege" in reporting them. Statements made by MPs or others outside parliament in the course of an election do not attract this privilege; indeed Section 10 of the Defamation Act of 1952 "specifically excludes defamatory statements published by or on behalf of candidates" (Crone, 1995, p. 172). It is, therefore, especially in these days of so-called negative campaigning, important for editors to check very carefully what is said about any of the candidates.

Traditionally the reporting of elections on British broadcasting has been governed by the Representation of the Peoples Act 1983 (RPA). The Act contains certain guarantees and guidelines on how parliamentary elections should be covered by the media and under what conditions political parties and candidates have the right to access the national media.

Amendments to the RPA that relate to television have recently been in-troduced and replaced with codes of practice. The amendments came into effect in March 2001 and replace Section 93 of the RPA with guidelines that provide for a new set of rules to be adopted by broadcasting authorities, who are required to consult the views of the Electoral Commission in con-sidering both the drafting of the rules and any proposed modifications. The Electoral Commission does not have the powers to actually intervene in the decisions of the relevant regulatory authority.

In terms of radio and television, the rules of coverage are contained in a number of instruments, the first being the 1990 Broadcasting Act and the second, a set of more detailed guidelines established by the Independent Television Commission (ITC) for commercial broadcasters, the BBC's Pro-ducer Guidelines, and the Radio Authorities' (RA) guidelines for commer-cial radio stations.

PROGRAM GUIDELINES AND CODES

The BBC, ITC, and RA have all developed comprehensive guidelines for broadcasters who are required by the 1990 Broadcasting Act to cover elec-tion campaigns. As soon as an election is called, the guidelines are invoked for the express purpose of covering the election campaign, which requires broadcasters to remain within certain parameters of how they cover the parties involved. There is an extra impetus during this period for the regu-latory authorities to ensure that broadcasters achieve fairness, balance, and objectivity in their reporting of election-related issues.

Chapters 33 and 2 of the BBC's *Producer Guidelines* (2002) set out the guide-lines that BBC program producers should follow at times of elections. The guidelines are based on the BBC's Royal Charter and Agreement and require the BBC to provide for comprehensive and impartial news coverage, sup-ported with informed and fair reporting. The agreement also explicitly ex-cludes the BBC from expressing the Corporation's own opinion. This, however, does not mean that the BBC is constrained within a completely sterile and neu-tral straitjacket. Correspondents are free to make judgments but this is re-strained to the point where a broadcaster's personal views should not be ap-parent on air, according to Section 5.1 of the Royal Charter and Agreement.

The ITC and the RA also have similar features in their guidelines, which apply to all terrestrial broadcasters in the UK. The broadcasters are obliged to adhere to the codes, and failure to do so can bring a variety of penalties to offending companies.

Section 3.3 of the *ITC Programme Code and Guidelines* (2001) on "major matters" covers the general rules pertaining to terrestrial broadcasters' coverage of issues of national importance that includes "significant legislation currently passing through parliament." The rules state that broadcasters should provide for a full range of views and ensure that due impartiality is achieved at all times. Complementing Section 3.3, Section 4 of the code deals explicitly with coverage during election campaigns. The rules require that terrestrial broadcasters give adequate and appropriate coverage of the major parties in the election and maintain impartial and nonpartisan coverage of the elections and the parties involved. The RA has a similar set of rules for commercial radio stations to adhere to. Additionally the guidelines provide for clear signposting of party political broadcasts in order to distinguish them from other parts of the schedule. Clear labeling of party political broadcasts that resemble a format in the television schedule, for example, news, is required and where actors are used this should also be clearly pointed out to the viewer.

Combined, the BBC's program guidelines together with the ITC and RA codes provide for the central regulations on how television and radio should cover the elections. Balance, impartiality, and equal access to candidates from the major political parties are a fundamental principle, and at election times these principles are rigorously enforced by both the broadcasters and where relevant the regulators.

PARTY POLITICAL BROADCASTS AND POLITICAL ADVERTISING

The current rules on access for candidates to television and radio impose a strict ban on paid political advertising. Instead of paid political advertising, a system of party political broadcasts has been created that can be traced back to the very beginnings of broadcasting in the UK. The first recorded party political broadcasts were in 1924 on the BBC, when broadcasts by the three main party leaders were aired on radio (Electoral Commission, 2001). In 1951 the tradition was carried through to BBC television and as television expanded into what is commonly referred to as a duopoly, with regulated commercial television being introduced, the commercial broadcasters belonging to the ITV network also took on the tradition of allocating airtime to political parties for their party broadcasts.

The long tradition of airing party political broadcasts that allow qualifying political parties free access to airtime in order that they can convey to the general public party manifestos and party policies has been very much a part of the television tradition in the UK.

However, the 1990 Broadcasting Act was the first piece of legislation that actually incorporated the tradition of broadcasters providing airtime for party political broadcasts into UK media law. Sections 36 and 107 of the 1990 Broadcasting Act grant the ITC powers to require the terrestrial broadcasters licensed under Part I of the Broadcasting Act (C3, C4, and C5) to carry party political broadcasts as well as to respect the rules for party political broadcasts determined by the ITC. The Act also grants the ITC powers, under Sections 36 and 107, paragraphs 2a and 2b, to determine which political parties are granted airtime and the length and frequency of airtime that any such political party is allocated. The terrestrial commercial broadcasters are therefore required under the terms of their license to broadcast to comply with the ITC guidelines.

Section 4 of the ITC code contains guidelines on a wide range of issues that ensure that terrestrial commercial broadcasters cover the elections within the parameters of acceptable standards. The allocation of airtime for party political broadcasts, the scheduling, and frequency, are all set down clearly by the ITC.

The BBC is not required to air party political broadcasts by the Broadcasting Act and there is no formal legal obligation on the BBC to make time available for the purposes of party political broadcasts, but it has nevertheless provided, as part of the institution's understanding of its remit, airtime according to the same qualifying grounds as the ITC and the RA. Chapter 36 of the *Producer's Guidelines* provide guidelines for party broadcasts on the BBC. The rules stress that the BBC is not editorially responsible for party broadcasts, but it does retain the responsibility that these broadcasts remain within the parameters of the law on libel, violence, and racial incitement.

Despite the reform in the legal framework mentioned earlier, all free-to-air broadcasters continue to provide for party political broadcasts in program guidelines and they remain an important part of the British audiovisual landscape during the election campaigns and at other important junctures of the British political calendar such as Budget day. However, the majority of party political broadcasts are predictably transmitted during the official election campaign. Parties may choose a length of 2 minutes, 40 seconds, or 4 minutes, 40 seconds, and the broadcast should be transmitted normally between 5:30 P.M. and 11:30 P.M. (the BBC has a similar policy). Election broadcasts by major parties must be broadcast in peak time, that is, between 6:00 P.M. and 10:30 P.M.

The allocation of party airtime is free to the political parties that qualify for access to broadcast, and responsibility for the editorial content of the program remains with the relevant political party. The costs of production are also carried by the relevant political party and they are considered to be independent from the broadcasters, who only act as a vehicle for the broadcasts. As long as they comply with the law and taste and decency standards then the broadcasters are obliged to air the programs. However, broadcasters remain legally responsible for the program as the broadcaster, and therefore have the right to ensure that party political broadcasts conform to legal guidelines. All party political broadcasts must also be clearly labeled as such, in order that the audience are fully aware that what they are watching is in fact a broadcast from a political party.

There are also laws applicable to the press on political advertising that aim to regulate the amount of funds individual candidates spend in the course of a campaign. Newspapers can publish advertisements for candidates only if they are authorized by the candidate or his or her agent. Those from supporters or well-wishers, whether praising the candidate or criticizing an opponent, for example, would be illegal. It is possible, however, for supporters to place general advertisements about broad policy issues that do not relate directly to any particular candidate. In the past, because of its close ties with the Trades Union movement, the Labour Party has benefited from this.

A change in the law in 1984 restricted that practice and the trades unions are only allowed to fund actions of this sort from the so-called "political levy." This is part of a member's union contributions that they have specifically agreed in advance can be used for political purposes. Apart from this last change, most of the detail of election law is concerned with individual contributions, as in the restrictions on advertising.

BALANCE AND IMPARTIALITY

Given the different approaches of consecutive governments to the two sectors, the press and broadcast media have very different rules and guidelines as to how they should cover the elections and this is no more so than in the area of impartiality and balance.

It is instructive that the PCC does not concern itself with questions of political balance or bias (Section 1:iv of the code specifically asserts the right of newspapers to be partisan) but with issues of privacy, harassment, intrusion, the reporting of children, payments for articles in criminal cases, and similar matters.

In the absence of either restriction or obligation with regard to political coverage, it might be asked what kind of a free market of ideas has the press provided? In June 2001, in what was perhaps the most striking feature of the whole campaign, Labour candidates were endorsed by 14 daily and Sunday national newspapers, representing 64% of total circulation (Deacon, Golding, & Billig, 2001, p. 109). This was an improvement on the 1997 election, which itself saw unprecedented press support for Labour. Previously, it had often been observed that the mass-circulation press in Britain as it developed from the mid-nineteenth century onward has been very much weighted ideologically to the right, the dependence of newspapers on revenue from advertising being argued as one of the main factors causing this imbalance (Curran, 1986). The demise of left-of-center papers such as the

Daily Herald in the 1960s meant that the Conservative Party, both in terms of the number of titles and circulation figures, has enjoyed a distinct advantage over Labour. Newspapers also tended to be unequivocal in support of their favored party. This remained up until 1992, though some commentators detect a lessening of partisanship from this point (Seymour Ure, 1997). Change was apparent by the time of the 1997 General Election, when Labour enjoyed the support of the majority of newspapers for the first time, as 6 out of 10 national dailies gave their support to the party.

Whether or not this heralds a permanent shift in support from Conservative to Labour, only time will tell. However, it has been argued that what this switch truly demonstrates is a move away from wholehearted support for any party. As of the 1992 election, when political party support was generally voiced without reservation, with only three titles showing any indecision, what has been called a "skeptics circle" of newspapers, has widened considerably. By 1997, seven papers were caught between fear (of Labour) and loathing (of the Conservatives). These shifts in loyalties may of course merely reflect a greater volatility among the electorate, but changing attitudes within the press cannot be ignored.

The Labour Party's list of supporters in the national titles in June 2001 was impressive—with the *Guardian,* the *Times,* the *Sun,* the *Star,* the *Daily Mirror,* the *Express,* the *Observer,* the *Financial Times,* the *News of the World,* the *Sunday People, Sunday Mirror, Sunday Express,* and *Sunday Times* all supporting the incumbent Prime Minister Tony Blair. Only the *Telegraph, Sunday Telegraph,* and the *Mail On Sunday* remained loyal to the Conservatives. The *Independent* did not endorse Labour but cautioned against voting Conservative, and the *Independent On Sunday* and the *Daily Mail* advocated tactical voting to prevent a Labour landslide.

However, as Table 7.2 indicates, many of the papers that supported Labour were far from uncritical and endorsements varied from the enthusiastic, in the case of the *Mirror, Sunday Mirror,* and the *Sunday People* for Labour, and the *Telegraph, Sunday Telegraph,* and *Mail On Sunday* for the Conservatives, to others, such as the *Times* and *Sunday Times,* that supported Labour but with some reservation, as the least worst option for the electorate.

From the table it can be seen that in 1 week of the campaign, the *Guardian,* for example, published more than three times as many articles that were critical of the party as were in favor of it. The *Telegraph,* in the same week, was almost even-handed in its opinion of the Conservatives, whom it backed. Both papers were highly critical of their political "opponents," but hardly gave their chosen party a ringing endorsement.

In the 2001 election, nine national newspapers, representing over 50% of total circulation, were either equivocal about their choice or did not make one at all. This represents not a realignment from Conservative to Labour as has been argued, but a "de-alignment" (Deacon et al., 2001, p. 111); news-

TABLE 7.2
Balance of Coverage—Number and Description
of Articles on the Two Main Parties

	Labour			Conservative		
Title	Favorable	Unfavorable	Neutral	Favorable	Unfavorable	Neutral
Sun	39	27	34	23	42	35
Mirror	53	9	38	5	76	19
Star	69	8	23	9	18	73
Mail	7	76	17	23	2	75
Express	50	40	10	39	45	16
Telegraph	11	38	51	22	17	61
Guardian	11	34	55	6	35	59
Times	12	20	68	7	27	67
Independent	19	30	51	21	38	48
Financial Times	36	34	30	44	30	28

Note. Table first appeared in McArthur, B., *The Times,* May 16, 2001, p. 14 and was based on an analysis of articles appearing in the previous week by independent researchers Echo Research.

papers now perhaps have abandoned their old partisanship and any support they now give is qualified and contingent, with the press maintaining "a skeptical distance from all parties."

The divide between broadsheet and tabloid papers in terms of news values and interests was clearly displayed in the extent and type of coverage of the election by the newspapers. Broadsheets maintained a more or less steady interest throughout, with a slight decrease in coverage during the middle of the campaign period. Tabloids rapidly tired of the campaign, with "red top" (*Sun, Daily Mirror,* and *Daily Star*) titles halving coverage by the last week. Overall, only one third of their lead front-page stories related to the campaign in contrast to 78% in the broadsheets.

This is in line with the observation that tabloids tend to remain more firmly wedded to normal news values at election times, reporting what is interesting to them, rather than following the campaign with what has been described as the almost religious devotion to duty displayed by the broadsheets (Deacon et al., 2001). This is endorsed by Peter Hill, editor of the tabloid *The Daily Star,* who claimed his newspaper's (attenuated) coverage was very successful: "We gave them [the readers] about as much election coverage as they really wanted. Whereas the other papers tended to do what they felt they ought to do, rather than what was realistic in this election, because it was just not an inspiring election" (Mills, 2001, p. 3). This is not to say that tabloids do not have an influence, at least according to themselves. Trevor Kavanagh, of the *Sun,* which has endorsed Labour for the last two elections, claimed recently that his paper was the first read each day in Downing Street, for the (entirely plausible) reason that, "Political parties need our readers. They include the floating millions who help to decide elections" (Kavanagh, 2002, p. 15). The Labour Party has indeed, to the consternation of many of its natural supporters, tended to focus its energies on this group of voters.

Both parties eclipsed the Liberal Democrats. Campaigns focused on the leaders, with a presidential aspect becoming more pronounced. The increasing management of election campaigns has led to complaints from journalists that press conferences, for example, are so tightly controlled by the parties that they are unable to ask supplementary questions, or that only favored journalists are invited to ask questions in the first place (Blackburn, 1995).

All broadcasters are required to be impartial in their coverage of the elections and adhere to the principles of due impartiality and balance. The guidelines stress that in order to achieve the aforementioned goals coverage should give appropriate weight to candidates of the main political parties—in the UK this consists of the candidates of the Conservative, Labour, and Liberal parties. Each of these parties is entitled to be invited to participate on a program that deals with their candidate's constituency. Full-length reports should also include a list of all candidates standing for election.

In the Foreword of the 1990 Broadcasting Act, it states that the ITC has a statutory duty to ensure that broadcasters that come within its regulatory scope comply with certain measures to ensure due impartiality in its programming. Due impartiality does not mean, however, that broadcasters are rigidly tied to across-the-board rules and it allows the rules to be applied in the context of a specific program's subject area. It does not mean that a broadcaster has to retain strict neutrality in terms of times allocated to opposing views, but requires broadcasters to provide for balance in viewpoints. At times when a program does not allow for balanced representation, a series of programs as a whole can be calculated as a measure of balance. However, it is not sufficient that other channels represent opposing views; it must be achieved within individual channels either within programs or through a series of programs.

The BBC's commitment to fairness at election time has traditionally not been governed by the RPA, but by the provisions of impartiality stated in the Royal Charter, which requires that certain conditions be met by the broadcaster that ensure that the BBC follows a similar set of guidelines as the other terrestrial broadcasters.

EQUAL ACCESS TO BROADCASTING

The allocation of airtime for political parties is drawn up collectively by the BBC, ITC, S4C, and RA, and the process is based on the right of political parties whose number of candidates standing at an election crosses a certain threshold to have access to the public to present its public policy and ideological issues.

Prior to 1998, the allocation of airtime to political parties for the purposes of party political broadcasts was determined by the parties' performance in the most recent past election and was decided upon by a combination of broadcasters and members of the main political parties, who combined to form the Committee on Party Political Broadcasting. Access for the two main parties, the government and opposition party, has been restricted at election times to five party political broadcasts for each party. Traditionally any party contesting a minimum of 50 seats in a general election has been allocated at least one slot for an election broadcast. Recent changes in the qualification for airtime for party political broadcasts have established a threshold that political parties must contest at least 110 seats to be granted access to a party political broadcast. Parties in Scotland and Wales must be contesting at least a sixth of seats to qualify for an election broadcast in their respective countries only, according to the regulatory bodies' guidelines.

In the 1997 election airtime was allocated to eight political parties under the 50-seat threshold rule and this included the Green Party, the Referendum Party, the Natural Law Party, the British National Party, and the Pro-Life Party, as well as the two main parties and the Liberal Party. In the 2001 General Election, a total of 11 parties in England, Scotland, and Wales qualified. The Socialist Labour Party and the Socialist Alliance qualified for airtime in all three nations, whereas the Green Party qualified for the threshold in England and Wales. Plaid Cymru, the Scottish Nationalist Party, the Scottish Socialist Party, and the Pro-Life Alliance were granted airtime only in Scotland or Wales. In Northern Ireland six parties produced party political broadcasts.

Before the amendments to the RPA the law stated that candidates could participate in an election campaign program about their constituency only if their rival candidates took part or agreed that the program could take place. This meant that if candidates either refused to allow a program that they participated in to be broadcast or refused to participate in a program, the broadcaster would have to abandon the entire discussion. Today this statutory requirement has been withdrawn and replaced with a comprehensive set of guidelines that, although similar to the original rules, allow more flexibility. Under the new rules it is no longer required that the consent and/or involvement of all candidates is mandatory before the transmission of a program that relates to a particular constituency is aired. Three criteria replace the old rules: The candidates of the three major parties should be invited to participate, there should be some participation of significant smaller parties, and the program should provide viewers with a full list of candidates standing for election in the constituency.

PUNITIVE MEASURES

The 1990 Broadcasting Act Section 110(2) sets the financial penalty for national license holders at 3% of the qualifying revenue for the last complete accounting period. However, the Act raises this ceiling to 5% for additional offenses. Section 110(3) sets the maximum penalty for local license holders at GB Pounds 50,000.

The PPC has certain restricted measures that it can employ if violations to the code of conduct are judged to have occurred. Offending papers are obliged to carry "in full and with due prominence," in the words of the Code of Practice, any criticism that the Commission may have of them. Alternatively, they may be asked to correct any inaccurate information they have published, or to publish an apology. Recent criticism, even from within sections of the press itself, is that the PCC acts more as a conciliator than a regulator and that, starting from a very low absolute number of complaints, only one in a hundred results in a critical adjudication (Rusbridger, 2002).

CONTROVERSIES AND RECENT DEBATE ABOUT REFORM

In the 1997 election, a number of challenges to the allocation of airtime were submitted to judicial review. The Referendum Party objected to its allocation of 5 minutes airtime whereas the Pro-Life Alliance broadcast was heavily edited on taste and decency grounds by the broadcasters, and both Sinn Fein and the British Nationalist Party objected to cuts made by the broadcasters on grounds of legal uncertainty.

The guidelines for party political broadcasts also include compliance measures in terms of libel, obscenity, and incitement to racial hatred, together with privacy, taste, and decency. This has led to a number of challenges to the right of broadcasters to censor material to be aired. The Pro-Life party has sought judicial review on a number of occasions against the decisions of the broadcasters to refuse to transmit the content of their election broadcasts, which were adjudged to breach standards. In the 1997 election, the Pro-Life Alliance submitted a case against the BBC when the BBC together with all of the other broadcasters refused to air one of their party political broadcasts on taste and decency grounds. The case was finally resolved by the Court of Appeal and the European Court of Human Rights, who failed to support Pro-Life's complaint against the broadcasters—with a decision that stated the Pro-Life Alliance had no case to argue on human rights grounds. Summarizing the opinions of the Court, the judge found that broadcasters had a right to balance an important duty with an important right and it was therefore justifiably within their terms of reference not to air material that could be deemed offensive or potentially distasteful to the public, under the obligations imposed on the broadcasters under Paragraph 5 of the BBC's agreement with the Home Secretary and in the case of the commercial broadcasters Section 6(1) of the 1990 Broadcasting Act.

A similar case arose in the run-up to polling day during the 2001 election when the Pro-Life Alliance party sought judicial review in order to overturn a BBC decision not to broadcast a party political broadcast consisting of images of aborted fetuses. The BBC, supported by other broadcasters, ruled against airing the program based on taste and decency grounds and the offense the images would cause to the viewing public.

However, and in an important challenge to the previous judgments, the Court of Appeal judged in favor of the Pro-Life Alliance party and against the BBC (*Regina v. BBC,* 2002). The Court of Appeal concluded that the ban was unlawful and the broadcasters had infringed on the right of a registered political party to exploit their right to access their agreed amount of airtime. The case raises a fundamental and potentially far-reaching issue of how to address the balance between the role of the broadcasters to ensure that taste and decency are maintained and the right of political parties to have access to the medium.

VOTER APATHY

Directly after the June 2001 election that witnessed another Labour landslide against an increasingly divided Conservative opposition party, a debate over party political broadcasts was ignited by the Labour Party. The concern over low voter turnout at the elections has raised concern about the level of public engagement with politics in general and more specifically with the media coverage of election campaigns. One such critic, a former advertising adviser to the Labour Party, has claimed that party political broadcasts are an anachronism and should therefore be replaced with spot advertisements.

The general election of 2001 was characterized by the lowest voter turnout recorded in the UK, with an overall turnout of 59.4% of the eligible voting population voting. According to a report by the ITC, this was reflected in how television audiences perceived media coverage of the event. The television audience for election night coverage fell by well over half, down from nearly 19 million viewers in 1992 to 7.6 million in 2001. The report continues to suggest that 52% of viewers had hardly seen any coverage of the election and those that had were largely male and over 65 (ITC, 2001). The nature of the coverage in the mass media generally demonstrates an interesting fascination with the election coverage itself, rather than details of party policies and manifestos. Golding and Deacon (2001), monitoring the

2001 elections, recorded that 62% of election items in the schedule dealt with the actual processes of election. This was reduced by half toward the end of the elections, but at the same time it was pointed out that only 43.7% of appearances of the political party leaders was invested in describing and explaining their parties' policies, whereas a large part of the coverage consisted of party leaders criticizing the policies of the other parties.

Apathy toward the political process is a trend seen across Western democracies, but the case of the UK, with turnout down from a postwar high of 83.9% in 1950 and averaging nearly 76% from 1955 to 1992, is particularly severe (Electoral Reform Society, 2001). Among 18- to 24-year-olds, it has been estimated that it was as low as 39%. In an election, as in 2001, where the result was from start to finish seen as a foregone conclusion, it may well be difficult to engage the voting public, but could the nature of the campaign itself or the way it was reported have been factors?

The ITC report showed that there was wide support for party political broadcasts despite what is seen as widespread voter apathy. Though 63% of the poll suggested that they considered the broadcasts to be important and 67% that they helped raise political awareness of the parties' manifestos, the actual number of viewers tuning in to the coverage was extremely low.

U.S.-style political advertising has recently been considered by the Electoral Commission as a way to modernize how elections are covered by broadcasters. The idea that a more dynamic type of system should be introduced to spice up election campaigns has come under fire from a number of quarters as an attempt to further decrease the quality of the nature of coverage of politics in the UK and simplify an important part of the political tradition. The consultation process following a report on party political broadcasts under the initiative of the Electoral Commission about the future of party political advertising demonstrates that there is continued support for the traditional ban on paid-for political advertising and the continuation of the tradition of party political advertising, which may be extended to other channels beyond the main terrestrial broadcasters, where channels enjoying a significant audience share will be required to broadcast party political broadcasts.

NEW MEDIA

The role of new media and the Internet in elections has as yet had very little impact at election times, despite the government's information technology policy looking into issues such as online democracy. *Guardian Online* editor Emily Bell claimed that the election on the Internet was, however, "an unrivalled hit," with traffic on the newspaper's politics Web site quadrupling during May 2001. More disinterested observers were not so enthusiastic, noting that although, as in 1997, this election was widely proclaimed to be the first Internet election, it was in Internet terms "a disappointment," being mainly used as another form of political marketing, or as in Emily Bell's case just mentioned, a new outlet for an existing media organization. A few attempts were made to creatively use the Internet by, for example, setting up Web sites to encourage more tactical voting, but there was little evidence of any use of interactivity to create "a new, more participatory style of politics" as an antidote to voter disinterest. However, we may come to regard the entry of the Internet into the electoral process in 2001 in the same way we do that of television in 1959, where a new medium was being tried out, with neither the broadcasters nor the politicians quite sure what to do with it. By the next election in 1964, they were already working it out (Coleman, 2001).

OPINION AND EXIT POLLS

Opinion polls play a significant part in elections, especially in the UK, where they appear with greater frequency and prominence than in any other Western democracy, for instance, in the 1992 campaign at a rate of two new polls for each day of the campaign. Opinion polls are intrinsically newsworthy and popular with readers and journalists alike. During the 1992 campaign, polls were seen by newspapers as the most significant news to be reported. When commissioned by newspapers themselves, they provide a ready-made "exclusive"; otherwise newspapers republish polls already in the public domain. Ivor Crew has commented that the reporting of polls allows static campaigns to be described as being full of "flux, change and excitement" (cited in Blackburn, 1995). However, the consistent inaccuracy of the polls in 1992, and again in 1997, has cooled their ardor somewhat, and the number of front-page news stories based on opinion polls diminished from 12% of the total in 1997 to 2.5% in 2001 (Golding & Deacon, 2001). Interestingly, opinion polls are not regarded as accurate in Northern Ireland, as people are wary of making public their true political beliefs.

Despite their recent fall from grace, so great has been the concentration on the publication of and comment on opinion polls, that it is regularly argued that they not only predict but in fact influence the results of elections and therefore should be prohibited. As with other proposals for restraint, this has not succeeded, opinion being that the damage thus done to freedom of speech would be greater than any occasioned by the polls themselves (Blackburn, 1995). The only legal restrictions on polling come into force once voting has actually begun on election day itself. A change in the Representation of the People Act 2000 meant that exit polls or any information based on information from voters may not be reported until after the polls have closed. This is to avoid polls predicting the wrong result and possibly affecting the outcome of an election. Broadcasters, publishers of evening newspapers, and operators of Internet news sites were warned of the dangers prior to election day in June 2001.

CONCLUSION

The rules that apply to mass-media coverage of elections in the UK diverge considerably in the press and broadcasting sectors, to an extent that there is a clear difference in how the media cover election campaigns. The strict obligations imposed on broadcasters to ensure due impartiality, equal access for qualifying party candidates, and objectivity are balanced with a highly partisan and politicized press sector, though it should be pointed out that the intensely political nature of the press is not necessarily a reflection of the depth or quality of the election issues as they are portrayed in certain sections of the newspaper industry.

Overall, the British media collectively cover the elections to a reasonable level and certain regulatory codes and principles ensure that broadcasters perform their public-interest function at election times. However, it is by no means perfect. Large sections of the popular press fail to cover the election campaigns in any depth that could be understood as rational and considered, and much of it does not inform the reader about the complexity of the political issues the voters will vote for in the final analysis.

Voter apathy is a growing concern, although it is not possible to determine with any degree of certainty to what extent the way the elections, and politics generally, are reported has contributed to this. Over the years there has been an increasing professionalism in the approach of political parties not only to the business of election campaigns but to political communication generally. Campaigns are more and more shaped by staged events, theme-based press conferences, meaningless photo opportunities, and the like, as the parties have sought to wrest control of the reporting of politics away from the journalists and toward themselves. As Ivor Gaber (2001) observed, "in a political discourse in which presentation substitutes for policy, and tomorrow's headlines are more important than next year's policies, problems will follow" (p. 18).

If politicians experienced difficulty in engaging the electorate in the election in 2001, most of the press found sales declining through the campaign with only a minority such as the *Guardian* and the *Financial Times* seeing slight increases. Broadcasters found it similarly difficult to hold audiences, and this could create problems as the UK audiovisual market becomes more competitive. Given the expansion of television channels, coupled with a relaxation of public service obligations on commercial channels, broadcasters may feel that political coverage is an unnecessary expense. An option might be to make the whole campaign more attractive to viewers, but this might be at the expense of the quality of the political process. That said, the regulatory framework for broadcasting works well but the extent to which the press, especially the tabloids, provides adequate coverage, holding as they do a large part of the newspaper market, is debatable and needs to be seriously judged against the normative requirements of democratic government. Given the traditional reluctance of politicians, of whichever party, to intervene in matters of newspaper content, it seems unlikely that any change will come from parliament and it will be left to newspaper editors and proprietors to decide whether or not satisfactory political coverage meets with their essentially commercial interests.

REFERENCES

BBC. (2002). *Producer Guidelines.* London: Author.

Blackburn, R. (1995). *The electoral system in Britain.* London: Macmillan.

Coleman, S. (2001). Online campaigning. In P. Norris (Ed.), *Britain votes 2001* (pp. 115–124). Oxford, England: Oxford University Press.

Crone, T. (1995). *Law and the media.* Oxford, England: Focal Press.

Curran, J. (1986). The impact of advertising on the British mass media. In R. Collins et al. (Eds.), *Media, culture and society: A critical reader* (pp. 309–335). London: Sage.

Deacon, D., Golding, P., & Billig, M. (2001). Press and broadcasting: Real issues and real coverage. In P. Norris (Ed.), *Britain votes 2001* (pp. 102–114). Oxford, England: Oxford University Press.

Electoral Commission. (2001). *Election 2001 review programme—Party political broadcasting review discussion paper 2001.* London: Author.

Electoral Reform Society. (2001). *Election 2001: Unfair and unrepresentative General Election report for the Electoral Reform Society.* London: Author.

Gaber, I. (2001, November 30). Political circus fails to attract the big crowds. *Times Higher Education Supplement,* p. 18.

Golding, P., & Deacon, D. (2001, June 4). Broadsheets soldier on as tabloids wilt. *Guardian Election 2001,* p. 18.

Independent Television Commission. (2001). *The ITC Programme Code and Guidelines.* London: Author.

Kavanagh, T. (2002, March 21). The sun also rises. *Prospect,* p. 15.

McArthur, B. (2001, May 16). Mirror cheerleaders hit their stride. *Times,* p. 14.

Mills, M. (2001). Media: Keep taking the bananas. *Guardian Media,* pp. 2–3.

Regina v. BBC. (2002, March 14). BBC accused of censorship over political broadcast. By Jessica Hodgson, *Guardian.* Accessed on 8/4/2003 http://media.guardian.co.uk/broadcast/story/0, 7493,667217,00.html

Robinson, G., & Nicol, A. (1992). *Media law.* London: Penguin.

Rusbridger, A. (2002, February 18). Taming the beast. *Guardian,* pp. 2–3.

Seymour Ure, C. (1997). Newspapers: Editorial opinion in the national press. In P. Norris & N. T. Gavin (Eds.), *Britain votes 1997* (pp. 78–100). Oxford, England: Oxford University Press.

8

Notes From an Election Observer

Karin Junker

The collapse of the two blocs of the Cold War period signified a new direction for all foreign-affairs relations between the East and West, and the North and South. It also deprived the nonaligned states of their role in the context of global geopolitics and the political landscape in the world's developing regions changed significantly.

One-party systems mutated around the globe, sometimes at breathtaking speeds, to real or apparent multiparty systems of governance. Developmental cooperation was no longer based on the primary intention of making the recipients favorably disposed to the donors of the respective system. Ambitious expectations were addressed to the governors of the transitional countries, which included huge reform of their systems with a whole range of human rights and political freedoms underpinning reform. This included democratic elections and accountable government, respect for the rule of law, protection of minorities, gender equality, press and media freedom, independent judiciary, the protection of human rights, and so forth.

With the benefit of hindsight, all of these objectives amounted to excessive demands on the countries concerned, and excluded the self-interests of all participants as well as the continuation of one-sided dependencies. Consistent with the theme of this book I would like to focus on the issue of elections as one part of the package of reform in transitional countries, and outline some issues from a practical vantage point, based on my experiences gained monitoring elections in a number of transitional and developing countries.

THE EUROPEAN UNION AND ELECTION MONITORING

In this turning point of world politics, characterized by democratic aspira-tions, the European Parliament took the decision to participate in the respective "first democratic elections," in the countries in transition. Par-ticipation took the form of courtesy visits and should have served to strengthen democratic movements. The real acid test, however, did not come with the first democratic elections, but later with the outbreak of power struggles and conflicts of interest that revealed significant defi-cits, which frequently resulted in election chaos. Above all else, at this moment in time it was a matter of providing political and logistic support, checking the correctness of procedures, providing protection through having an international presence, making a picture, *in situ*, of the political balance of powers, and being informed of the progress of developmental political cooperation.

With reference to the European Parliament's aforementioned decision, for a long period all invitations and applications related to election observa-tion were dismissed until finally pragmatism triumphed and participation was allowed here and there. However, this was unsatisfactory because a co-herent concept was missing and political decisions were not based on fixed criteria, resulting in different or contradictory approaches.

For some time now this has been remedied piece by piece. In 2000 the European Commission presented a Communication (European Commis-sion, 2000), in which previous experiences were built upon. In this context, it should be pointed out that the European Commission as a bureaucracy can and should carry out long-term tasks for the preparation and execution of elections (with the support of the European Union's local delegation of-fices), whereas members of the European Parliament (MEPs) can be ap-pointed only for a short period of time around the election days.

As a result, and in many cases, although not covered by the rules, an MEP is nominated to "chief observer" status, which makes sense, according to some relevant committees, because the meaning of an election, as a process of democratic participation of the citizens of a country or a region, can and should be best monitored by establishing a leading role for elected political representatives.

As stated before, the experiences gained through election observation had previously not been compiled systematically and it became clear that an ad hoc approach no longer seemed appropriate to make the best use of re-sources. Therefore, the European Parliament requested the European Com-mission to assess EU participation in election observation missions in the preceding years in order to contribute to a definition of a coherent European policy line through a consistent approach involving a strategy and methodology, taking into account lessons learned from previous experiences.

THE EUROPEAN COMMISSION'S PROPOSALS

The European Commission's 2000 Communication started with trying to define what *election assistance* means. According to the Communication, election assistance may be understood as the technical or material support given to the electoral process. It may imply professional help to establish a legal framework for the elections. Moreover, election observation is the political complement to election assistance. Consequently, the European Commission defined election assistance as the "purposeful gathering of information regarding an electoral process, and the making of informed judgements on the conduct of such a process on the basis of the information collected, by persons who are inherently authorised to intervene in the process" (International IDEA, 1997; cited in European Commission, 2000, p. 4).

The Communication stated clearly what most of us in the European Parliament thought or experienced ourselves. Although the European Union (EU) had gained significant experience in election observation and assistance in the preceding decade, approaches had been diverse and the wheel had sometimes been reinvented. Some progress had been made on the criteria to decide on EU electoral observation missions and a code of conduct for observers and criteria for recruiting them. But there was still the need for a coherent strategy for handling election observation and assistance.

With regard to the legal framework, the Communication proposed future EU election assistance and observation to be undertaken exclusively under the first of the three pillars of the EU, that is, under the rules of the European Community (mainly under regulations governing relations with third countries, but also using new human rights regulations). In relation to the institutions, the European Commission promised to study the opportunity of establishing an Elections Desk with horizontal coordination and planning tasks, including ex-ante evaluation, to assist geographical desks and delegations and cooperation with EU institutions and other bodies. In addition, the Communication stated that appropriate arrangements on electoral observation missions should be agreed upon among by the Council of the European Union, the European Parliament, and the European Commission. The European Commission concluded that the EU should adopt a strategy that allows for case-by-case decisions to support and observe elections, promotes national capacity and sustainability, and promotes pluralism and support for local nongovernmental organizations (NGOs) and local observers (in order to improve the quality and effectiveness of the EU's involvement in promoting free and fair elections and a transition to sustainable democracy by building on the varied experience of EU involvement so far, and the expertise of other agencies).

THE COUNCIL OF THE EUROPEAN UNION'S REACTION

Approximately a year following the European Commission's Communication, the Council of the European Union set out its objectives on the subject of election support and observation and outlined some general principles on election support. In particular, the Council underlined the importance of an early dialogue with the national authorities, and the fact that consistency must be measured between election support, the Country Strategy for each partner country, and the objectives of the Common Security and Defence Policy. According to the Council, election support may contribute to increase the confidence of the electorate in the election process, reduce the possibility of fraud, and present the opportunity to make recommendations for improving election systems in a spirit of partnership. Support may also contribute to conflict prevention. Effective EU support requires a coherent approach through mutually reinforcing use of both European Commission and Common Foreign and Security Policy instruments. Furthermore, the Council stated that the effectiveness of electoral assistance programs and observation missions could be considerably increased if they are backed up by clear messages expressed through the EU's political dialogue with the relevant government.

The Council also found it constructive to differentiate between electoral assistance and election observation. The need for coordination and time limits varies considerably. The EU needed to develop different, but complementary approaches. The Council suggested that loose coordination between the European Commission, the Council of the European Union, the European Parliament and Member States in the preelection assessment and analysis of the political context important. In addition, the ministers promised to seek to establish jointly with the Commission a list of elections in which EU intervention was considered a priority. The list should then be discussed with the European Parliament. These priorities should be kept under regular review throughout the year to ensure that political developments are taken into account.

On the issue of election assistance, the Council stressed that specific actions should include institutional capacity building with regard to organizing future elections including assistance in support of regulatory framework agreements for political parties and election finance, training and education of local staff, awareness campaigns for the rights of individuals to vote, setting up of election sites, support to domestic civil society organizations active in the election field, and support for the media.

In terms of election observation, the European Commission was encouraged to provide training for observers and follow up on creating adequate instruments to allow a timely response to provide accelerated decision making and recruitment in urgent situations. The practice of appointing an experienced member of the European Parliament as the chief observer of an EU election mission was encouraged. On assessment by missions, the Council of European Union called for an independent assessment that should be delivered to Council itself, the European Commission, and the European Parliament. Under no circumstances should preliminary results be delivered beforehand. The European Commission should further develop policy in this area, and particularly, impact indicators. The Commission was instructed to undertake an overall evaluation of EU election support within 3 years.

The European Parliament stated in the Fava report (Fava, 2001) that election observation and election assistance are key elements of the EU's global strategy for the respect of human rights, the strengthening of democracy and the rule of law, and the promotion of development in its relations with third countries. The election period is supposed to be a democratic expression of political pluralism and must be organized in accordance with internationally recognized standards. Although the number of elections worldwide has been increasing over the last decade and 60% of the world's countries have held elections within this period, the fact remains that many governments describe themselves as democratic, despite the fact that this flies in the face of social realities, whereas in many countries democracy remains novel and fragile.

The European Parliament suggested the establishment of a European Parliament "Election Coordination Group" composed of representatives of the Committee on Foreign Affairs, Human Rights, Common Security and Defence Policy, the Committee on Development and Cooperation, the European Parliament members of the ACP-EU Joint Assembly, and representatives of the Interparliamentary Delegations. The first meeting was held on March 11, 2002. The Group should cover all phases of observation including the preparations for the elections in the country, the election campaign, the counting of votes, and the official declaration of the results. Because members of the European Parliament will usually be present for only a limited period, their role should be different from other short-term observers because, as elected parliamentarians, they provide a particular political perspective, expertise, and experience.

THE ELECTION OBSERVATION MISSIONS

Parliamentary Elections in Cambodia

The parliamentary elections on July 26, 1998, and the resulting election observation mission probably was the most expensive and most elaborate of its kind, due to Cambodia's history, which, because of constraints on space, I cannot explain here in any detail. Even so the EU undertook a massive mission; but because specific rules were missing for the European Parliament, it had to sit at the children's table.

Unfortunately, the participation of delegates of the European Parliament in election observation at this point in time has not been awarded adequate importance by Parliament's Bureau. Ten places were offered by the European Commission, but the European Parliament limited participation to three, of which, finally, due to the incredibly short time notice of the decision, there remained only one observer, thus resulting in a narrow experience basis.

For the designing and planning of the operation, the Commission appointed a consulting company that, from a parliamentarian perspective, were extremely inflexible, which may work for service travelers, who are delegated by, for example, authorities, but not for Parliament delegates. This inflexibility could possibly be the main reason for the fact that, apart from Glennys Kinnock as special envoy of the European Commission, I traveled late to Cambodia as the only delegate representing the European Parliament.

Preparation for the Operation. Here, one has to deplore shortcomings, which could have been avoided. Many participants in the observation of the elections had only a very vague idea of the situation, culture, and society of the guest country and knew absolutely nothing of the conditions that they would meet during the operation. I make the following proposals for standard preparation as a response to the very lack thereof in the Cambodian operation:

1. Draw up a dossier with the most important data not only on population, living standards, the economic and political situation, culture, religion, and the like, but also on health care, hygiene conditions, and climatic conditions, differentiated according to regions if necessary and connected with practical references as to the following:

   • How much water one must drink.
   • What should not be eaten due to medical reasons.
   • Whether it is a malaria district and whether a mosquito net is needed.

- Where to find access to communications.
- That a torch can be useful.
- What basic necessities are unavailable or difficult to purchase.

2. Beyond that, special references for the respective operational area should be provided regarding:

- Geographical conditions.
- Characteristics and deviations from the usual (e.g., ethnic minorities, political characteristics, geographical specificities, etc.).
- Standard of accommodation and the environment that should be expected (e.g., distances to the next biggest city with supplies, missing electricity supply and/or lack of flowing water, modest sanitary installations).

Some participants were not prepared for conditions such as those just listed and lacked basic necessities like towels or toilet paper. Furthermore, they did not count on the fact that they had to eat at market stands, which were not particularly inviting, due to the lack of simple restaurants, and that there would be neither cold beverages nor bread or coffee. With some luck, however, one thing or the other could be purchased in the town markets.

The Cambodian Team Members. The quality of the support staff such as drivers and interpreters was varied, as the reports of the different teams demonstrated. The language skills of the interpreters were often limited, which can be attributed to the fact that there were not enough qualified language teachers and almost no native speakers in the team. An introductory course for the interpreters, in particular on terms related to the topic and instruction on the election procedures, would have been invaluable. Only some acquired the necessary knowledge on their own initiative. The low interest may also result from the fact that drivers and interpreters were excluded from the election turnout, because on the election day they were not at the place of their registration as set down by law. The EU should have provided for an adequate solution.

The Operation in the Province. With my team partner, a young French scientist, I was appointed to the southern province of Takeo, close to the Vietnamese border, and we were assigned the observation of the elections and counting in three villages. After the introductory lectures in the capital Phnom Penh, we along with eight other teams first headed to the province's capital, also named Takeo, to cover the different districts of the province Takeo.

We received no information about the city or the province nor any useful map material. I found a brief description of the region in my personal travel guide, which was in any case better than nothing. By chance during dinner we met the British project manager of the EU-funded project Prasac, who privately made available to us modest maps of the province with its districts, so that we could plan our route and at least imagine the conditions of the province. The day we arrived in Takeo, with only a modest food supply, there were not enough rooms and no breakfast. Moreover, only at this point in the mission did the teams learn where they would definitely end up. It is not clear why instructions about the operational area and the particular conditions could not have been given in Phnom Penh, where one would have still had the opportunity to make additional preparations and arrange the necessary provisions. In Takeo it was too late and once in the villages even more so. The two courtesy visits with the officials of Takeo could also have been scheduled for during the journey through the region without any problems.

Whereas the briefing days in Phnom Penh covered an exhausting 10-hour program, with some of the lecture content being partially irrelevant and difficult for many participants to follow if only because of jetlag, we now had enough time. We stayed in the city of Takeo on Thursday, then continued the journey to our assigned districts on Friday. Once there, there was little we could do before the actual election day. We visited the local counting centers, which were typically schools or pagodas, so that we would not have to locate them on election day. There we were able to ensure that all necessary materials had been duly and completely received and were only awaiting further distribution to the polling stations, which was done mostly by horse carts and ox trucks. There were no cars, at best a few mopeds. On election day we visited 14 polling stations of the almost 30 located in the three municipalities, which were in close proximity to one another, thus keeping the loss of driving time to a minimum (the conditions were difficult logistically and we had to navigate muddy roads full of potholes and water holes filled with the monsoon rains, herds of cattle, and numerous other obstacles).

The Election Day. On the election Sunday at 6:40 A.M., we arrived at the polling station in the school in Romenh, where groups of people wanting to vote had already arrived. We followed the opening instructions of the election committee and the first voters were allowed into the polling station at 7:00 A.M. sharp. People were jostling while waiting in front of the doors, full of impatience to come to the ballot boxes. The atmosphere remained good to cheerful, despite the crowded conditions. Crowds of curious people also observed the voting procedure through the open windows.

As is a common European approach, a system had been designed to provide the people waiting with a number and then call them according to numerical order. After a short period, this system broke down, because it was completely alien to the voters. However, it did not result in chaos; the election committees remained resolute and consistently allowed only two voters into the area (there were in each instance two polling booths). In one case a member of the election committee blocked the entrance with her leg, putting it on a stairway handrail as a barrier to ensure that the two-voter rule was observed.

Whole families gathered before the polling stations and women supplied the crowd with beverages. As far as I was able to observe, the security forces held back discreetly and did not interfere with the process. Whether there was any intimidation of voters before the election day was, for obvious reasons, unascertainable to us. On the election day itself, I did not sense anything of the kind in my field of observation.

On the contrary, it was remarkable that many young women took part in the election consciously without needing any assistance. Help was, however, necessary for some elderly people, who experienced difficulties with the procedure. These people, as well as invalids, were assisted by the chairman of the election committee. We could not observe any clear violation of the secrecy of the ballot. Whether in individual cases verbal indications as where the cross was to be made could have been given, was incomprehensible to us, if only because of language reasons. However, in my opinion, no serious infringements of the rules took place.

In all of the polling stations, observers from independent election observation commissions were represented. In addition there were also many party representatives. The neutrality requirement was in no case violated. Whereas the party representatives were almost exclusively men, there was a relatively strong participation of women in the election committees. Young women were also the majority among the national election observers.

In accord with regulations, posters were hung that explained in front of the polling stations, the election procedure in a comprehensible way to voters. Also posters delineating the 39 competing parties were hung, although not all parties were candidates in all provinces. This was also true for Takeo. On the ballot papers only the respective local candidate parties were listed, therefore no errors could result in this regard. Election references could also be found in other places in the villages, for example, the market in Romenh. I did not notice any party's activities or emblems in proximity to polling stations, which would infringe on the rules, except for a CPP T-shirt that a cyclist, who was watching some ballplayers, was wearing.

We were received everywhere we visited in a friendly and respectful manner. The local organizers made paths for us through the waiting voters, carried chairs, and provided us with any information that we requested. This was not just politeness; we were really welcomed. In one polling station as well as at a counting center, I was allowed to take plenty of photographs, so there is also impressive documentation of the mission.

Nobody at the polling stations could prepare themselves for our visits, because we visited stations without notice and at unpredictable hours to maintain an element of surprise. In some cases we visited the same polling stations several times without forewarning. By 10:00 A.M. and at the latest 11:00 A.M. the worst of the crowds had passed through and the participation at that time was already over 90%. In some cases only four or five voters were missing. Under these circumstances, who can blame the Election Committees, observers, and party representatives for leaving the muggy polling stations with a temperature of 39°C in the shade instead of just killing time, waiting bored in front of the entrances to the stations? We also longed for closing time. There was simply nothing happening anymore. However, the opening times were strictly adhered to and the stations finally closed at the planned 4:00 P.M.

We were a bit surprised that the polling stations contained far more ballot papers than the number of registered voters. Actually, for each polling station only one to four substitute ballot papers were needed, which was noted as per regulations. Here, in fact, was the possibility for falsification by adding more ballot papers; however, this was largely irrelevant due to the high election turnout. The fact that the ballot papers were numbered made complete control possible. People from the parties and national observers counted meticulously so that any suspicious incidents could be detected. However, this fact should be taken into account for future election support. A smaller election turnout could have created problems for the whole election process.

The training courses for the election committees should cover not only the correct process of the election procedure, but also, in more depth, the evaluation of the validity ballot papers. It was not only the uncertainty about the expressed will of the voters that led to nullifications. Ballot papers could be declared invalid partly just because they were folded in a different way than was established, even though they contained an unmistakable mark for a certain party. Because all ballot papers went through several hands before they were assigned to a party and finally declared valid or invalid, and all this happened under observation of the inspectors, manipulation at this stage was highly unlikely.

The fact that the expensive ballot boxes donated by Japan were supposed to be folded in a complicated way in order to be transported to the counting centers was not understood and, after checking the appropriate guidelines, was not even put into practice, as it was too troublesome. The lesson to be drawn from this is that the material must be solid and resistant but not too costly. Otherwise, the handling of the materials did not result in any special difficulties. Before counting, the ballot papers from several boxes were mixed, so that any allocation to polling stations was rendered impossible.

The Counting. Work in the counting centers was done according to the regulations as well. Every movement was observed by national observers and party representatives, and every vote and every incident was noted. When requested, everybody confirmed the correctness of the election and, based on this fact, there were no complaints whatsoever. The participants countersigned the protocols, even though they were not obliged to do so. At least for the most promising parties, observers were present and monitored one another, securing plurality in the polling stations and counting centers. Irregularities would have certainly attracted attention and protests.

We visited all three assigned counting centers in our allocated region. In two of them we observed the opening of the ballot boxes and the preparations for counting. The procedure was carried out according to the rules. In two counting centers, likewise, we witnessed the closing of counting. We observed the final counting with the respective final result, the proper closure of the ballot papers and protocols for further transport, and no complaints were made.

The Postproceeding Period. When returning to Phnom Penh we had the chance to exchange opinions and views with the other teams. Mirroring our own experience, most of them did not have any complaints. Some of them reported some small arguments, which, however, were not considered as relevant. All in all 96% of EU observers and 93% of the other international observers allocated marks between "very good" and "good," the rest rated the election process from "satisfactory" to "adequate." No one gave the process the worst mark.

The Reactions. Even before any results were published, the later winner of the elections, CPP-Hun Sen, announced his victory with an unrealistically high number of seats in parliament and just that quickly charges of cheating were leveled by the competing parties FUNCINPEC and Sam Rainsy. Taking the 3 million CPP members, compared to only 4.7 million registered eligible voters, into account, the Hun-Sen Party was clearly to become the strongest parliamentary party, but without achieving an overwhelming result. The royalist party FUNCINPEC, which was one step ahead in Phnom Penh and some other provinces, acquired (together with its separation party Sam Rainsy) more votes than CPP did almost everywhere. In addition, CPP benefited indirectly from a relatively high number of votes for "other" parties that did not result in parliamentary seats.

In conclusion, the Cambodians voted pluralistically. Finally, FUNCINPEC lost its ability to win a majority through the split of votes for itself and the Sam Rainsy party. The determination of seats was fiercely controversial. Three different systems of calculation were in use, with one being apparently unfavorable to the underdogs. But, according to FUNCINPEC and Sam Rainsy, this system was applied, inappropriately. I was not able to learn a satisfactory conclusion to this matter of dispute.

Assessment of the Elections. The eligible voters demonstrated a democratic maturity and were not affected by pressure applied from one direction or another. The voters were able to witness an election that was conducted peacefully and was widely free and fair, at least on election day. As important, voters had access to a system that supported their right to secrecy and confidentiality in the voting process. Although there was some pushing and a degree of light discussion in front of the polling stations, voting was conducted inside the polling booth and in privacy.

In order to run a constructive policy in government and opposition, it would have been desirable to witness the parties emulate the voters in terms of their democratic maturity. The people in Cambodia were noticeably tired of violence, war, and political and economic instability. They wanted peace and development. It would have been a great moment to see the politicians not mutually blockading or accusing one another, but fulfilling their mandate to govern the country in the public interest.

In my opinion, the Cambodian election of July 26, 1998 was a prime example of democracy. The participation of thousands of national election observers supported the mobilization of civil society as an important support for democratic development. The successful training of thousands of Election Committees, which worked effectively, should also have an important and positive effect for the future of democracy in the country. Evidence of considerable falsification of the elections results was absent, though intimidation of voters before the election might have been possible. It remains unclear whether these acts led to a distortion of the polling or the elections.

As much as the eligible voters welcomed us, there were some groups that questioned the role of the observers. The international observers were declared incompetent by Sam Rainsy, for instance, long before the results of counting were available. National observers were even attacked by him later on. This particular political class needs to learn how to gain at least the same political maturity as the voters showed and therefore fulfill their responsibilities as political representatives.

The world press followed the election with great attention, resulting in heightened pressure on the political classes, and therefore their input should be considered positively. The low number of about 500 foreign observers for about 7,000 polling stations was frequently criticized by the European-based media. They reported that the number of observers was too low to monitor the elections throughout the region. However, the number is considered quite sufficient to form an evaluation of the process, particularly because they were not the only teams active on the ground. In this respect, little or no attention at all has been paid to thousands of national observers, although they ensured an areawide overview. With international support they gained extensive training and preparation for the election day. Supporters were, among others, European-based NGOs whose task is to promote democratic development, as, for example, the German Friedrich-Ebert-Stiftung. In the final analysis there was no serious evidence that the election rules were undermined by the actors involved, and the election result was accepted whether the results were pleasing or not.

Parliamentary Elections in Zimbabwe

At the beginning there was chaos—accreditations for the parliamentary elections on June 24–25, 2000, were rejected, made more difficult, or certified according to hardly transparent criteria, and were changed shortly before the elections.

Nominations of NGOs like the German political Friedrich-Ebert-Stiftung and the *Weltkirchenrat* (World Council of Churches) were rejected, though the latter was later accepted. On the other hand, everyone, regardless of status, could travel freely and look up contacts or visit events, as far as logistically possible. Observers from the European Parliament were not recognized as members of the EU delegation but instead as assisting the embassies of the member states, which made possible their accreditation as national observers with the appropriate formalities.

The six MEPs plus two staff members were well equipped with four cars plus drivers. The internal organization worked well. The preparatory venues were visited, partly decentralized, partly together, for example, a visit to a German tobacco farmer whose farm was occupied and who received wide coverage by the media in Europe, because he stood firmly on the side of the reformers.

The Electoral Campaigns. Remarkably there was almost no publicity of the government party ZANU (PF) in the whole country. On the other hand, there was considerable publicity for the oppositional party MDC (Movement for Democratic CHANGE) in the form of leaflets on thorn bushes or paintings on the back of traffic signs. The MDC published full-page election announcements in daily papers before the election days.

According to the observers, election meetings/events of the ZANU (PF) were rather sparsely visited, although substantial pressure was exerted. On the contrary, the MDC, on the other hand, had good support although dates and the locations of events (in both cases) were difficult to agree upon. It was probably a new experience in the country that candidates not only introduced themselves in public and in black and white but also fought together for change. The ZANU (PF) canceled at short notice the planned talk/meeting with the MEPs, so that there was only one meeting with the MDC.

The analysis was unanimous: Farm occupations did not have to do with the race question and the land problem, but with power preservation. The squatters were not perceived to be defenders of liberty, but rather paid unemployed people and other groups of desperate folks, not to mention even thugs and criminal elements. A lot of terror and violence occurred on the farms. Not only were White farmers murdered, but also numerous Black opposition candidates. There were probably more victims of violence than it is possible to assess, because causes of death were hushed up and acts of violence went unreported. The country was brought to the brink of ruin as tourism came to a standstill, investors withdrew, and the economy of the neighboring countries was more and more affected. Foreign exchange shortages and the oil crisis were also contributing to the worsening situation. Tobacco production and tourism were the main sources of Zimbabwe's income and both were badly damaged by the events.

The presence of election observers contributed very much to an atmosphere of enhanced security as well as to a de-escalation of violence. The MDC people were not the only group to state such feelings as "[it's] so good that you are here." As somebody told us, the very fact we were seen and that we encouraged the democratic process of election was positive, and therefore we should only simply make ourselves visible in public.

After the journey of Harare via Kadoma to Gweru, I spent one of the two election days in the industrial area of the Midlands in a sprawling rural constituency in the east of Gweru. Here I visited 10 polling stations together, which were scattered and often difficult to find. There only directional signs were in very close proximity to the polling station, thus making it possible that some people wanting to vote did not actually find their polling place. Furthermore, the list of the polling stations was not published, they were hard to find, and there were undoubtedly irregularities with the registration process, possibly to a very large extent. Voters who were registered received no confirmation, contrary to former times, so that they could not submit a polling card in the polling stations.

With regard to the election day, I can report the following. The polling stations opened on time. The election committees worked neutrally and correctly. Voting irregularities were not apparent. Election observers of MDC and ZANU (PF), whose participation was debated in the run-up to the elections, were universally represented. Here and there other parties were also present. Also the MDC agents confirmed that the procedures had been trouble-free. We were received everywhere in a friendly fashion by the police and the election committees, obtained all requested information, and allowed to inspect everything we wished to.

An Unexpected High Turnout of Voters. The polling stations that I visited were almost exclusively in schools, though some were in villages, others in farm areas, and one in the cafeteria of a big prison (prisoners were disqualified from voting). There were large crowds at 9 of the 10 polling stations. At the opening time, long queues were already partially formed. The voters let all procedures patiently wash over them and behaved in exemplary fashion and according to the instructions. They appeared determined and fearless, to the extent that the whole atmosphere of terror that surrounded the elections did not seem to have any effect on them. The MDC agents were partially overjoyed. They had never experienced such an election turnout and had not expected it. In two cases I was prevented by the police from taking photographs. In other cases photography was permitted or tacitly tolerated. Voters did not complain at all; many expressed sympathy with surreptitious signs and greetings and farewell gestures were always friendly.

In only one polling station did a gaping void in participation occur without any clear reasons for it. The leader of the election committee assumed it could be due to the cold morning air, the long distances, or the fact of having two election days. Our driver, who was close to MDC and very helpful, assumed that it could also be due to a transportation problem because the school was situated in an isolated area far away from any settlement in the middle of a farm area and with bad access ways. A series of pickups packed with many people wanting to vote drove to other polling stations. There was a donkey truck as well. But most of the people came by feet and often walked for miles. The employees of many farmers were brought to the polling stations by truck, not distinguishing between ZANU (PF) or MDC supporters. To let the MDC people vote without intimidation was the main issue.

I experienced only one case of irregularity, which was based on a mistake and was remedied later on. I took the opportunity to speak with the waiting farmers, who were obviously marked by terror. One of them reported violent occupations; another one was spared this trouble, though he reported huge degrees of intimidation of his workers. Their exhausted conclusion was "We survived." They had great expectations for the election and did not want to be prevented from participating under any circumstances. A high level of suppressed frustration and rage was also clear. They also thanked us explicitly for our presence there.

Conclusion. Despite all the repression, more than 5 million out of 12.4 million Zimbabweans have registered to vote, which may also be the result of the relatively high educational level in Zimbabwe compared to other African countries. Even among the elderly voters, there were only a few who were illiterate, and those who could not read and write were assisted in the correct manner. It can be concluded that the procedures in the run-up to the election days made a free and fair election already impossible. Nevertheless, the elections were held unexpectedly peacefully, with high turnout for the vote.

Parliamentary and Presidential Elections in Peru on April 8, 2001 (First Round) and June 3, 2001 (Second Round of the Presidential Election)

Background to the Elections. Peru has had a checkered political history, characterized by political instability that has included long periods of military rule. In 1985 Alan García, of the Aprista party (Socialist), was elected president in a democratic poll. His regime was tainted by corruption and economic mismanagement. In 1990 Alberto Fujimori defeated his principal opponent, Mario Vargas Llosa, by a small margin. President Fujimori instituted economic reforms and put the Peruvian economy on a sounder footing. However, faced with terrorism from the Sendero Luminoso and other paramilitary organizations, a serious drug-trafficking problem, and ongoing corruption, in 1992, acting totally unconstitutionally, Mr Fujimori dissolved Congress, convened a constitutional Assembly, and drafted a new Constitution. In April 1995 Fujimori was reelected president with 64% of the votes, and his party obtained a majority in Congress. For the next 5 years Fujimori maintained complete control over Peruvian political life, with the support of the army. During this time he largely muzzled the media.

Fujimori's economic stabilization program, which eliminated most government subsidies, reduced the level of inflation. His market-oriented reforms included privatization of mining, electricity, and telecommunications. As a result of important foreign inward investment, with the support of the IMF (International Monetary Fund) and the World Bank, growth was strong between 1994 and 1997. In 1998 and 1999, growth was undermined by factors such as the impact of El Niño, economic instability in Brazil, and the economic problems in Asia.

In the meantime the Fujimori government enjoyed considerable success in the fight against armed groups and terrorism. The Tupac Amaru Revolutionary Movement (MRTA) was greatly weakened by the arrest of its leader, Miguel Rincón Rincón, in 1995, though it did carry out the attack on the Japanese ambassador's residence in Lima in 1996, when, following a 4-month siege, military commandos stormed the residence, killed the rebels, and freed the hostages. The other main rebel movement, Sendero Luminoso, was also effectively defeated. Its leader, Abimael Guzmán, was captured in 1992, and its second-in-command, Oscar Ramínez Durand was taken into custody in 1999. This seriously affected the operational ability of the MRTA. As a result the country is now much more peaceful. However, the government forces, both army and police, frequently acted in a brutal manner, disregarding human rights.

Border disputes between Peru and Ecuador, which had led to armed conflicts in 1941, 1981, and 1995, were finally solved in 1998 by the negotiation of a settlement. In the period after 1992, effective power was exercised by President Fujimori, his principal adviser Vladimiro Montesinos, head of the National Intelligence Service (SIN), and General Hermoza, Commander in Chief of the Army. Montesinos became enormously powerful through his control of the SIN.

Despite a constitutional provision restricting the president to two terms of office, President Fujimori was able to run for a third term in the April 2000 elections. This was criticized by opposition parties, who also brought a series of complaints regarding serious election irregularities to the National Electoral Commission. In the run-up to the elections, President Fujimori greatly increased spending on social welfare programs. By effectively buying votes in this manner, his popularity increased and he obtained the largest number of votes, though not an absolute majority. Because of electoral irregularities observed by both independent Peruvian organizations, including Transparencia, and international observers, Fujimori's main rival, Alejandro Toledo, refused to take part in the second round of elections held on May 28, 2000. Despite complaints from several countries and organizations, including the EU, the second round of the elections went ahead. The EU decided not to send observers to the second round, which Fujimori won in the absence of any serious opposition.

Meanwhile, a major political scandal broke out. Vladimiro Montesinos had organized a widespread net of corruption that covered a gamut of illicit activities, including the bribing of politicians, senior business people, and media figures. In September 2000 a video showing Congressman Alberto Kouri Bumachado receiving $15,000 (U.S.) from Montesinos was broadcast on television. This was the start of the "Vladivideos" scandal. It transpired that Montesinos had videotaped a large number of transactions in which senior figures accepted bribes. These videos were shown to the public following Montesinos' flight to Panama on September 23, 2000. When Panama refused to grant political asylum, Montesinos returned to Peru on October 23, and subsequently disappeared. Meanwhile the Swiss government agreed to freeze three Swiss bank accounts in Montesinos' name, with deposits totaling $48 million (U.S.). A subsequent investigation showed that other large sums had been deposited in various foreign banks.

As a result of these revelations, Fujimori announced the reduction of his presidential mandate and called for new elections to be held on April 8, 2001. He also disbanded the national intelligence service. As the crisis deepened Fujimori fled to Japan (it appears that he held dual Peruvian and Japanese nationality as his parents were Japanese). On November 21, 2000, he was impeached by Congress.

In the same month Valentin Paniagua, President of Congress, was chosen by Congress as interim president. Paniagua had no links with the Fujimori administration. As interim president, Paniagua chose an interim government to rule Peru until the new president and government took over on July 28, 2001. The new Cabinet was a mixture of technocrats, experienced politicians, and notable figures including the former UN Secretary General, Javier Perez de Cuellar, who was appointed prime minister and minister for foreign affairs.

The main objectives of the interim government were to organize free and fair presidential and congressional elections, to pursue as much political reform as possible, and to maintain economic stability.

The Paniagua administration had made the electoral bodies more independent and had renewed almost 80% of the staff of the ONPE (Oficina Nacional de Procesos Electorales). It increased media freedom and was in the process of purging the armed forces and the judiciary of elements known to be close to Fujimori and Montesinos. It was significant that the armed forces had reaffirmed their commitment to the political authorities.

Election Organization. The Peruvian Constitution provides for a directly elected president who may be elected for two consecutive terms of office. The president appoints the Council of Ministers, directed by the prime minister, which is the principal executive body. There is a unicameral parliament, the Congreso, consisting of 120 members, which can be dissolved once during a presidential term. Under the new parliamentary system, the country is divided into 25 electoral districts, one for each department and one for the constitutional province of Callao. The 120 seats are distributed according to population. This replaces the former National List System and is intended to make members of congress more responsible to the electorate.

All Peruvians between the ages of 18 and 70 are obliged to vote and failure to do so results in a fine. Peruvians over 70 are entitled to vote if they wish to do so. If the obligation to vote is disregarded, high fines can be imposed by the authorities.

Elections in Peru are organized by three permanent electoral agencies:

- The Registro Nacional de Identificación y Estado Civil (Reniec) is responsible for preparing the register of electors and issuing national identification cards, (and also for registering births, deaths, and marriages).

- The ONPE is responsible for organizing and implementing the elections, including preparing and distributing ballots and related voting materials, running the elections on polling day, and reporting the results of the counts.

- The Jurado Nacional de Elecciones (JNE) is responsible for overseeing the entire electoral process, including administering justice on electoral matters, maintaining the registry of political organizations, inscribing candidates, and proclaiming the results.

Each polling center *(colegio)* is divided into a number of polling stations *(mesas),* with not more than 200 voters for each *mesa.* Each *mesa* is run by a president, a secretary, and a third member of the *mesa.* These are selected by drawing lots from among the voters who have a certain minimum standard of education. Three supplementary members of the mesa are also selected should the selected members be unable to fulfill their tasks. Not more than one representative *(personero)* from each political party presenting a candidate may be present in each *mesa* during the proceedings and at the count. Votes are counted in each *mesa* immediately after the close of voting, at 4:00 PM.

The results are then entered on an *acta electoral* (electoral minutes). Six copies of this acta are made, signed, and then sent to the JNE, the Jurado Electoral Especial (JEE), the Oficina Descentralizada de Procesos Electorales (ODPE), the ONPE, the Armed Forces, and the public and political organizations (this copy is in fact kept for public inspection if necessary). The large number of copies is intended to make falsification of the result more difficult, as each copy of the acta is signed by the members of the *mesa* and by the *personeros* present. The results are collated in each department (administrative unit), using a computerized system, and are then sent to a central computing center in Lima. If no candidate for the presidency gets more than 50% of the valid votes cast, there will be a second round of presidential elections not more than 28 days after the formal announcement of the results of the first round. There is only one round of voting for the Congreso.

The Conduct of Elections in the First Round. All the parties signed a pact committing themselves to mutual fair treatment and to respecting the results of the elections. Despite different accusations by the parties as a result of relatively minor irregularities, the pact was generally respected and the electoral campaign went remarkably well. There was no evidence of intimidation.

However, despite a legal obligation to do so, none of the political parties or presidential candidates provided information regarding the sources of their financing or of their campaign expenses. On this matter all the parties were uniform in their noncompliance.

All parties had access to the electronic media. Under a system known as the Franja Electoral, approved by the JNE and published in the *Gazeta Oficial* of January 19, 2001, political groups have at their disposal 10 minutes each day on the television and radio channels, both privately and state owned. This cost-free space is available from 60 days before polling day to the day before polling. If a political group does not submit material for its allotted spot, the ONPE will use the space for voter education.

A serious controversy blew up in the weeks before the election concerning the publication of the results of exit polls. According to the law such results could not be published until 10:00 P.M. on polling day (voting closes at 4:00 P.M.). Finally, a last-minute decision by the Constitutional Court to revoke this clause enabled the rapid publication of exit polls and quick counts.

The first round of the presidential elections provided an unexpected result. Alejandro Toledo of the Peru Posible Party came out on top with 36.51% of the votes; second place went to Alan García of APRA, a former president of Peru, with 25.78% of the votes. In third place came Lourdes Flores of the Unidad Nacional Party with 24.30% of the votes, even though most opinion polls had placed her second ahead of García. The fourth-place candidate was Fernando Olivera of the FIM Party, with 9.85% of the votes. All other candidates got less than 2% of the votes. As stated earlier, these results required a runoff election.

The Conduct of the Elections in the Second Round. The candidates for the second round were Toledo and García. As 8 weeks separated the two rounds of the elections, due largely to delays in finalizing the results of the first round, there was time for relations between the two candidates to deteriorate. The final weeks of the campaign were marked by personal verbal attacks and a notable lowering of the general tone. This was referred to by the Peruvian media as the *guerra sucia* (dirty war). However, the attacks remained largely verbal, and there was remarkably little physical violence, except for a small number of deplorable incidents such as the planting of a bomb outside the JNE offices. Such acts were most likely perpetrated by nonconstitutional political activists and not by representatives of the mainstream political parties.

Many Peruvians were afraid that Vladimiro Montesinos, the former head of the security services under ex-President Fujimori, was still in a position to pull strings behind the scenes. There seems to be widespread fear of a Montesinos-controlled network. Both candidates strongly pressed for a campaign to clean up corruption and spoke frequently in favor of human rights.

Certain supporters of candidates that had not gone through to the second round, as well as disgruntled Peruvian citizens who disapproved of both candidates, called for a count of blank or spoiled votes. At the final tally, however, the number of blank and spoiled votes was not excessive, with 11.06% spoiled votes and 2.75% blank votes (total invalid votes: 13.81%).

The transitional government of President Paniagua remained scrupulously objective and neutral throughout the campaign and is held in very high esteem. Several commentators expressed the view that if Valentín Paniagua were to have stood for president, he would have been elected easily. Despite the candidates' personal attacks on each other, the campaign for the second round passed off smoothly.

As there were only two candidates in the second round, the system was much easier to operate and less open to error. Similarly, counting, which took place in polling stations immediately after voting closed at 4:00 PM, was much simpler than in the first round, and so the results were released much more quickly. Not only was the quick-count estimation carried out by Transparencia remarkably accurate, but the official results themselves were available within 12 hours of the close of voting.

Conclusion. The transitional government was to be congratulated on its neutrality and independence. It went to great lengths to ensure that the elections were carried out correctly, without government interference. By purging the electoral organizations of elements close to the former regime, they ensured much cleaner and more transparent elections than in the past. In general, the congressional election and both the first and second rounds of the presidential election were well conducted, free, and fair. There were, however, some problems.

Many *mesas* did not open on time, due primarily to the way in which *mesa* officials were selected, which was on a lottery basis. Particularly in poor areas, some selected officials did not turn up on election day, preferring instead to pay the fine as they felt incapable of fulfilling the obligations imposed on them. This was particularly true of less educated *mesa* presidents and secretaries. In some areas more than half the selected presidents and secretaries failed to appear and had to be replaced by deputizing members *(suplentes)* or, where these were not available, by people chosen at random from the voters' queue.

Especially in the rural regions of the Amazon area or the Andes the lottery system met exclusively illiterate election committees, which were not capable of managing their task. For future elections, it is therefore necessary to assure that at least one literate member belongs to each election committee.

Some irregularities were observed when, on occasions, *personeros* were coopted as *mesa* staff, mainly because they knew how the system worked. This appears to have been an ad hoc solution to an immediate problem rather than an intentional violation of the neutrality of polling station officials. As no more than 200 persons voted in any one *mesa,* late opening did not prevent the public from being able to cast their votes.

The general level of training of *mesa* staff was inadequate. Many did not really know how to conduct operations. While those observed by the delegation were well intentioned, and were even-handed in their approach to the different political parties, many were not fully familiar with the complex procedures, notably regarding the count. The congressional count was particularly complicated (see later discussion), and more intensive training for all involved would have been required. Similarly, in the case of illiterate voters, the absolute secrecy of the ballot could not be guaranteed. However these are problems encountered in almost all elections in developing countries.

As in the first round, all electoral material was only in Spanish. This made it difficult for populations of remote areas, who only spoke local languages, to understand instructions. Also, the programs in the electronic media that were supposed to inform the public about the elections were produced exclusively in Spanish. In future elections, these programs should be broadcast in the local languages as well as in Spanish, particularly because radio is the most important and most widespread medium, reaching even the illiterate population in the most isolated villages.

As mentioned previously the system of selecting candidates for the Congreso was excessively complicated. This is evidenced by the fact that there were 1.29 million spoiled votes in the congressional elections, whereas, with roughly the same number of voters, there were only 396,000 spoiled votes in the presidential elections, in which voters simply placed a cross on the symbol of the candidate of their choice. A simpler system for the congressional balloting would lead to less confusion and would facilitate the count.

The lists of polling stations provided to observers by ONPE was not always accurate. For example, in the department of Loreto the list for colegio CE60071 (Indiana) indicated 14 *mesas.* In reality the colegio had 26 *mesas.* Similarly for colegio CE60084 (Mazan) 6 *mesas* were listed in the ONPE document when there were in fact 13, and for colegio CE60304 (Mazan) only 5 *mesas* were listed though there were 11. This appears to be due to clerical inefficiency rather than any attempt to defraud.

The proportion of women voting was remarkably high, with no appearance of discrimination in this regard. Special attention was paid to disabled voters. Cards printed in Braille could be placed over ballot papers to assist the blind, and persons in wheelchairs were carried into polling stations by the police when ramps were not available. It is regrettable that many *mesas* were on the upper floors of schools, thereby causing problems for disabled persons and giving the police extra work.

The special precautions for disabled people were in practice to a large extent restricted to the big cities. In the villages by the Amazon or in the Andes, many old and disabled people did not even find their way to the polling stations due to the difficult conditions.

Despite the threat of fines in the case of people not respecting their electoral obligation, there were areas where turnout was far lower than in the cities; in the region of the Andes, for example, the poll was comparatively low. These people living below the poverty line in difficult and isolated areas really have nothing to lose. And in reality it would also be difficult to collect the money paid in fines from all the villages in the mountains or by the river. In fact, most are not really affected by the threat of punishment.

It is very important to distinguish between the role of the *personero* and polling station staff. In cases where *personeros* are dynamic and polling station staff less so, the distinction can be blurred, and on occasions *personeros* played an excessively prominent role. The overall conclusion of the European Parliament delegation was that both rounds of the election were well conducted in a transparent manner that corresponds to recognized democratic norms, and can consequently be considered free and fair.

Parliamentary and Presidential Elections in Sierra Leone

Background to the Elections. The 2002 presidential and parliamentary elections, postponed from March 2001 to May 14, 2002, due to instability in the country and to allow sufficient time for preparations, were viewed as a key element in the peace process. The president, Alhaji Ahmad Tejan Kabbah, had formally declared the end of the 10-year civil war on January 16, 2002 and the participation of the former rebels of the Revolutionary United Front (RUF) as a political party (RUFP) was considered vitally important to contribute to lasting peace.

Election Administration. The administration of the elections was the responsibility of the National Electoral Commission (NEC), an independent organization that faced accusations of political bias from opposition parties during the course of the campaign. Relations between the NEC and the opposition parties improved as the campaign went on. The Electoral Laws Act, adopted on February 7, 2002, set a deadline of April 2 for the nomination of candidates.

The Electoral System. The presidential election, in which 9 of the 11 political parties took part, required a candidate to receive more than 55% of the vote in order to win outright. In the event of no candidate reaching this figure, a runoff election would be held between the candidates occupying first and second place after the first ballot.

The parliamentary elections, in which 10 of the 11 political parties fielded candidates, was organized according to a district block system of proportional representation. The country was divided into 14 electoral districts, each of which was allocated a block of eight seats. Individual candidates' names were not mentioned on the parliamentary ballot-papers as voters were to select a political party rather than candidates. In addition to the 112 members of Parliament elected in this way, 12 paramount chiefs were to be elected indirectly by Chiefdom counselors representing the chieftaincies. These elections were to take place before election day but were postponed until afterward.

Special voting, for those whose occupations would make it impossible for them to vote on election day, was scheduled for May 11, 2002. Election day itself was May 14, 2002, and counting was to take place in the polling stations as soon as the polls closed. Following this count, ballot boxes were to be transferred to regional centers for a second stage of counting and regional collation. Collation was also to take place at the national level.

Voter Registration. The electoral registration process had been fraught with difficulties, many deriving from administrative and logistical problems such as an insufficient number of registration offices and lack of supplies, particularly cameras and film to take voters' photographs for their electoral registration cards. Opposition parties ascribed political motives to the problems surrounding the registration process and alleged that they would benefit the ruling Sierra Leone Peoples' Party (SLPP). They continued to voice this complaint as campaigning progressed, leading to the conclusion that either they considered the registration problems particularly grave or they had considerably fewer complaints about other aspects of the electoral process. In fact, the logistical problems faced by the NEC at the time of voter registration probably gave them useful experience for the logistical operation of election day itself.

Voters who registered in one place and then wished to cast their vote in a different place had to make the request in writing using a special form and would be given a paper entitling them to vote at the new polling station. Each polling station was to be provided with a list of voters who had transferred in this way.

Media Coverage. The EU Election Observation Mission monitored the political parties' access to the media, including radio broadcasting, which is by far the most important form of mass media in Sierra Leone. Each political party had been allocated a quota of electoral broadcasting time and the Electoral Laws Act required that parity should be maintained in the amount of coverage given to each. However, this rule was to be policed by the state broadcaster, Sierra Leone Broadcasting Service (SLBS), giving it responsibility for regulating its own activities. And indeed, SLBS radio and television news programs and political commentary programs gave far greater airtime to the SLPP than to other parties.

Voter and Election Officer Education. Training of polling station officers was not sufficiently thorough and on polling day many were unclear about whom they should permit to vote. This problem was particularly evident in the case of voters who had registered at other voting stations, of whom there were many in those polling stations serving as camps for internally displaced people.

Voter education had started late and was notably deficient. Although earlier concerns that much of the country was unaware that an election was taking place appear to have been addressed before the election day, many voters remained very unclear about voting procedures.

Party Organization and Resources. In Sierra Leone, parties tend to be formed for the purpose of fighting elections and largely disappear at other times. In this election, most parties lacked organization and nationwide structures and few had any significant resources to finance campaigning. Election posters were, in the main, very basic and some candidates did not even have vehicles. The SLPP was the notable exception. Members of the delegation observed various election materials during a visit to their offices and there were numerous reports, highlighted by opposition parties, of their using official vehicles for campaign purposes.

Violence and Intimidation. Election campaigning was remarkably peaceful, especially considering the violence that has accompanied past elections in Sierra Leone. However, opposition parties reported incidents of voter intimidation by the ruling SLPP, particularly on the part of paramount chiefs who traditionally had complete control over their communities. Representatives of political parties reported instances when these chiefs had made it difficult for them to hold meetings in their communities. Most notably, there were numerous reports from Kono District in the east of the country that voters had been intimidated to such a degree that they were obliged to leave their homes and move to the central town of Makeni. However, opposition parties registered few official complaints with the NEC, with some explaining that if they did so no subsequent action would be taken.

On May 11, the final SLPP campaign rally took place in Freetown, centering at the town's sports stadium. Very large crowds of SLPP supporters gathered at numerous points in the city to travel together to the event. In most places the crowds were good-humored and there was a party atmosphere, but this was not the case at the RUFP office where representatives of the former rebels' party clashed violently with the SLPP supporters. The

RUFP office was ransacked during the disturbance, and the violence soured the atmosphere prior to the poll.

Election Observation. The largest mission of international observers was that of the EU, which had a 7-member core team, 20 long-term observers, and 56 short-term observers in addition to the European Parliament delegation; 5 Swiss observers also worked with them.

The elections were also observed by 11 Commonwealth representatives, 20 delegates from the Economic Community of West African States (ECOWAS) and 10 from the Organization of African Unity (OAU), along with 20 from the Carter Center and 15 from the World Council of Churches. Among the national observers there were 2,000 from the National Election Watch and 1,500 from the Sierra Leone Council of Churches.

The Observation of the Poll and the Counting. The extremely difficult logistical challenge presented by conditions in Sierra Leone, coupled with low levels of experience and organizational capacity, hampered the smooth running of the elections. However, polling day was peaceful and in both the voting and the counting procedures, members of the European Parliament delegation observed relatively few irregularities.

Attempt at Undue Influence. Only one attempt to influence the vote was observed by members of the delegation: At a polling station on the outskirts of Freetown, the presiding officer engaged in voter education to the extent of indicating exactly where voters should mark their ballot papers. Party agents present in the polling station objected vociferously and a serious altercation erupted, which came close to violence before it was ultimately diffused by the policeman assigned to that polling station.

Administrative and Organizational Problems. I observed a dangerous situation when opening a polling station in Freetown, where there were insufficient facilities to control the large crowds of voters forming outside. Particularly, there were too few police officers present. The pressure of the crowd caused the gate to give way and some people were injured. I was unable to obtain help for one woman, who was bleeding profusely, because all the police officers were at the entrance of the polling station.

Lack of organization was also evident at the polling station in the Kissy District of Freetown, opened by another member, where there was a large, orderly queue of voters who had registered to vote at that place, very many of whom discovered they had been allocated polling stations at a considerable distance, some located on islands in the bay. There was a great deal of anger among voters when they discovered this. The observer reported the growing tension to the long-term observers for Freetown.

Halfway through the morning of election day, the NEC changed the election rules by way of a press release advising polling station presiding officers that voters should be allowed to vote at the polling station where they registered, regardless of whether their names were on the register of voters held at that polling station. This notification was aimed at addressing some of the difficulties that arose at the beginning of the poll, such as that encountered by one member. However, it was worded in an ambiguous way and was given very different interpretations by presiding officers in different polling stations. Some continued to turn away all voters whose names were not included in the register; others allowed voting by people who had registered in completely different places. This problem was particularly noticeable in polling stations serving as camps for internally displaced people.

Members of the European Parliament delegation observed very many polling stations that had not received the list of transferred voters but whose presiding officers allowed people with valid transfer voter forms to cast their ballots. There were also a number of polling stations with more than 1,000 registered voters that had not received the duplicate sets of equipment that had been promised to all polling stations of that size. In cases where duplicate sets of equipment had been received, the premises were sometimes too small and sometimes voters had difficulty finding the second polling station. Similar confusion arose in places where numerous polling stations were located in the same room. Sometimes up to eight polling stations shared the same space and the distribution meant the secrecy of the ballot could not be guaranteed, although in these cases no deliberate attempt to violate the secrecy of the vote was observed. Mr. Corrie discovered two polling stations that had not opened at all as their materials had not been delivered; their presiding officers had pragmatically arranged for their voters to be accepted by adjacent polling stations that had opened.

Police presence was generally discreet, although it was sometimes insufficient. One member observed some polling stations at which there was no security presence at all. The attitude toward international observers was very welcoming and friendly. Polling station officers, voters, and police officers were very willing to assist members of the European Parliament delegation with their observation work and were happy to answer all questions.

The Counting. Counting began in polling stations immediately after the close of the poll, in the presence of the party agents and any national or international observers who were in the polling station at the time. Following the count in the polling stations, collation was carried out in two stages, at the district level and the national level. The counting and collating procedure took 2 days longer than the 72 hours that the NEC had set as its target.

The Results. The results of the election were declared on Sunday, May 19, 2002. The incumbent president, Ahmad Tejan Kabbah of the SLPP, was reelected with 70.1% of the vote. In the parliamentary election, of the 112 ordinary members of the House of Representatives, the SLPP gained 83, the All People's Congress won 22, and the Peace and Liberation Party won 2. All other parties polled insufficient votes to gain seats. The party of the former rebels, RUFP, polled 1.7% in the presidential election and 2.2% in the parliamentary election.

Conclusion. Although there were shortcomings in the voter registration, the campaign, and the electoral process, the achievement of peaceful elections in Sierra Leone should not be underestimated. The high turnout demonstrated the commitment of the people to the democratic process and in the main they were able to express their political preferences at the ballot box without intimidation or hindrance.

In general, members of the European Parliament delegation found that the polling station presiding officers were professional and impartial, and that they and their staff were assiduous in respecting electoral procedures. They also supplied voter education in an appropriate, politically neutral manner, when the deficiencies in this area became evident. In most of the Freetown polling stations observed by the European Parliament delegation, there were representatives of a variety of political parties as well as a good presence of national observers. Their presence increased transparency and reduced the likelihood of political bias tainting the polling procedures.

During the count, members of the European Parliament delegation observed that presiding officers made every effort to apply the rules fairly and to achieve a consensus among party agents where doubts arose. Between polling stations, however, there were inconsistent interpretations of the rules on such matters as void ballots.

In some places outside Freetown, EU observers reported that district election officers had difficulties understanding the complicated calculations involved with the distribution between the parties of the eight parliamentary seats available in each district and that there was confusion in the collation of polling station results.

The European Parliament delegation viewed the elections as a very significant contribution to the process of pacification and democratization in Sierra Leone, but shared the general concern of the EU Election Observation mission that this process remains fragile.

In conclusion, the European Parliament observation delegation considered that, despite obvious irregularities in the lead-up to the election and administrative imperfections on polling day, it would be appropriate to view the election results as a reasonably accurate reflection of the wishes of the Sierra Leonean electorate.

SUMMARY AND CONCLUSION: ELECTION MONITORING CONTRIBUTES TO DEMOCRATIZATION

The whole world's interest in election monitoring is diverse and unfortunately often less well-developed where there is a regional gradient. The Zimbabwe case made more headlines than the Sierra Leone one and the British press, of course, paid more attention to both cases than did the German press, for instance. Also the European Parliament is not free of subjective impulses. Therefore, the proper course was to develop a formal procedure for the decision-making process in which delegates of different allocations and groups are involved. This also prevents one-sided favoritism toward certain regions.

Media coverage of elections in our part of the world focuses mainly on the question of who won or lost and whether any irregularities, acts of violation, or other scandals have occurred, issues on which election monitoring also focuses. But there are a whole range of other issues that election monitors also address. First, information and facts in the run-up to the elections are collected and reviewed. Have there been any threats or intimidation? Have votes been "bought" (with promises like the assignment of jobs or allocation of land, for instance)? How have the media represented the candidates and parties? What was the predominant notion in the media's coverage? Did the opposition have a fair chance? Have the electoral registers been manipulated?

Second, election monitors must also be informed about the respective electoral laws and the selection and training of election committees. Furthermore, it is essential to check that all materials and facilities (ballot papers, registers, ballot boxes, polling places, etc.) are delivered and operational in time for the election process to take place.

Attending electoral meetings and talking to a large number of members of different parties and groups of civil society as well as to the police and other authorities help to build a clear picture of the atmosphere in a country. Besides evaluating the electoral results after the election day, it is important also to draw a balance of what went well or badly and to determine constructive suggestions for improvement.

Even if a government is suspected of manipulative intentions, it is assumed that outright ballot rigging does not occur if election observers are in the country. Therefore, more subtle methods of influencing the election outcome are sometimes used in the run-up to the elections, for example, during the registration of people entitled to vote, as those are often more difficult to prove afterward. However, in Zimbabwe, campaigns of intimidation by the opposition that led to the murder of more than 30 constituency candidates were indeed obvious.

Election-monitoring missions stand to a certain extent for protection against disruptive actions during the election day(s). The presence of international observers draws higher public attention not only in the election country, but also in the countries of origin of the observers. Election monitoring enables elections to take place in the eyes of the whole world's public. To what extent this causes positive effects cannot be measured, but I am convinced that the operations are not completely useless, even if the election results are unpleasant.

The necessity for monitoring election stems from the historical and political context of a country, clearly illustrated by the case of the Peruvian elections. With the examples of Cambodia and Zimbabwe, however, I have emphasized instead describing how monitoring is performed in actual practice, in particular in the provinces.

Everything worked quite well in Cambodia, Zimbabwe, and Sierra Leone, whereas chaos ruled in Peru during the first round. This was due to logistic difficulties as well as, and mainly, to the "lottery" selection of election committees, which had little or no training and were in many cases illiterate.

Another barrier was sometimes the electoral system itself. Often it consisted of only one simple electoral action, for instance marking the ballot with only one cross in Cambodia, Zimbabwe, and for the presidential ballot, Sierra Leone. But in Sierra Leone, the ballot process for selecting the parliamentary seats presented a certain degree of difficulty, which should concern the voters. And the electoral system in Peru was peppered with difficulties. Besides the ballot papers for a presidential candidate and for a party for the parliamentary elections, there was another system altogether for the election of constituency candidates existed. Not only did the voters have trouble with the system but so too did election committees when they tried to count the votes later on. The rate of invalid or blank ballot papers was particularly high in the Andes region, where a huge part of the population cannot speak Spanish, but only the regional languages. This can lead to distorted election results, without any intention of fraud.

Based on observer experiences, the following conclusions can be drawn with regard to electoral process:

- Attention should be paid to current conditions and events during the run-up to the elections, for instance, intimidation or manipulation at registration.

- The members of the election committees should be paid attention to, to ensure that they are able to accomplish their mission. Furthermore, at least one member of each committee should be literate.
- The party representatives and the representatives of the national monitoring committees should be well instructed.
- Electoral laws should be simplified as necessary, to avoid confusion or errors.
- Advertising for elections in the media should be divided fairly between competing parties or candidates.
- Information campaigns should be presented in regional as well as national languages, to ensure that everyone has access to information about the election and the candidates.

Finally, it is important to point out that election monitoring limited to capitals and big cities reflects only a partial picture. The standard of education and living is clearly higher in these areas than in the more solitary rural areas, a fact that came into light particularly in Peru. Even if one lives in one of the poor slums in a capital, the chances for children to attend a school and the opportunities for adults to struggle through are much better.

To come to an appropriate assessment, then, the monitoring delegations must spread out into the provinces as well. The monitoring mission in the provinces may be full of privation, but impressions of the real situation in the country cannot be gained better anywhere else than there. Only in this way, can many political attitudes be comprehended. The observers get to know the capitals anyway, as the international airports are located there and are therefore their starting points. In short, monitoring missions contribute to democratization in an increasingly globalized world, even under less favorable conditions.

REFERENCES

European Commission. (2000). *Communication from the Commission on EU Election Assistance and Observation* (COM [2000] 191 final). Brussels, Belgium: Author.

Fava, G. C. (2001). Report on the Commission Communication on European Union Election Assistance and Observation (A5-0060/2001). Brussels, Belgium, and Strasbourg, France: European Parliament.

International IDEA. (1997). *Code of conduct for the ethical and professional observation of elections.* Stockholm, Sweden: Author.

9

Conclusion

David Ward

Periods when elections take place represent a litmus test for the media at a time when incumbent and potential political representatives rely on the media to communicate a whole range of political and social issues to the voting public. The platform that the mass media provide during election periods is essential to allow citizens to gather information concerning the candidates and political parties who will represent them in the political sphere for the coming term of office. Without the information that the media provide, democratic and fair elections on a national or regional scale would take an extremely different form. Indeed, where elections are judged to be unfair and unequal the media are usually held up as an integral institution that underpins imbalance or discrepancies.

Elections are a system for narrowing down the participants in the political sphere on the basis of a manageable and representative formula. Two major factors are seen to ensure that this system of representation works. The first is the fact that citizens periodically vote for their representatives and have the right to vote based on the availability of an accurate and balanced range of information communicated through the mass media. The second is the scrutiny of both the candidates and elected representatives that the media perform in order that the viewers and readers can critically engage with issues that are raised at election times.

As is evident from the national case studies in this book, each nation-state has a different set of socioeconomic, political, and cultural traditions that have in many respects created a different set of nationally specific rules and regulations for the mass media. These are more finely tuned during election periods, and the rules that are employed during elections provide a valuable set of national reflections as to the perceived importance of the mass media and the role of the state in developing and supporting certain measures to ensure fairness and media freedom.

IDEAL VERSUS REALITY

Normatively the idea that elections should be free and fair, and that the mass media have a crucial role to play in ensuring that the candidates have access to the mass media, is fundamental to all of the national rules that govern the election process and the mass media's coverage of elections and election campaigns. At the same time, there are important differences in the political systems that are central to an understanding of how the media play out their role during election periods. There is a set of key principles that underpin a notion of media freedom and access for candidates to ensure that the electorate are able to access information about the parties and candidates standing for election under certain conditions. Citizens are therefore seen to be empowered to make an informed decision about who will represent them in the political sphere. Each political system demonstrates differences in its structure and the mechanisms employed, and in many ways the regulation of the mass media is a reflection of these different political traditions.

There are a number of basic principles that are essential to guarantee that elections are conducted in the mass media according to principles of fairness and nondiscrimination. These include fair and equal access for the candidates and political parties, responsible journalism, wide coverage of the issues and the candidates, and professionalism. These factors do not act in a vacuum and the structures of the mass media and the civic culture that supports public debate in the public sphere that the mass media provide is crucial to understanding the quality of the relationship between politics, elections, and the media, and through the media the public. Like any other profession, journalists work within certain structures and as a result free and fair coverage of an election is only possible when the media are independent, and this means, when they enjoy stable economic conditions and can operate at arms length from external forces to undertake to work in the public interest. The question of how the media are therefore regulated by the state is crucial in guaranteeing these conditions.

Equality is technically achieved in all of the countries in this study and the principle of nondiscrimination is legally established across the range of systems. However, the manner in which this principle is applied varies both between countries and between mass-media sectors. Independence does not only mean different things in different countries, but perhaps paradoxically it can mean different things to different media sectors. In none of the countries studied in this book is the organization of elections via the mass media a perfect model and it is possible to identify certain areas where failings in the systems have occurred and will continue to do so in the future. Many of the authors point to imperfections in the national systems; some of these are profound and are seen to undermine the democratic process, whereas others may not have the same impact, but are nevertheless still important.

How nation-states regulate their media systems based on the legal framework they have adopted is of considerable importance as to the success or degree of failure in ensuring that elections are contested between candidates according to certain conditions. This holds both generally and during election campaigns when special provisions are employed to account for the exceptional circumstances of the election campaign period to ensure fair and equal coverage between the candidates.

NATIONAL NUANCES

Whereas the legal requirement for free and fair elections is a universal one in democratic systems of governance, the interpretation of these rules and the mechanisms employed to distribute the rights of candidates, journalists, and the public vary considerably among countries with different philosophical and political traditions. They also vary between media, and in the majority of cases the press and broadcasting sectors are governed by a different set of regulations and requirements. Legal freedom, however, does not always translate into real freedom and the liberty of the media does not always equate to a responsible, independent, and balanced approach to the elections. This is no more so than the differences in the regulatory and legal apparatus that lays out the ground rules for the press and broadcast media in countries that employ a system of public-service broadcasting. In this context the public broadcast media have detailed requirements placed on them to ensure that certain thresholds of access and fairness are guaranteed, both under normal circumstances and even more stringently at times of election campaigns.

The regulatory model adopted for the broadcasting sector in the United States differs considerably from the public-service model and broadcast media are generally regulated in a parallel way to the press sector and the free-market model, with minimal regulatory requirements. In the U.S. approach, access to the mass media is essentially acquired by the candidates through purchasing slots to place political advertising. Although the principle of equal access underpins this, there is nevertheless a question of financial advantage granted to the larger parties who can afford to invest, as the U.S. chapter demonstrates, huge amounts of money to promote themselves through the mass media.

The most common alternative to the paid-access one is the provision on television of free access for parties and candidates to ensure that the whole campaign process is independent from commercial imperatives. Regulatory instruments impose rigid rules on the broadcasters to ensure that candidates are entitled to broadcast party political programs and reach the electorate through television. This is seen as a public service provided by the broadcasters and is subsequently understood to be a major obligation usually imposed on the public-service broadcasters. In some cases these rules are laid down in laws, whereas in other cases the rules are worked out in an agreement between broadcasters and the parties. And sometimes they are included in the regulation worked out by an independent electoral body, in agreement with the political parties or by a regulatory authority in charge of the media.

Both of the systems share the principle that party political broadcasts should be editorially free from the broadcasters and should be signposted clearly so that a distinction can be made by the viewer between party broadcasts and normal programming. In this sense, whether broadcasters are required to provide access free of charge or sell airtime to political parties or candidates, the editorial responsibility for the party broadcasts lies with the political parties; although in the case of the UK, the broadcasters have the right to refuse a party political broadcast on taste and decency grounds.

On top of the provision to provide a window for political parties and candidates to communicate to the electorate, the media also have a role to play in their overall coverage of the elections. The regulatory framework in France is perhaps the clearest example of this distinction, and there is a clear dividing line between party political broadcasts and normal editorial coverage of politics and political issues. Again, the press and broadcast media in the United States are characterized by a very different regulatory regime that has developed, and the print and broadcast media are relatively free of positive content constraints and obligations under the protection afforded by, and interpretation of, the First Amendment.

The public-service broadcasters are, as part of their obligations to provide a public service in broadcasting, required to provide a set of services based on notions of balance. This is defined in a number of ways and can include either due impartiality, full representation, balance, or fairness, and more often all of these principles. This is not always realized by the broadcasters themselves, who at times can come under pressure from external forces, but it is nevertheless set out in national laws and regulations.

BROADCAST AND PRINT

There are a whole different set of rules employed by countries that apply to different kinds of mass media. The press, for instance, enjoys minimum regulation, which enables them to embrace an editorial policy in support of a particular candidate or party, and the philosophical notion of a patchwork of different proprietors is seen to provide pluralism. There is of course no direct link between the number of outlets and plurality of opinion of news, and the high costs of publishing a newspaper is prohibitive for all but the very select members of any society. It has nevertheless acted as the guiding regulatory principle and the press are effectively self-regulating; this is, as McNicholas and Ward point out in the chapter on the UK, not without certain problems and limitations. As a result a very different regime has been developed for newspapers, who, in contradistinction to the broadcasting industry are usually partisan in their approach to the political parties, which is accepted as a standard and unproblematic characteristic of the print media that has its roots in the 19th-century concept of the liberty of the press.

The broadcasting sector has been approached in the majority of cases examined in this book in an extremely different manner. This is not to say that broadcasters are nonpolitical, but they are nonpartisan and are required to remain an impartial and disinterested platform or fully representative of social groups, based on a model of public service in broadcasting. A similar set of rules have been employed in South Africa, where similar provisions and requirements are placed on the public broadcaster.

However, it should be stressed this is not always a perfect model, and the case of Italy is perhaps a poignant reminder of some of the difficulties that public broadcasters have experienced arising from their historical roots. There is also a further distinction between commercial and public broadcasters that supports a further split, with the commercial broadcast media having fewer and lighter touch regulations. Indeed, this model of regulation is probably the most extreme in the United States, where, as the Kaid and Jones chapter demonstrates, the broadcast media have little or no content regulation. This is becoming increasingly common around the world in countries where a dual system has developed with a clear line between commercial and public or state broadcast media.

At the other end of the scale is the control by the political classes of the mass media and the continuing dominance of the mass media across both print and broadcast media of this elite group. The case of Russia described by Skillen in this volume demonstrates the complex nature of the transition from the state communist system to a system of liberal democracy. The relationship between politics and the media is characterized by widespread abuse of the mass media, and the relationship between the media and politics remains one with fundamental problems in realizing a healthy and stable mass media that operates in the public interest.

LEVELS OF REGULATION

The regulation of the media at election times can therefore be understood in terms of the depth of regulation and both positive and negative regulatory instruments. Regulation not only defines what the media should not do, but also in some cases what it should undertake to do. In this respect there are levels of regulation as well as different kinds of regulators that are tiered according to the degree that each sector has obligations imposed on them by the public authorities. The model of regulation for the press is one of self-regulation and this is supported by codes of conduct and best-practice guidelines that journalists and editors follow. There is minimal state involvement with the print media in most countries and the courts are usually responsible for legal principles of defamation and slander in cases that seriously breach the law. Although there are some obligations placed on the print media in some countries, for instance, a ban on political advertising, the restrictions are minimal and the press at election times functions in very much the same way as they do in normal periods, though there is a natural focus on elections at election times.

On the other hand, television and radio are understand to be media that require greater public regulation and far more positive regulation. This is especially pronounced during election times, when broadcasters are required to fulfill certain regulatory objectives, on top of their normal obligations. It is important that these obligations are developed within a nonpolitical framework that accounts for the principles that should guide politicians, parliamentarians, and policymakers. The increased prevalence of private broadcasters that operate under different imperatives invokes yet another set of rules that are far more similar to the press model.

CONCLUSION

The whole area of media and elections has become a central issue over the past two decades in terms of trends in both developed democracies with a long history of democratic elections and independent media, and developing constitutional democracies. In established democracies, a set of concerns have arisen revolving around a variety of aspects of how the media report national elections and the relationship between the media and political parties, in the context of the requirements of parliamentary democracy to have fair elections, governed by certain basic principles. Developing constitutional democracies, where traditional election coverage associated with Western models of democracy have developed, in countries that have less mature democratic and accountable structures, a different set of problems arise for journalists who report on elections where freedom of information remains closely guarded.

The media and political standards are entwined together within the borders of nation-states and in many cases the quality of political citizenship is reflected in how the media are regulated during election periods to ensure that certain standards are maintained. In all cases where a democratic system is employed, media freedom is enshrined legally or constitutionally as a fundamental right. Although there are indeed a set of core principles that act as both the philosophical and moral foundation of liberal democratic systems of government, there are also strong national specificities that must be taken into consideration. The style and nature of how elections are approached by the mass media varies not only between countries, but also within countries, and depending on the media sector. In this respect the historical conditions under which the media sectors have evolved within have indelibly shaped the approach that nation-states have taken toward print and broadcast media. There are in most cases, subsequently, very different approaches taken toward the two sectors when it comes to obligations and requirements on the sectors during the election period.

One thing is very clear, however, and this is that where there is an unstable media environment, the reporting of elections according to the principles of fairness and nondiscrimination becomes far more problematic. The media's role in elections must therefore be understood within the wider package of media freedom and responsibility that provides an enabling environment for journalists who are allowed to work with certain reassurances that they will not suffer from intimidation. Economic security and independence are therefore crucial conditions for quality and autonomous journalism that provides a public sphere for debate and argumentation to ensure that plural and diverse opinion underpin the democratic process, no less so at election times when the electorate take advantage of their right to elect representatives to govern.

Elections must be supported by a dynamic civil society that is constructed upon public argument and debate in the public sphere that is independent of external forces. The mass media must be recognized as a central institution in this process and must therefore be supported and required to provide a platform for the candidates and parties that meets legal and normative standards clearly set out and enforced by independent authorities. Legal and normative principles set down in a body of law can only be achieved through the development of robust institutions that are resistant to external forces. The imposition of norms and standards from developed democracies is not always practical or workable within the specificities of national conditions and must be considered within the context of the socioeconomic conditions of developing nations. In this context legal recognition must accompany institution building and developmental policies that encourage good practice and solid economic foundations.

10

Media and Elections:
Some Reflections
and Recommendations

Bernd-Peter Lange

This chapter is based on the first edition of the *Media and Elections Handbook* published by the European Institute for the Media (EIM; Lange & Palmer, 1995), on the many reports on monitoring missions of the Institute and the experience of the different monitors. The chapter is not in the first instance a scientific analysis but a practical set of recommendations built on many experiences. It provides a checklist and benchmarks of best practice in order to help establish democracy and the legal and institutional framework for free and fair elections, as far as the media are concerned.

HISTORICAL BACKGROUND

The last century in Europe has been dominated by the struggle of three antagonistic models or ideologies for the organization of political and societal systems:

- Liberal democracy with different political parties and free-market economy ruled by fair competition.
- One-party dictatorship and communism.
- Extreme nationalism and fascist dictatorship and imperialistic attempts to suppress other sovereign countries.

At the beginning of the 21st century, liberal democracy and the free-market economy have prevailed and regained ground. Luckily, in a worldwide perspective, dictatorship is on its retreat. However, even in well-established democracies the fair play between majority and minority, between ruling parties and opposition, is not to be taken for granted. Elections are a rivalry concerned with power and privilege. The struggle for dominance has to be regulated by the rule of law and by transparency, provided by independent media and professional journalism.

We have just experienced in the so-called well-established democracy of the United States in the elections for the presidency in the fall of 2000, wherein the application of the rule of law was not well accepted by the two competing candidates' camps and the media played an undue role in stating "facts" before the counting of votes had come to an end. There was the problem of machine or hand counting of votes, the premature declaration of a *winner* by the media, pressure from one candidate on the counting teams and the different courts. These facts illustrate that democracy and a free-market economy are never well established unless defended and sustained in a day-to-day struggle.

The lesson that can be learned from this controversy over the electoral system in the United States and its proper application is that the rule of law and the fight for the application of democratic rules by engaged persons, in an adequate institutional framework, is the main prerequisite of a living democracy. In this respect, independent media have an obligation to work in the *public interest* on the side of the citizens to ensure that the will of the people expressed in free and fair elections is recognized in the results of elections.

Fourteen years after the fall of the Berlin wall, after the collapse of the Soviet Union and the subsequent abolishment of the one-party systems of communism in Central and Eastern Europe, it is time to evaluate the progress of democracy, of the development of independent and responsible media, and of a market economy not only in these countries, but also in other countries engaged in the struggle for democracy and free and fair elections and the struggle against governmental control over the media, such as the former Yugoslavia, Peru, Zimbabwe, and Pakistan. In so many countries, it is continually necessary to evaluate the election processes.

---

1 Today, in countries of Eastern and Central Europe, but also in many countries in Africa, Asia, and South America, and even in the United States, it is evident that the process of establishing and sustaining democracy and a free-market economy is still a challenge in this era of globalization and needs substantial support from both inside and outside these countries in transition.[1]

---

[1]Concerning the challenges for democracy in general, see Weidenfeld (1996).

THE CONCEPTS AND NORMS FOR DEMOCRACY
AND A FREE-MARKET ECONOMY

The well-established democracies like the United States, United Kingdom, France, or the Scandinavian countries differ in the organization and interplay of the political and societal powers—that is, different constitutional powers of the parliament, the president of the republic or the prime minister or chancellor, different powers of the Constitutional or Supreme Court, the role and organization of political parties, and the associations of business enterprises and unions.

---

2 Even acknowledging the different historical and constitutional backgrounds of the well-established democracies, they all have in common the respect for human rights, the division of powers with checks and balances, the rule of law, and the guarantee of freedom of press and broadcasting.

These common basic norms are laid down precisely in the respective constitution, the Charter of the United Nations, the Convention of Human Rights of the Council of Europe, and the different treaties of the European Union.

These norms, fundamental for functioning, living, and sustainable democracies, have their basis in the commonly accepted philosophy of the period of enlightenment spread throughout Europe and North America in the 18th century, and found increasing acceptance worldwide in the period that followed. Fighting the Mafia and corruption, controlling the military, preventing the build-up of political dynasties, and so on, is only possible in a democracy: Political power can only be exercised under the rule of law and for a limited time in a fierce but fair competition between majority and opposition in Parliament, and between different parties and political figures. Therefore, prerequisites of a functioning democracy are regularly organized elections conducted according to well-established rules, applied by independent institutions, and *supervised* by independent and professionally run media.

---

3 Democracy as the basis of a civil society and a free-market economy can only function when complemented by free and independent media as a countervailing power to the political and economic powers.

The European Institute for the Media (EIM), a nongovernmental organization, subscribes to these norms and has helped to put them in place by monitoring the media coverage of elections since 1992 across the former

Soviet Union, now called the Commonwealth of Independent States (CIS) and Central and Eastern European countries. The European Commission has provided financial support for these initiatives, although they have been undertaken with strict independence (see the list of monitoring missions conducted by the EIM in Appendix C). The EIM is well prepared to perform these monitoring missions based on its Pan-European perspective, its independence, its professionalism, and the comparative approach it takes in its research work.

CONCEPT OF THE ROLE OF THE MEDIA

A civil society, an open and democratic political system, and a market economy, based on civil rights and liberties and personal accountability, cannot exist without media—mainly press and broadcasting as mass media, but recently also the new media, like the Internet as interactive media—that are widely available and accessible to the general public at costs affordable to everybody.

---

4 The media have to independently reflect the pluralistic structure of such a society; they have to inform, *enlighten,* and educate the public. They have to provide a platform and forum for controversial societal debates, and because of this, are an important factor in forming public opinion. They have to comment on the personal behavior of politicians, military personnel, business people, representatives of churches, union leaders, scientists, and so on, and they have to evaluate crucial developments inside the society and in the world.

Public opinion has to be understood in a very broad sense: It concerns political, economic, societal, cultural, religious, and scientific questions as well as the speeches and actions of public figures.

As democracy cannot live up to its standards without a free press, a market economy as well cannot develop its potential of invention and innovation, on the one hand, and of fair competition concerning the quality and prices of goods and services, on the other hand, without a free press providing well-researched information and background material. Citizens as well as consumers rely mainly on the press and broadcasting before they make their decisions both in the political process and on the changing markets. And politicians as well as business people base their judgments and actions mainly on the information and commentaries that put that information into context by the political and the economic press respectively. Therefore, the process of forming public opinion has to embrace all relevant developments in politics, economics, science, religion, culture, sports, and society as a whole. Political democracy will not endure without a free-market economy and vice versa, and both will serve the citizens, the working professionals, and the consumers only if they are accompanied and challenged by free and independent media. Therefore, a civil society cannot tolerate media that are dominated or controlled by one-sided powers, be they political, economic, or social.

The constitutional division of political powers—legislative, executive, and judicial—and their checks and balances is further elaborated by the fourth estate or the countervailing power of independent media, separate from the political and economic process.

---

5 It is widely agreed that the media have to fulfill the role of watchdog on the side of citizens, working professionals, and consumers to make sure that the norms of a civil society and the rules of fair competition are observed in both the political and economic spheres. The media have to make sure that these norms are not only articulated in writing but are observed in reality.

MEDIA AND ELECTIONS IN GENERAL

The media have a crucial role in covering the political process and in shaping and contributing to the formation of public opinion, as expressed most importantly in the time of campaigning before elections and during elections themselves.

---

6 The watchdog function of the media is especially crucial during times of electoral campaigns and elections themselves. For ordinary people, the press and broadcast media are often the sole source of information on the candidates, their former achievements, and future programs and on issues under current debate.

Biased media will lead to judgments and actions that are not self-determined by the otherwise sovereign people. Media coverage has become such an important element of the run-up to elections and for elections themselves that, if the media coverage in the press and on television is not free and fair, the results may be prejudiced to an extent that the elections as a whole, even if the formal process of voting has been organized correctly, may be judged not to have been free and fair.

Media scholars argue that the media in our complex societies of the 21st century gain in significance during these periods of campaigning and voting; the professional functioning of television is therefore of utmost importance for free and fair elections.

---

7 The concept of information has to be understood in a broad sense: Television can give you as a voter an idea of how trustworthy candidates are, how they communicate/connect with the people, how they behave under stress, for instance, when challenged in public by a contender or a well-prepared professional journalist, how they sell their program, or what they stand for.

The scientific debate on the impact of the media on personal behavior, mainly discussed in the context of violence in media programs or in films and its impact on children, reaches the conclusion that although there is no direct link between media content and behavior, the objective presentation of information is the only way to ensure free and fair elections.

---

8 A direct line cannot be drawn between the content of the media on the one side and the personal behavior of the viewers and listeners or readers on the other side when casting their vote. Nevertheless, a negative impact by biased programs can be avoided only when the information is presented to the voters as objectively as possible by independent media. Only then can sovereign decisions be made by citizens. And only then can elections be qualified as free and fair.

We cannot ignore the content of the media because, at least for some groups in society, who are, for example, unable to clearly distinguish between content in the media and reality, there is a potential risk for negative impact.[2] The other argument in favor of independent media and professional journalism, unbiased toward candidates and parties running for elections, concludes that—regardless of potential direct impact of media content on voters—the information presented has to be as objective as possible for the voters so they can make a knowledgeable choice on their own, directed by neither the interested parties, interested journalists, nor interested groups behind the journalists. Therefore, the proffer of unbiased information via independent media is a prerequisite for sovereign decisions by citizens and consumers. This is a fundamental notion about which there is no dispute. In

---

[2]See Groebel et al. (1995) with regard to impact research concerning violence in TV programs.

their book *Television and Elections,* Mickiewicz and Firestone (1992) stated that: "The cornerstone of credible news coverage of campaigns and elections is journalistic autonomy. The media must be known to be free of interference from representatives of the government, a political party or a particular candidate in shaping the programme content."

Therefore, everything must be done to integrate media freedom and professional journalism in the respective constitutional and legal systems, make it part of the adequate institutional framework and—and this is most important—to make it a societal and journalistic culture. Otherwise, democracy with regular voting and a market economy will not only be a distant goal, but will never even overcome a horrible past and show up on the horizon.

MEDIA SYSTEMS

Media freedom and professional journalism have to be secured from different but interrelated angles in a complex media system.

---

9 Independence of the media under the rule of law and professional journalism can be secured only in an elaborate media system that embraces:

- Constitutional guarantees for free speech and research and for freedom of the press and broadcast media.
- Laws that specifically articulate (a) the organizational framework for the media including licensing procedures, financing, taxes, ways of distributing, and so forth, and the rights and responsibilities of the media especially in relation to politics (i.e., access to information, the right of journalists to protect their sources of information, the clear definition of state secrets, and data and privacy protection), (b) the obligations of regulatory authorities, (c) the access to printing facilities and audiovisual productions, and (d) the organization of infrastructures to disseminate books, journals, and newspapers and to air broadcasting programs.
- Independent regulatory authorities that apply the laws, enforce the protection of minors and antitrust laws in the field of communications and the media, stimulate quality programs and innovations, and foster media literacy among all groups of society.
- Clear rules together with elaborate guidelines in the media organizations concerning the ethical culture of the institution, specifically (a) the guarantees for reliable research and information (e.g., which methods have to be observed in researching and covering scandals), (b) the kind of material suitable for publication, (c) the kind of programs that can and cannot be broadcast (i.e., violence, pornography, slander, rumors), (d) the training of journalists, and (e) the functioning of self-regulation.
- The standards of the journalistic profession concerning the distinction of news coverage and commentaries, unbiased news coverage itself, and research.

Weak points in a media system have to be compensated by strong points in other areas. Otherwise the interplay between the different levels will not conform to democratic needs, especially in times of elections.[3]

Media have to function not only on the basis of regulations or the institutional framework, but also in relation to professional journalistic standards; and they have to be evaluated not only concerning the written legal framework, but also in relation to the enforcement of this framework and in relation to the real work done by the journalists *under* the regulations and using their qualifications.

Media systems, mainly in Western Europe, are characterized by a so-called dual broadcasting system, the rivalry between public-service and commercial broadcasters, both organized as far as possible from either political influence from political parties or the government or vested economic or societal forces. This, though never ideal but desirable, dual system is still a goal for many countries of the CIS, Africa, Asia, or South America.

---

10 Still very crucial in many countries is the transformation of state-owned and -controlled media, mainly in the field of broadcasting, to public-service media or to commercial media via privatization. Management should be appointed on a contractual basis with different time frameworks than the respective period of the parliament or the president. Positions should not be held by government officials, members of governmental agencies, or leading members of political parties.[4]

In this respect, the funding of the broadcasters in a dual system is of crucial importance. Political forces like the majority in the parliament or in government tend to use decisions on the augmentation of the license fee for public-service broadcasters or the extent of advertising allowed in commercial programs as a leverage for their influence.

---

11 The financing of government-owned or public-service media should be organized on a legal basis, not out of the state budget, and in such a way that politicians cannot use the financing (e.g., the increase of the license fee) as a leverage for egoistic influence on the personnel of the institution or on media content.[5]

---

[3]See European Institute for the Media (1995).

[4]See, for example, Berner (2000).

[5]The introduction of a special index, automatically regulating the amount of the license fee, could be helpful.

12 If at all, subsidies to the media should be distributed only on the basis of neutral criteria and for only a meaningful period of time as part of the transition from state media to self-sustaining independent media. Subsidies should be distributed only upon the decision of a body that is separate from the government and the parliament and that represents a variety of viewpoints and professional experiences.[6]

In a dual broadcasting system, depending how it is organized and how the revenues are regulated, competition can extend to rivalry over the advertising revenues, affecting the programming as a favorable framework for the interests of the advertisers to attract mass audiences with high bargaining power, or, if the sources for financing are well separated, can concentrate on the quality of the programs broadcast. Then the public-service broadcasters financed like the BBC, by license fee only, can be the benchmark in quality programming.

13 A stable dual broadcasting system, with public-service broadcasters mainly financed by license fees and commercial broadcasters financed by advertising revenues and sponsoring, has the potential for quality programming on the one hand and innovation in the programs on the other.

Market forces alone do not guarantee fair competition in a dual broadcasting system. Nor do they guarantee quality press in the newspaper market or quality programming in broadcasting. Market forces tend, if they are not regulated, toward a process of media concentration, limiting the choice of the readers, listeners, and viewers, because in a capitalistic media market, the owner still has the right to decide what is published and with which political leaning it is published.[7]

14 There is a need for a legal framework for the fair competition in the field of a free press and a dual broadcasting system. This should include the prevention of undue media concentration in the sphere of commercial broadcasting; for example, by mergers, takeovers by foreign capital, or the formation of vertical and conglomerate alliances. This should also include the sources of financing and the limits of income from advertising

---

[6]Sweden, for example.

[7]Cut-throat competition may lead to "bad" journalism, trying to augment the readership via sensationalism, slander, (invented) scandals, and so on. See Groebel et al. (1995).

(how often a program can be interrupted by ads, how the ads have to be announced, etc.).

For the free market of information and ideas to function, publishers' and/ or broadcasters' access to the sources of information (the news agencies, press conferences, and party congresses, etc.), to the markets of necessary supply including paper and printing machines for newspapers and cameras, videorecorders, and so on, for broadcasters, and to the infrastructures of distribution has to be free and unconditional.

---

15 The distribution, printing, and paper supply sectors as well as the authorities to award scarce frequencies, and so on, should be demonopolized at a national level, and the free flow of information and of the hardware and software for printing and channeling of content across national borders should be guaranteed.[8]

This is true with regard to cable and satellites as well as to the Internet.

MEDIA COVERAGE OF ELECTIONS

Different countries have different histories, cultures, and experiences. In an attempt to understand and evaluate the respective media system and its functioning especially in times of campaigning for elections, this context of a special development has to be acknowledged. Understanding, though not in all cases accepting, differences is possible only by always reading the special context of a situation.

---

16 In general, media coverage of elections has to take into account the special sociocultural or sociopolitical context of the respective society: How far is the education in schools advanced to better understand political processes? What about the rule of law and its application? How well functioning is the interplay between ruling parties and the opposition? How often have the citizens exercised their political choices by voting? How well established is the electoral system? Do we have a media system built on independence, sustainability, and professionalism? There is a general obligation of journalists to foster political culture in this respect.

---

[8]See McCormack (1999b).

In neither the East nor the West is the organization of elections ideal, nor does it live up perfectly to all the generally accepted norms of free and fair elections in a democracy. This is also true for the organization and regulation of media coverage of electoral campaigns. This necessitates an in-depth evaluation of norms and regulations and their application, keeping in mind the specific stage of development in a country, especially in a time of dramatic transition.[9] This does not mean, however, the granting of *bonuses* for failures or neglect or bias in organizing or covering elections. To understand a specific situation does not include accepting it. On the contrary, journalists and editors, as *watchdogs* on the side of citizens, have the duty to criticize undemocratic behavior of politicians, to make public maneuvers to manipulate elections, to educate the general public in respect of democracy, and to secure a fair and balanced coverage of elections.

The media coverage of elections has to be adapted to the specific organization of the respective elections: what kind of elections take place, which rules apply to political advertising, the funding of the campaign, and the voting itself.

---

17 The organization of independent media coverage of elections is two-fold, inter-linked with both the organization of the campaign and the voting process itself. On the one hand, the media have to take into account the kind of elections that take place:

1. Parliamentary elections require the following:

   - If political parties run for election, journalistic coverage has to concentrate on party programs, the performance of the party in the past, the reliability of its candidates, the financing of the party, and its campaign—the vested interests behind the scenes, potential coalitions, and their probable efficiency.
   - If personal candidates run in local/regional constituencies, the journalistic coverage has to concentrate on the evaluation of the political record of the respective candidates, their achievements in relation to their past promises, their credibility, and their links to specific political, economic, religious, and other interests.
   - If a second round of elections takes place, the voters have to be well informed of their specific choices and perspectives in this limited time period.

2. Presidential elections require:

   - Journalistic coverage has to provide an insight into the constitutional powers of a president, his or her achievements and failures as an incumbent president, his or her credibility, his or her performance under stress, be it from an internal or external crisis or by the undis-

---

[9]See McCormack (1999a). See also the chapters on individual countries in this book.

guised lobbying of vested interests. The journalistic coverage of a presidential race has especially to distinguish the acts of incumbent presidents in exercising their duties from the events they "create" to promote their campaign to prevent their getting an unfair advantage over their contenders/opponents.

On the other hand, media coverage has to take into account the organization of the elections themselves:

- If there is in place a strict rule concerning campaign financing, especially the financing of political advertising, the journalistic coverage has to embrace questions concerning the compliance with these rules. If such rules are not in place or are not enforced, journalistic coverage has especially to guarantee the fairness of the campaign by eventually counterbalancing the power of financially well-equipped candidates or parties.
- If free access time in broadcasting or free space in newspapers or journals is granted, it is not as important for journalists to arrange roundtables with competing candidates than it is if no such free time or free space is made available.
- In the case of virtually no limits to campaign financing and paid political advertising and no free time granted (as in the United States), it is especially important to have (a) a professional journalistic coverage of the campaign and (b) well-organized and unbiased debates between candidates, led by the best journalists that can be found.
- Taking into account the experiences of the recent presidential elections in the United States, it is advisable for the media not to publish local or regional results before all voting stations (especially in a country with different time zones) are closed and not to declare a winner before the counting process has officially ended.
- The media have to provide precise information concerning an eventual obligation for registration as a condition for voting, the opening times of the voting stations, the rights to get a leave from the employer when voting takes place on a working day, and how to avoid using ballots that can be excluded from counting.

The norms of journalistic coverage of elections are universal. But their application varies in relation to public-service media without external competition on one hand and commercial media competing in the marketplace of ideas and for funds for advertising or subscription on the other hand. A public service broadcaster has to guarantee internal plurality of information and commentaries; therefore it has to adhere to strict political neutrality and balanced reporting in relation to the competing political parties or candidates. With media competing in the marketplace, the plurality of opinions shall be guaranteed by competing commercial enterprises with more or less specific political leanings and thereby giving the public a choice of sources for information, especially in times of the run-up to elections.

18 The benchmarks for the media during election campaigns are different for the respective parts in a dual system: Public-service media, funded by a license fee, have a special obligation to represent the views of the competing parties and the public in an unbiased way, whereas commercial media may have political leanings as long as the pluralistic system of competing private media represents more or less the whole political and societal spectrum. Nevertheless, commercial media are also required to keep a clear distinction between news reporting and commentaries, the latter to be identified as the responsibility of specific persons.

The time after elections is the time before elections, which is to say that politicians are campaigning all the time. Nevertheless, let us say that a year or a year and a half before elections, a specific time period, a precampaign period begins in which the campaigning of the parties and/or politicians becomes more intense and, through their statements and attacks on their rivals, more focused on the upcoming elections. In some countries, however, this precampaign period is much shorter because the prime minister (like in the UK) or the president (like Yeltsin did in Russia by his resignation) have the opportunity to call for early elections.

The period after the precampaign period and just before the elections, the official campaign, is normally governed by special rules for media coverage.

19 The coverage by the media on an election campaign goes through three different stages:

- The precampaign period.
- The campaign.
- Reflection period/silence time directly before the voting day.

To the precampaign period apply the general rules of news coverage and reporting, rules that are standard for the journalistic profession worldwide.

For the campaign period, often defined by the electoral law, special rules may apply, such as the reporting of opinion polls is not permitted, the expenditures on political advertising are limited, or no candidates running for office may appear on talk shows of the entertainment sector of TV programs.

During the campaign period, there are three types of coverage:

- Free access to the media.
- Paid direct access.
- Editorial coverage.

Different rules in the specific campaign period may apply to the offering of free access to the media, and via the media to the public for the parties or candidates. If well organized, free access can help to provide a direct impression of the contenders, their achievements and plans, their trustworthiness, their standing, and so on. Take for example the presidential elections in the United States, where practically no limits exist, in relation to either the private funding of political ads or their content. Mighty economic, religious, or societal groups, therefore, have the ability to support their candidate in the media and to defame the opponents, so free access is of utmost importance. In the United States, free access is granted by presidential debates (but only for the candidates of the Democrats and Republicans), which are organized by the public-service system PBS and led by journalists known for their integrity.[10]

FREE ACCESS TO THE MEDIA

---

20 If in a country vested interests are very strong or if professional journalism is not well established, free access to the public via the media is especially useful:

- It can better ensure equality in the public representation of political parties and candidates because the amount of money available to a party or candidate is irrelevant. Moreover, because the resources of political paid advertising are often provided by special-interest groups, free access to time on TV or radio or space in a newspaper is a way to diminish or balance the dependence of politicians on such groups.
- Free access avoids the risk of biased journalism.

Free access has to be organized intelligently to avoid the line-up of boring statements read to the camera by inexperienced politicians, and to guarantee equal access between the different political groups and over the time of the campaign. This last aspect is especially important, because many undecided voters make up their mind for whom to vote at the last minute and therefore the political desire of contenders or parties to be present in the media in the last days of the campaign is overwhelming.

---

21 Free access must be distributed equitably to the running parties and/or candidates. Two principles can be applied:

- Proportional distribution or the recognition of the respective importance of parties or candidates: (a) a general ambition to create balance be-

---

[10]See the U.S. chapter in this book.

tween major political blocs, right and left (France), (b) a parties' representation or nonrepresentation in parliament, whereby those who are already in parliament get free access in proportion to their actual representation and "new" parties get much less (Germany), and (c) the number of candidates, running for a party.
- Strict equality. All parties/all candidates get exactly the same time, as they are running for the future and do not deserve a bonus for the past.

"New democracies" tend to choose this second criterion in the distribution of free time/space because of the number of new parties and the lack of criteria on which to base reasonable proportional access (e.g., 1998 parliamentary elections in the Czech Republic).

Especially in countries of the East, broadcasting often is the main source of information. So, the administration of free access is mainly important for television. The answer concerning the funding of free access has to differentiate between public-service broadcasters and commercial channels.

22 In all Western European democracies, the public-service broadcasters are required to make free time available to the parties/candidates, either fully for free or in compensation for production or distribution costs; sometimes this rule applies also to private broadcasters. In this case, they should be reimbursed for their losses.

There are commonly accepted rules on how to organize and regulate free-access time/space as an equally distributed means for political advertising directly by the running politicians or parties.

23 Free-access time/space should be clearly separated from editorial material under the responsibility of journalists. Therefore, specific announcements before and after each broadcast or the printing of a "free-access statement" should be broadcast or published. These slots for free-access publications or audiovisual statements should be scheduled throughout the campaign and at times when they are likely to reach the largest audience. Nevertheless, the breakdown of the free access into many different slots for each party or candidate may cause too much repetitions, becoming very boring for the readers/listeners/viewers.

New parties or fresh candidates tend to read statements directly to the camera. They should learn from their experienced counterparts in the West how to create a spot professionally to better catch the awareness of the public. The opportunity to communicate with the potential voters via free access to the media would be left unused if professional help would be excluded. This is not a call for sophisticated spin doctors, which might translate political messages into the language of brand-name promotion and thereby overdue political campaigning. This is a call for professionalism in political communication on both sides: that of politicians and that of journalists.[11]

---

24 The order of slots should be randomly determined by lot by the independent electoral regulatory body with journalistic experience. Fair distribution to the different contenders should obviously be the ambition and thus, for example, the first on radio might be the last on TV and vice versa for the sake of balance. Schedules should be available before the start of the campaign, should not be changed during the campaign, and should be well advertised in the programs and the TV guides.

Intelligent organization for the distribution of free access is needed in order to guarantee balanced allocation. It should be clear also, in the announcements of free-access statements, who has the responsibility for the content and which kind of redress is possible.

---

25 The parties/candidates are solely responsible for the text or the audiovisual program that is printed or broadcast in respect to their free access. But there should be a mechanism, for instance redress and sanctions, in regard to items published or broadcast that contain false allegations or contravene laws on racism, xenophobia, or the protection of personal integrity. Therefore, free access should not be permitted after the time when the right of reply can no longer be granted.

There is a need for an independent body to organize and supervise the distribution of free access to the applying candidates or parties.

---

26 A powerful independent regulatory authority is needed to regulate free access and to guarantee immediate obedience to the rules during the campaign.

The solving of disputes within the time of the period of the campaign is of utmost importance to guarantee the equal chances of competing candidates and/or parties. Mighty contenders tend, especially in a close race, to come out with unproven allegations against their rivals in the last minute of

---

[11]See, for example, European Institute for the Media (1994).

a campaign, hoping that the accused politician or party has no more time to answer or to prove the contrary and that nobody can judge the allegations before the voting takes place. In this respect, a day of campaign silence just before the voting day may help. In respect to very serious one-sided allegations, the regulatory body may grant redress even on this day and may make public its decision at the last moment.

The regulation of free-access time or space should be laid down as clearly and transparently as possible so that there exists a strict framework for the campaigning parties or candidates and the public is well informed.

---

27 There are different sources of organizational/institutional rules establishing the respective allocation of free-access time: In some cases they are articulated in laws or intergovernmental treaties; in other cases the rules are worked out in an agreement between broadcasters and the parties. Sometimes they are included in the regulation worked out by an independent electoral body, in agreement with the political parties or by a regulatory authority in charge of the media.

PAID DIRECT ACCESS

The direct buying of votes by various possible means is a hot topic in relation to the organization of free and fair elections. There exist reports that the minister for agriculture in Hungary offered food for free in order to gain votes. Other reports tell us that in a campaign in Egypt a rich entrepreneur and politician used white goods as give-aways in exchange for votes. Less obvious forms of buying votes exist, such as when incumbent presidents like the former president of Croatia schedule the opening of reconstructed roads or schools just before the election date.

Economic science has analyzed the political cycle of augmented subventions and reductions of taxes and other financial contributions (like payments for social services) in the year before elections and collecting back the "social benefits" in the years after the elections.

Journalists are part of the different manipulations to buy votes when they write articles or make television features under their journalistic name, in reality getting paid for it by the favored politician or party. This has been a common practice in countries of the former Soviet Union where in times of communism journalists had to be the spokespersons of the one-party system and where, after the collapse of the regime, journalists could not make enough money from their "normal" work.

The worldwide accepted norms of the journalistic profession state that journalists have to make public all forms of direct or indirect buying of votes. Only by doing this they can help the public to make an independent, well-informed judgment when voting.[12]

The possibility of direct access to the public via the media through paid political advertising can also be judged as an undue form of buying votes.

---

28 The question of whether paid direct access to the public in the form of political advertising should be allowed at all or, if allowed, where the limits should be drawn is answered highly controversially in the different countries. This debate is closely linked to the question of campaign financing (see the actual debate in the United States, where $3 billion (U.S.) have been spent on the presidential campaigns), concerning on the one hand the controlling of soft money, sponsoring either candidate, and concerning public financing of campaigns.

The arguments against paid access stress the inequality of opportunity between the *have* and *have-not* parties/candidates and that the high costs would create dependence of politicians on their sponsor. The arguments in favor stress that paid access in a country of free speech and market economy is part of the freedom of individuals to express themselves as they wish. Nevertheless, there is a widely recognized common ground in Western societies that there is a need for at least some regulative framework for paid access.

If paid access is granted, it should be balanced by extended free access and professional journalistic coverage on the one hand, and limited with regard to the time and money that can be invested and marked as such on the other.

---

29 Regulation should be in favor of transparency and state that paid time must be clearly marked or announced and not placed in editorial programs themselves.

To limit paid direct access of political parties/candidates to the media, strong regulations and powerful regulatory authorities are needed.

---

30 Regulations should limit the time in which paid political advertising can be broadcast and the prices; the broadcaster may ask for paid access. The prices should be affordable to the majority of parties and should be below normal commercial rates in order to limit the leverage of parties with greater financial capacities.

---

[12]Journalists have to be trained to adhere to these norms and they must have acceptable financial conditions to be able to follow the norms. See the section Editorial Coverage: The Responsibility of Journalists.

Regulation not only has to limit paid direct access and control the prices, but also has to guarantee equal access. This is especially important in a commercial press or broadcasting environment with acceptable political leanings of the respective journals or broadcasters. These may offer space or time for political advertising, but only if it fits with their editorial philosophy.

---

31 If paid access is allowed, regulation has to make sure that it is granted on the basis of equal opportunity to all of the contenders.

In order to avoid the possible negative effects of one-sided paid political advertising, it has to be transparent to the public and the amounts paid and by whom should be open to journalistic scrutiny.

---

32 In the same way in which campaign financing has to be transparent, media expenditures for realizing paid access should be transparent, and the regulatory authorities have to make sure that the payments to the media are made through official channels that have been defined in the electoral legislation.

It should also be transparent that the responsibility for the content of the political advertising lies not with the journals or broadcasters, but solely with the persons/institutions that paid. This is the consequence of the clear distinction between the editorial part of the media on one hand and political and other ads on the other. This distinction has to be made all the time, but especially in times of campaigns. Of course, the interest of political parties/candidates leans toward blurring this borderline: They want to have a favorable journalistic environment for their ads in order to maximize the effect. This is true not only for political advertising but also for ads for goods and services offered in the marketplace. Therefore, regulation and the exact supervision of its application by powerful, independent, and professional regulatory authorities is needed.

---

33 Responsibility for the content of the paid political advertisements should be with the parties/candidates that have ordered it. But as with free time, there should be a regulatory mechanism, for instance, redress and sanctions, against paid ads that contravene the regulation, for example, not observing the financial limits, not clearly announcing the political propaganda, working with false allegations, or breaking laws on racism or xenophobia.

---

34 Especially for the application of paid-access regulation, there should be a strong and independent regulatory authority, otherwise the rules are not the worth the paper they are written on.

EDITORIAL COVERAGE: THE RESPONSIBILITY OF JOURNALISTS

Apart from free and paid access, the most important role of the media in times of electoral campaigns is journalistic coverage.

35 The responsibility of journalists and how they exercise their profession can be judged only in the broader context in which media operate and against the background of the current standards and traditions of journalism in a country. The experience of monitoring the media coverage of elections in the last 10 years in many countries in Eastern and Central Europe demonstrates that journalists are often unwilling to engage in a proactive and critical analysis of candidates and issues and lack developed understanding of the role and functions of political journalism.

36 In relation to free and paid access for parties and candidates to the general public via the media, unbiased editorial coverage is of the utmost importance. Therefore, the primary responsibility for good campaign coverage rests with the professional work of journalists and editors. Editorial coverage has to be distinguished in relation to:

- Journalistic reporting.
- Journalistic commentaries.
- Journalistic organizing of roundtables/debates between candidates/representatives of parties and/or between representatives of societal groups like scientists, artists, members of associations and unions, and so on.

37 The quality of the journalistic or editorial coverage is closely linked to the conditions under which the journalists work and the rules that apply. In this respect, codes of conduct as part of self-regulation either in an enterprise (newspaper, journal, or broadcaster) or of the journalistic profession are important.

38 Concerning journalistic reporting, we have to specify the meaning of full, free, and fair information:

- The coverage has to be impartial and balanced in relation to the issues to be addressed and the political choices facing the electorate. This should apply not only to the information that is available, for example, via the press releases of the parties, candidates, and press agencies, but also to new information researched by the journalists themselves. A proactive attitude on the part of journalists is required in order to present as much relevant information and background material as possible to the potential voters.
- The journalistic responsibility includes making choices and setting priorities in order to best serve the public—the journalists in this respect are duly setting agendas in challenging the parties and candidates.
- The fairness doctrine mainly has to deal with the critical coverage of incumbents still running for the next term. Candidates occupying official positions should not gain undue advantage from additional coverage when exercising their functions; a good journalist has to determine whether an incumbent is using an event just to reinforce his or her position generating special awareness in the media or is really performing his or her official duty. (A recent example was in Russia in the spring of 2000, when Putin, acting president and also running for election, declared that he would not take part in the campaign yet at the same time got most of the media coverage, in both quantity and quality, merely by being mentioned positively during the campaign time.)[13]
- News and current-affairs programs in the form of both news coverage and analytical reports or programs have to be based as far as possible on well-researched and -checked facts. Rumors and sensational assumptions should be avoided. Only then can the traditional distinction between serious press and tabloids be maintained. And only then can we continue to speak about quality papers.
- Hidden advertising, for example, paid-for articles by parties or candidates disguised in the form of journalistic presentations, have to be avoided by strict editorial control.

Full, free, and fair coverage is only possible when the media are independent, and this means, when they enjoy stable economic conditions on their own so they can fight against a commercial, secret buying-up of the media.

Freedom of the press and broadcasting can only be enjoyed when it is balanced by responsible use. This requires the internal self-regulation of

[13]nSee European Institute for the Media (2000).

the journalistic profession. At the same time, the external framework has to guarantee these freedoms, which means the abolishment of censorship and the refraining of politicians to penalize media outlets or journalists with whom they do not agree. These penalties, in order to muzzle the media especially in times of political campaigns, can take different forms:

- Reject wishes for interviews.
- Withdraw paid political advertising.
- Threaten journalists with court procedures.
- Intervene against journalists through their employer.

---

39 Media should not be penalized for articles or programs of any of the competing parties/candidates. The abolishment of censorship not only has to be written into law but has to be practiced in the day-to-day interaction between state authorities and the media, and, as a last resort, enforced by independent courts applying the rule of law and understanding the importance of free press and broadcasting for the functioning of democracy and a free-market economy.[14]

However, any candidate or party making a reasonable claim of being defamed and thereby harmed should be granted the opportunity to reply or be entitled to a correction. The responsibility to correct inaccurate information should be left to the media; only if the editor refuses the right of reply should there be an outside arbitration, ideally by a journalistic self-regulating body or a press council.

---

40 Another question concerning the responsibility of journalists is whom the journalists are representing in their coverage of elections and political affairs in general—the public or the politicians? As mediators, journalists must enable both to have a voice, but in interviews, news coverage, commentaries, and organizing debates it is clear that journalists have a role to play as representatives of their audiences and their readership.

Having said that, it is important that journalists do not automatically cover politics as an attempt by politicians to deceive the electorate. Cynicism should not be a credo for journalists.

---

[14]See European Institute for the Media (1996): "In fact, Armenia, Georgia and Azerbaijan all have a media law and a constitution which state freedom of speech and deem censorship impermissible. The incorporated exemptions—protection of state security, social order, mores of society, slander etc.—can apparently be subject to opportunistic interpretations" (p. 126).

41 Journalistic commentaries have to be distinct from the normal news coverage and they should be signed by the name of the journalist to make clear that a personal opinion is being published or broadcast. A public-service broadcaster has to make sure that in a specific time frame, for example, every week of the campaign, the different commentaries (taking them collectively) are giving a balanced view of the political spectrum in the specific campaign.

The role of journalists varies not only in relation to editorial coverage on the one side and commentaries on the other side, but also in relation to the organization and leading of political debates between representatives of different parties.

42 The organization of roundtables/debates between candidates should be guided by two main principles:

- The equality of the invited participants. Here the same applies as concerning the distribution of free-access time (see Box 27).
- The rule that the journalist(s) are the persons leading the debate, not the candidates. (Here the U.S. example of public debates between presidential candidates is a good one: The highly respected, well-experienced journalist is the only person in the debate to put forward the questions, selected only by her or himself; she or he decides to whom to give the floor; she or he controls the adherence to the time limits, and so on. This of course functions properly only when the leading journalist is absolutely neutral and acting in the interest of the whole electorate.)

There should be 1 or 2 days before the election day for a reflection period without campaigning.

43 A reflection period is usually decreed in an election law or has been agreed on in a bipartisan accord and starts at the end of the official campaign—often on a Friday evening to the start of voting on the following Sunday. During this period, any election propaganda, programs promoting candidate/party, as well as the publication of opinion polls are prohibited. This is in order to prevent the voter to be swayed by last-minute propaganda, when there is no more time for other parties to react or for the media to comment.

Journalists have to offer their services in the free marketplace. They are hired and fired by private enterprises or public service broadcasters on a contractual basis. They have to make a living by exercising their profession.

---

44 The most important factor in guaranteeing journalistic independence as a prerequisite for them to live up to the standards of responsible, professional journalism in advocacy of the general public is the income they get for this work on a stable contractual basis. If the income is not sufficient to make a normal living, journalists are especially vulnerable to payments from interested parties. These very sensitive factors relate to the general economic situation of specific media in a country, and this one particularly is dependent on the general economic situation in a country.

---

45 All the efforts to improve journalistic professionalism and performance by better qualification, codes of ethics, and so on, will fail if the economic basis of their work is not sound.

INSTITUTIONAL FRAMEWORK

Media markets and job markets for professional journalists have to rely on self-regulation in order to prevent interference in their independence and their critical work, highly important to all kinds of power structures. Nevertheless, they can only live up to the norms of fair coverage of campaigns and elections and of professional journalism when their limits are defined by a regulatory framework.

Conflicts with political or economic power structures, conflicts with specific political interests, and conflicting interpretations of the norms of professional journalism all have to be solved by independent third parties.

---

46 It is not sufficient that the norms of editorial coverage of an electoral campaign are made explicit in laws, agreements, codes of ethics, and so forth. To guarantee their application, their transformation in day-to-day practice so that a specific culture of democratic coverage can develop, a strong institutional framework is needed by both regulatory authorities and the juridical system.

---

47 The regulatory body with authority over the media's coverage of elections, be it the body that normally regulates the commercial media or the whole dual system, or a special body established just to guarantee free and fair elections, should be apolitical in the sense that it is dominated by judges or should contain representatives from different interests or parties in order to guarantee its independence. Well-respected media professionals also should be represented.

The judges that have to apply media-related laws have to be specially trained to better understand and solve the conflicts. Apart from the normal juridical system and the application of the rule of law, the regulatory authorities have to be well equipped, need strong procedures in researching a case, need to hear the respective parties, and have to have the right to immediately express adequate sanctions in order to be well respected.

48 The regulatory authority has to act immediately so that its decision becomes effective during the campaigns. In the case of violation of electoral law or agreements concerning the media coverage of elections, the regulatory body should request that the media in question instantly to remedy the situation; in case of refusal, the regulatory body should pass the case to a judicial authority. Such a court should be independent from the acting government and have the capacity to impose severe fines or other forms of sanctions such as the publication of the decision of the court in a prominent spot in the newspaper or journal or the broadcast of it in primetime. Recording of the programs during the election campaign is certainly helpful when dealing with complaints.

The division of powers has to be observed between parties and journalists on the one side, and between active journalists in a campaign and members of a regulatory authority on the other.

49 During the campaign, journalists or editors of the media who also are candidates themselves or members of an election commission, should not be allowed by electoral law to produce news magazines or to otherwise participate in the coverage of the electoral campaign.

MIDTERM MONITORING

In order to make sure that a positive societal learning process takes place, the development of media coverage of elections should be closely monitored both inside and from outside a country in transition. By doing so, not only is a comparison in time possible but also a comparison between different countries that may have started from an almost equal position.

---

50 Finally, it should be stressed that in a midterm or long-term perspective the progress/regress of the standards of the media coverage of elections in a specific country should be monitored. Qualitative and quantitative methods have to be applied to guarantee an unbiased result:

- To compare the different situations for specific elections (e.g., Russia 1993/1995/1999 Duma elections, 1996/2000 presidential elections).[15]
- To compare the legal framework in progress.
- To compare the performance of the media in general and of the journalists specifically.
- To compare the respective institutional arrangements, how they function in reality and how they interact between each other and in relation to the government and the political parties.

In the perspective of worldwide watch of the processes of democratization in the different regions of the world, this monitoring could and should be a worthwhile contribution.

---

51 Such scientifically based but practical monitoring enables both the general public and the professionals in a country, in other countries, and in international institutions to inform themselves about the progress in the process of democratization throughout the world.

---

52 The intention of these guidelines is not to impose specific rules on specific countries, but to serve as both a checklist, developed from the experiences in different countries with a longer tradition of a democratic soci-

---

[15]The power of the Duma is limited, as are the governmental interferences in the campaign and in the media coverage; on the contrary, the power of the president is large, therefore the struggle to become president is more fierce, the interventions by the incumbent or the power structure more numerous, and the possibilities for the media to provide fair coverage more limited. In this respect, the democratization of Russia has not made a lot of progress. See also the chapter on Russia in this book.

ety and of freedom of press and broadcasting, and as a benchmark for the further development of a civil society.

ACKNOWLEDGMENTS

The chapter is based on the work of the EIM and in this respect G. McCormack and E. Chernyavska have to be mentioned and thanked for their very professional work for many years. Special thanks go to B. Berner for her systematic analysis of this topic and her continuing endeavors to support the media and democracy program of the EIM. The chapter has been edited by G. Parlmeyer. I want to extend my thanks to her for her excellent work.

REFERENCES

Berner, B. (Ed.). (2000). *Assessment of the Croatian state broadcaster HTV* (Final Report of the EIM). Düsseldorf, Germany: European Institute for the Media.

European Institute for the Media. (1994). *The 1994 parliamentary and presidential elections in Ukraine, monitoring of the election coverage in the Ukrainian mass media, Final Report.* Düsseldorf, Germany: Author.

European Institute for the Media. (1995). *TV requires responsibility* (Vols. 1 & 2: International Studies Bertelsmann Foundation). Düsseldorf, Germany: Bernd-Peter Lange, Runar Wold (Eds.).

European Institute for the Media. (1996). *Monitoring the coverage of elections in Armenia, Georgia and Azerbaijan, media in the Transcaucasus.* Düsseldorf, Germany: Author.

European Institute for the Media. (2000). *The media coverage of the March 2000 presidential elections in Russia, final report.* Düsseldorf, Germany: Author.

Groebel, J., Hoffmann-Riem, W., Köcher, R., Lange, B. P., Gottfried Mahrenholz, E., Mestmäcker, E. J., Scheithauer, I., & Schneider, N. (1995). *Bericht zur Lage des Fernsehens an den Bundespräsidenten* [The state of the art of television, report to the president of the Federal Republic of Germany]. Gütersloh, Germany: Bertelsmann Foundation.

Lange, J., & Palmer, A. (Eds.). (1995). *Media and elections: A handbook.* Düsseldorf, Germany: European Institute for the Media.

McCormack, G. (Ed.). (1999a). *Media in the CIS: A study of the political, legislative and socioeconomic framework* (2nd ed.). Düsseldorf, Germany: European Institute for the Media.

McCormack, G. (Ed.). (1999b). *Media management in the CIS: A basic guide with practical recommendations.* Düsseldorf, Germany: European Institute for the Media.

Mickiewicz, E., & Firestone, C. (1992). *Television and elections.* Durham, NC: The Aspen Institute and the Carter Center of Emory University.

Weidenfeld, W. (Ed.). (1996). Demokratie am Wendepunkt; Die demokratische Frage als Projekt des 21 [Democracy at a turning point; development of democracy as a project of the 21st century]. Berlin: Siedler Verlag.

A

Internet Sources for Electoral Legislation, Regulation, and Court Decisions

France

French Broadcasting Law No. 86-1067 of September 30, 1986 as revised by Law No. 2000-719 of August 1, 2000 *(Loi n° 86-1067 du 30 septembre 1986 modifiée relative à la liberté de communication)*
http://www.legifrance.gouv.fr/html/frame_lois_reglt.htm

Decree No. 2001-213 of March 8, 2001 on Presidential Elections *(Décret no 2001-213 du 8 mars 2001 relatif à l'élection du Président de la République au suffrage universel)*
http://www.legifrance.gouv.fr/html/frame_lois_reglt.htm

Electoral Code–Legislative Part *(Code électoral–Partie Législative)*
http://www.legifrance.gouv.fr/html/frame_jurisprudence.htm

Electoral Code–Regulatory Part, Decrees of the Conseil d'Etat *(Code électoral–Partie Réglementaire–Décrets en Conseil d'Etat)*
http://www.legifrance.gouv.fr/html/frame_jurisprudence.htm

Law No. 77-808 of July 19, 1997 on opinion polls as modified *(Loi n° 77-808 du 19 juillet 1997 modifiée relative à la publication et à la diffusion de certains sondages d'opinion)*
http://www.legifrance.gouv.fr/html/frame_lois_reglt.htm

Conseil d'Etat, Ruling Alain Meyet, June 2, 1999
http://www.conseil-etat.fr/ce/jurispd/index_ac_ld9906.shtml

Conseil d'Etat—Analysis of the jurisprudence, 1991–1999, Elections
http://www.conseil-etat.fr/ce/jurispa/index_ju_aj9911.shtml

Conseil constitutionnel—Decision No. 98-2552 of July 28, 1998
http://www.conseil-constitutionnel.fr/decision/1998/982552.htm

Conseil d'Etat, Ordonnance of February 24, 2001, M. Jean Tiberi
http://www.rajf.org/article.php3?id_article=61

CSA—Presidential Elections of April 21, and May 5, 2002
http://www.csa.fr/themes/television/television_elections_detail.php?id=
8190

CSA—Parliamentary Elections of June 9 and 16, 2002
http://www.csa.fr/themes/television/television_elections_detail.php?id=
8197

Germany

German Constitution *(Grundgesetz für die Bundesrepublik Deutschland)*
http://www.artikel5.de/gesetze/gg.html (in German)
http://www.uni-wuerzburg.de/rechtsphilosophie/material/the_basic_law.
pdf (in English)

Press Council *(Deutscher Presserat)*—Press Code
http://www.presserat.de/site/pressekod/kodex/index.shtml (in German)
http://www.presserat.de/site/service/lang_english/kodex/engkod1.html
(in English)

Agreement between Federal States on Broadcasting *(Rundfunkstaatsver-
trag)*
http://www.artikel5.de/gesetze/rstv.html

Law on Political Parties *(Parteiengesetz)*
http://www.bundestag.de/gesetze/pg/

Federal Electoral Law *(Bundeswahlgesetz)*
http://www.bundestag.de/gesetze/bwg/
http://www.iuscomp.org/gla/

Media Laws of the Länder
http://www.artikel5.de/links.html#rfr-laender (in German)

Decision of the Federal Constitutional Court of 1978 (Vol. 47, p. 198)
http://www.uni-wuerzburg.de/dfr/bv047198.html

Association of regulatory authorities for broadcasting *(Arbeitsgemein-schaft der Landesmedienanstalten)*
http://www.alm.de/index2.htm

ARD—links to the public service broadcasters
http://www.ard.de/ard_intern/sender/index_text.phtml

Italy

Law of December 10, 1993, No. 515, on the "Regulation of election campaigns for the Chamber of Deputies and the Senate of the Republic"
http://www.agcom.it/L_naz/L_515_93.htm

Law 28/2000 on "Instructions for equality of access to means of information during election and referendum campaigns and for political communication"
http://www.agcom.it/L_naz/L_220200_28.htm

Law 225/1999 Conversion into law, with amendments, of the Decree-Law of March 13, 1999, No. 131, on urgent rules on electoral issues
http://www.agcom.it/L_naz/L225_99.htm

Law 223/1990 on "discipline for concentrations in the radio and television sector"
http://www.agcom.it/L_naz/L223_90.htm

The Italian Communications Authority—AGCOM *(Autorità per le Garanzie nelle Comunicazioni)*
http://www.agcom.it/intro.htm

Parliamentary Committee for the aims of and vigilance over radio and television services *(Commissione parlamentare per l'indirizzo generale e la vigilanza dei servizi radiotelevisivi)*
http://www.parlamento.it/parlam/bicam/14/rai/

National Council Order of Journalists *(Ordine dei Giornalisti–Consiglio Nazionale)*–Codes of Ethics
http://www.odg.it/barra/etica/etica.htm
http://www.uta.fi/ethicnet/italy.html (in English)

National Federation of the Italian Press *(Federazione Nazionale della Stampa Italiana)*–Laws on Press and Press Regulation
http://www.fnsi.it/

Union of RAI Journalists *(Unione Sindacale Giornalisti RAI)*–Statute
http://www.usigrai.it/

Russia

The Russian Constitution
http://www.departments.bucknell.edu/russian/const/constit.html
http://www.uni-wuerzburg.de/law/rs00000_.html

Law on Mass Media
http://www.medialaw.ru/e_pages/laws/russian/massmedia_eng/massmedia_eng.html

Law on Information, Informatization and the Protection of Information (1995)
http://www.fas.org/irp/world/russia/docs/law_info.htm

Law "On Basic Guarantees of Electoral Rights and the Right of Citizens of the Russian Federation to Participate in a Referendum"
http://www.democracy.ru/english/library/laws/bg_law_eng/index.html

Federal Law "On the Election of Deputies of the State Duma of the Federal Assembly of the Russian Federation"
http://www.democracy.ru/english/library/laws/dumaelect_eng/index.html

Federal Law "On the Election of the President of the Russian Federation"
http://www.democracy.ru/english/library/laws/presidelect_eng/index.
html

Resolutions of the Central Electoral Commission
http://www.democracy.ru/english/library/cec/

Union of Journalists—Code of Ethics
http://www.ijnet.org/Code_of_Ethics2/Russia__Congress_of_Russian_
Journalists.html

Charter of Television and Radio Broadcasters
http://www.internews.ru/crisis/charter.html
http://www.msps.ru/eng/libr/rr/r_un_r6.html

South Africa

Constitution
http://www.polity.org.za/html/govdocs/constitution/saconst.html

Public Protector
http://www.polity.org.za/govt/pubprot/

Public Protector Act, No. 23 of 1994
http://www.polity.org.za/govdocs/legislation/1994/act94-023.html

Films and Publications Act (Act 65 of 1996)
http://www.polity.org.za/govdocs/legislation/1996/act96-065.html

Promotion of Access to Information Act
http://www.acts.co.za/prom_of_access_to_info/index.htm

Elections—Regulations & Legislation
http://www.gov.za/elections/legislation.htm

Electoral Act, No. 73 of 1998
http://www.gov.za/acts/1998/a73-98.pdf

Municipal Electoral Act 2000
http://www.elections.org.za/Documents/ACT27-2000.doc

Independent Electoral Commission
http://www.elections.org.za/

Media Development and Diversity Agency (MDDA)
http://www.gov.za/documents/2000/mdda/mdda4.pdf

UK

The Electoral Commission
http://www.electoralcommission.gov.uk/

BBC Documents and Policy (Guidelines)
http://www.bbc.co.uk/info/bbc/corp_info.shtml

BBC Programme Makers' Guidelines for the General Election Campaign
http://www.bbc.co.uk/info/genelection/

Producers' Guidelines (Chapter 34)
http://www.bbc.co.uk/info/editorial/prodgl/index.shtml

ITC Programme Code
http://www.bbc.co.uk/info/bbc/corp_info.shtml

Radio Authority—Codes and Guidelines
http://www.radioauthority.org.uk/regulation/codes/codes-main.html

Commercial Radio's Election Guidelines
http://www.radioauthority.org.uk/publications-archive/adobe-pdf/
regulation/codes_guidelines/election%20reporting.pdf

Press Complaints Commission Code of Practice
http://www.pcc.org.uk/cop/cop.asp

Representation of the People Act 2000
http://www.hmso.gov.uk/acts/acts2000/20000002.htm#aofs

Political Parties, Elections and Referendums Act 2000
http://www.hmso.gov.uk/acts/acts2000/20000041.htm#aofs

Broadcasting Act 1990
http://www.legislation.hmso.gov.uk/acts/acts1990/Ukpga_19900042_en_1.
htm

United States

U.S. Constitution
http://www.findlaw.com/casecode/constitution/

Federal Communications Act of 1934
http://www.fcc.gov/Reports/1934new.pdf

Federal Election Campaign Act of 1971 (FECA)
http://www.fec.gov/law/feca.pdf
http://aloe.csv.warwick.ac.uk/uscode/2/ch14.html

Federal Election Commission (FEC)—Campaign Finance Law Resources
http://www.fec.gov/finance_law.html

Bipartisan Campaign Finance Reform Act of 2002 (BCRA)
http://frwebgate.access.gpo.gov/cgi-bin/getdoc.cgi?dbname=107_cong_
public_laws&docid=f:publ155.107

Integrated Text of BCRA and FECA
http://www.bna.com/moneyandpolitics/bcra_feca.pdf

Commission on Presidential Debates
http://www.debates.org/

U.S. Supreme Court Judgments:

• *Bush v. Gore*, 531 U.S. _ (2000)
http://www.supct.law.cornell.edu/supct/pdf/00-949P.ZPC
http://caselaw.lp.findlaw.com/cgi-bin/getcase.pl?court=US&navby=case&
vol=000&invol=00-949

• *New York Times Co. v. Sullivan*, 376 U.S. 254 (1964)
http://eon.law.harvard.edu/ilaw/Speech/times.html
http://caselaw.lp.findlaw.com/scripts/getcase.pl?court=us&vol=376&
invol=254

• *Miami Herald Publishing Co. v. Tornillo*, 418 U.S. 241 (1974)
http://www.bc.edu/bc_org/avp/cas/comm/free_speech/miamiherald.
html

http://caselaw.lp.findlaw.com/scripts/getcase.pl?court=us&vol=418&
invol=241
- *Buckley v. Valeo*, 424 U.S. 1 (1976)

http://supct.law.cornell.edu/supct/cases/424us1.htm

http://caselaw.lp.findlaw.com/scripts/getcase.pl?court=us&vol=424&
invol=1

- *FEC v. Christian Action Network*, 1995

http://www.law.emory.edu/4circuit/apr97/952600.p.html

- *Maine Right to Life Committee v. FEC*, 1996

http://www.law.emory.edu/1circuit/oct96/96-1532.01a.html

- *Vermont Right to Life Committee v. Sorrell*, 2000

http://csmail.law.pace.edu/lawlib/legal/us-legal/judiciary/second-circuit/
test3/98-9325.opn.html

Campaign Finance—Key Court Cases
http://www.brook.edu/dybdocroot/gs/cf/courts.htm

Society of Professional Journalists—Code of Ethics
http://www.spj.org/ethics_code.asp

Radio-Television News Directors Association—Code of Ethics
http://www.rtnda.org/ethics/coe.shtml

American Association of Advertising Agencies—Standards of Practice
http://www.aaaa.org/inside/standards.pdf

American Association of Political Consultants—Code of Ethics
http://www.theaapc.org/content/aboutus/codeofethics.asp

Council of Europe

Council of Europe Recommendation No. R (99) 15 of the Committee of
Ministers to Member States on Measures Concerning Media Coverage of
Election Campaigns
http://www.humanrights.coe.int/media/

Media-Monitoring Organizations

The European Institute for the Media—Media and Democracy Programme
http://www.eim.org/MaDP.htm
Council of Europe
http://www.coe.int/portalT.asp http://www.humanrights.coe.int/media/

Internews.
http://www.internews.org/

Monitoring.ru Group (Media Monitoring and Surveys)—Russia
http://www.monitoring.ru/

Osservatorio di Pavia (Media Monitoring and Research)—Italy
http://www.osservatorio.it/

B

The European Institute for the Media—Media and Democracy Programme

The Media and Democracy Programme (MADP) was established in 1989 as a media-oriented response to the seminal changes taking place in Central and Eastern Europe. Its main task has been to monitor the media development in former one-party regimes and to assist the progress in establishment of the pluralist media in new democracies.

The MADP seeks to assist the establishment of the rule of law in new democracies as well as to raise awareness of the regulatory framework pertaining to the media and media self-regulation. The MADP has thus undertaken the specific task of distributing information on European policies in the media sphere and of know-how transfer, on both an organizational and an individual basis.

The MADP's activities include research and comparative analysis of media developments in European and Mediterranean countries undergoing political and economic transition. Of particular concern to the program is the contribution of the media toward diversity, participation, and accountability in society. The findings are disseminated in a proactive way so as to encourage debate, in society in general and the media community specifically, on ways and means of improving media performance.

In February 1996, the MADP started the Media Monitoring and Assistance Unit (MMAU) for the Commonwealth of Independent States (CIS) with the help of the European Commission (EC) which was geared toward monitoring media developments and assisting professional and democratic media and journalists in the countries of the former Soviet Union.

In July 1996, the MADP began a media-monitoring and legal-assistance program in former Yugoslavia, Albania, and Romania, which was funded by the European Union (EU). The program comprised workshops, consultancies, and internships, as well as publications, mainly related to media law. In April 2000, the EC approved a 3-year project for the countries of Central and Eastern Europe, which has provided know-how transfer to the media in the region, with a focus on new technologies, media law, and professional skills building in various areas of journalism.

To date, the MADP has:

- Monitored media coverage in more than 40 presidential, parliamentary, and municipal elections in 14 countries in Central and Eastern Europe and the former Soviet Union, with accompanying reports for each mission. Thus a unique database has been generated that serves as the starting point for further research, for instance, in the field of political communication, regulatory practices, and economic structures of media in countries undergoing transition.

- Provided information and analysis on media developments to various international governmental organizations, such as the European Parliament, the EC, the Council of Europe, the Organization for Security and Cooperation in Europe (OSCE), the United Nations Educational, Scientific and Cultural Organization (UNESCO), as well as international and local nongovernmental organizations (NGOs) that are involved in media assistance.

- Organized international workshops and conferences on a variety of issues, from media and elections to the legal framework of the media and perspectives of public-service broadcasting.

- In co-operation with the EIM's (European Institute for the Media) legal unit, the MADP has analyzed and prepared commentary on media legislation in Russia, Hungary, and Serbia, as well as drafted broadcasting laws for Bosnia and Herzegovina.

- Published several books: *Media and Elections* (1995, a revised version for the Council of Europe, 1997)—translated into seven languages; *Media in the CIS* (1997, second edition 1999); *Media and Conflict in the Transcaucusus* (1999); *Media Management in the CIS* (1999); and *The Current European Decisions and Recommendations on the Media* (2000) in Serbo-Croat, which are standard points of reference in discussions of media developments by local partners as well as an information source for Western policymakers.

- Published a monthly newsletter, *Media in the CIS,* incorporating information from EIM's correspondents in the 12 CIS member-states, *Russian Media Bulletin,* and *Ukrainian Media Bulletin.*

- Established offices in Moscow and Kyiv that monitor media developments in Russia and Ukraine as well as in the region, liaise with media organizations, the NGO community, academia and public authorities, and offer logistical support for EIM activities in the CIS.

C

List of Media-Monitoring Missions Conducted by the Media and Democracy Programme of the European Institute for the Media

Country	Election	Year
Albania	Municipal elections	1996
Armenia	Parliamentary elections	1995
	Presidential elections	1996
	Presidential elections	1998
	Parliamentary elections	1999
Azerbaijan	Parliamentary elections	1995
	Presidential elections	1998
	Parliamentary elections	2000
Belarus	Presidential elections	1994
	Parliamentary elections	1995
	Referendum	1996
	Presidential elections	2001
Bosnia and Herzegovina	Parliamentary, presidential, and cantonal elections	1996
	Municipal elections	1997
Croatia	Presidential elections	1997
	Presidential elections	2000
	Parliamentary elections	2000
Estonia	Parliamentary elections	1995
Former Yugoslav Republic of Macedonia	Parliamentary and presidential elections	1994
	Parliamentary elections	1998
FRY	Parliamentary elections (Serbia)	1992
	Parliamentary and presidential elections (Serbia)	1997
	Municipal elections (Kosovo)	2000
	Parliamentary elections (Serbia)	2000

(Continued)

APPENDIX C
(Continued)

Country	*Election*	*Year*
Georgia	Parliamentary and presidential elections	1995
	Presidential elections	2000
Hungary	Parliamentary elections	1994
Kazakhstan	Presidential elections	1999
Kyrgyzstan	Presidential elections	2000
Moldova	Parliamentary elections	1994
	Presidential elections	1996
	Parliamentary elections	1998
	Parliamentary elections	2001
Romania	Parliamentary and presidential elections	1992
	Parliamentary and presidential elections	1996
	General and presidential elections	2000
Russia	Parliamentary elections	1993
	Parliamentary elections	1995
	Presidential elections	1996
	Parliamentary elections	1999
	Presidential elections	2000
Ukraine	Parliamentary and presidential elections	1994
	Parliamentary elections	1998
	Presidential elections	1999
	Parliamentary elections	2002

Contributors

Arnold de Beer

Professor de Beer is Professor Emeritus, Department of Journalism, University of Stellenbosch, South Africa, as well as the research director of Media Tenor SA—Institute for Media Analysis. He is the founding editor of *Ecquid Novi,* a South African journal for journalism research, and a board member of *Journalism Studies.* He is also the Chair of the African Council on Communication Education Media & Society Division, and a member of the Appeals Board of the SA Press Ombudsman. He was the first recipient of the SA "Communication Educator of the Year Award," from the SA Public Relations Institute. Presently he is coeditor with John C. Merrill of *Global Journalism.*

Helmut Drück

Helmut Drück is the Chairman of the Television and Radio Advisory Council of the Goethe Institute and Chairman of the Studien freis Rundfunk und Geschichte. He has also been the Intendant of Rias Berlin and worked for Westdeutscher Rundfunk. He is a member of the board of governors of the European Institute for the Media.

Clifford A. Jones

Clifford Jones teaches at the University of Florida's Frederic G. Levin College of Law. His areas of interest include Election and Campaign Finance Law, Federal Courts, Media Law, and European Community Law. Clifford received his J.D. from the University of Oklahoma and his M.Phil. and Ph.D. are from the University of Cambridge. He is a former Fulbright Scholar (Senior Scholar Research Grant, Johannes Gutenberg University of Mainz, Germany).

Karin Junker

Karin Junker has been a member of the European Parliament (MEP) Culture, Youth, Education, Media and Sport Committee since 1989 and she is a member of the German Social Democratic Party. Karin has held many positions including the federal leader of the working group of social-democratic women; member of the German public broadcaster WDR's broadcast council (chairman of the program committee and chairman of AG foreign reporting); and deputy chairman of the Social Democratic Party's media commission.

Lynda Lee Kaid

Professor Kaid is Senior Associate Dean and Professor of Telecommunication College of Journalism and Communications. Lynda has published widely in the field of democracy and the mass media. She is an expert in U.S. elections and the media's coverage of U.S. party political campaigns.

Bernd-Peter Lange

Former Director-General of the European Institute for the Media (1993 to 1999); in 1995 he founded the European Centre for Media Literacy in Marl. He became a Professor of Economic Theory at the University of Osnabrück in 1973, where between 1985 and 1987 he was Dean of the Social Sciences Faculty. He has published extensively on the subjects of mass-media organization and regulation, economics, finance and concentration, and new information and communication technologies and their impact on society. He has served on several advisory bodies such as the Information Society Forum for the European Commission. Born in Hamburg in 1938, Professor Lange went on to study Law and Economics at the University of Bonn (1958–1966). In 1967 he was awarded a doctorate in Constitutional Law at the same university. He has worked as a Research Fellow at the Institute for Economic Concentration at the Free University in Berlin, where he became Assistant Professor after 4 years. He has been a member of the board of governors of the European Institute for the Media.

Elisabeth Mauboussin

Elisabeth Mauboussin has worked as Secretary at the college of the CSA, the French audiovisual regulatory body, since September 2001. From 1991 to 2001, she was regulatory assistant director at the CSA. She is a member of the editorial board of Légipresse, a monthly magazine of communication rights. She is cofounder of Angle Droit, a monthly magazine dealing with regulatory and economic questions of communication. Elisabeth Mauboussin is also the author of a book and many articles on audiovisual regulation in France.

Anthony McNicholas

Anthony McNicholas is a visiting lecturer at the University of Westminster and the London College of Printing where he teaches on a number of media-related courses at both the undergraduate and postgraduate level. Anthony McNicholas completed a PhD in Communications at the University of Westminster on the Irish immigrant press in mid-Victorian England in December 2000. He is currently a Research Fellow working with Professor Jean Seaton, who is writing Volume VI of the official history of the BBC.

Teresa Perrucci

Teresa Perrucci graduated with a degree in Political Sciences from the University of Perugia, Perugia, Italy, and subsequently obtained a Specialization in Communications Sciences and in Methodology of Social Reserch from the University La Sapienza, Rome, Italy. Currently, she is working on a doctorate degree in Communication Sciences at the University of Salerno, Salerno, Italy, and is a senior researcher at the Institute for Economic and Social Research, Region of Umbria, where she is carrying out research dealing with content analysis in both television and print. She has collaborated with the Authority for equal protection of Communications, in the field of Monitoring of Television Broadcasting, with particular emphasis on political pluralism.

Daphne Skillen

Dr. Daphne Skillen has worked as a consultant on Russian affairs for 20 years. She managed the largest media and elections training program in the run-up to the 1999 and 2000 elections in Russia for the International Foundation for Election Systems. She is currently working as a media consultant.

Marina Villa

Marina Villa is a Professor at the IULM University (in Political Communication), Catholic University (in Public Communication), and Milan University (in Public Communication). Her main interests include political communication, journalism, and mass communications. Marina has a PhD in Sociology and Social Research Methodology, has worked for the Italian communications regulatory authority, and has published numerous articles on Italian and French mass media and political communication.

David Ward

David Ward has been Deputy Director General, Head of the Communication Policies Programme, and Director of Research and Strategy at the European Institute for the Media. He is also a Senior Research Fellow at the Centre for Communication and Information Studies, University of Westminster. He has published a number of articles on European Union communication policy, democracy, and press freedom, which have been published in books and international academic journals. He has recently published a book on European Union television policy published by IOS Press.

Author Index

Subject Index

For the purposes of this index the terms such as democracy, elections, election campaigns, election candidates, government, journalism, media, politics, press and television are not indexed due to their frequent occurrence in the text, but instead they provide headings for related topics. The countries related to the chapter titles are also not indexed for the same reason of frequency of occurrence, but they form sub-categories under certain topics where this is considered useful to the reader.